Developing Communication Theories

SUNY Series in Human Communication Processes
Donald P. Cushman and Ted J. Smith, III, Editors

Developing Communication Theories

edited by
Gerry Philipsen
and Terrance L. Albrecht

STATE UNIVERSITY OF NEW YORK PRESS

Published by
State University of New York Press

Printed in the United States of America

For information, address the State University of New York Press, State University Plaza, Albany, NY 12246

Production by Bernadine Dawes • Marketing by Fran Keneston

Library of Congress Cataloging-in-Publication Data

Developing communication theories / [edited by] Gerry Philipsen and Terrance L. Albrecht.
p. cm. — (SUNY series in human communication processes)
Includes index.
ISBN 0-7914-3159-2 (alk. paper). — ISBN 0-7914-3160-6 (pbk. : alk. paper)
1. Communication—Philosophy. 2. Communication—Methodology. I. Philipsen, Gerry, 1944– . II. Albrecht, Terrance L. III. Series.
P90.D468 1997
302.2'01—dc20 96-10632
CIP

1 2 3 4 5 6 7 8 9 10

CONTENTS

ACKNOWLEDGMENTS

We would like to acknowledge the support of Ann Staton, who was Chair of the Department of Speech Communication at the University of Washington at the time of the lecture series that provided the impetus for this volume. She provided crucial administrative support to the project. We also are grateful for presentations in the lecture series by John Wilson, Edna Rogers, and Janet Bavelas. Our greatest debt is to the authors of the chapters, who have helped to provide here an important record of developing communication theories.

INTRODUCTION

GERRY PHILIPSEN AND TERRANCE L. ALBRECHT

For over 2,500 years, scholars have written and theorized about the process of human communication. The philosopher Plato, living and writing in fifth century B.C. Athens, initially attacked savagely the study of human communication, in his dialogue Gorgias. Then, in his later dialogue Phaedrus, he proposed that the subject be studied systematically, not only in the law courts and assemblies but in families and intimate relationships as well. Plato's colleague, Aristotle, is said to have conducted empirical research into verbal messages and their effects in civil affairs. Thus, these early scholars foreshadowed what was only much later to become one of the major research topics in the study of human behavior, the study of how humans engage in the process of communication, and the effects that various patterns of messages have in lives and societies.

Although there is a rich tradition of communication scholarship down through the centuries, it was not until the twentieth century that there has been a sustained effort to investigate empirically the processes and effects of human communication. In this century, communication—its models, theories, research methods, and pedagogies—has become one of the major topics of theory and research in contemporary scholarship. There is now a substantial body of empirical and theoretical writing that can be categorized as research into human communication. It appears that in terms of everyday life as well as in terms of scholarship, this is, as the philosopher Richard McKeon phrased it, "the age of communication" (McKeon 1956).

At first glance, the statement that we live in "the age of communication" looks like a cliché. Certainly, since McKeon's famous assertion of that idea was published (McKeon 1956), it has been repeated many times in print and it undergirds much that we read and hear about communication in these times. But those of us who study communication know that although the phrase is said over and over, it is not overused or trite because the more we study communication the more we discover how much there is to be known and how much remains unknown. For us, the compilers of this volume, the study of communication continues to be a fresh and exciting endeavor, and our efforts at study are repaid by a host of new and promising lines of research and theorizing about this fundamental aspect of social life.

Our belief in the importance of communication to human life, and in the possibility of learning something about the way communication works in human life, have led us to an interest in communication theory—to systematic statements about the nature and dynamics of human interaction. This volume is an extensive and thought-provoking expression of that interest.

The title of this volume, *Developing Communication Theories*, makes reference to substance and to process. The *substance* is communication theory. In this volume we present five theoretical essays about human communication, along with a concluding essay that provides a commentary on the overall corpus of works. Thus, we present a substantial body of original papers about human communication as an important human activity. The volume is also about the *process* of constructing communication theories. In presenting the theoretical fruits, as it were, of their work, each of the contributors has provided a chronicle of how their theoretical insights developed over time. The concluding interpretive essay thus addresses not only the substance of the theories presented, but also is a commentary on how these theories were constructed.

Each of the theoretical essays included here presents work that is well known to scholars in communication. Each of these authors was given the same commission—to write a chapter in which they set forth their own original ideas about communication and in which they also discuss explicitly how their theories were developed. We were particularly interested in the interplay of theory, concepts, and data. That is, we asked each author to discuss how existing concepts and theoretical insights informed each other, what problems they encountered (and solved or did not solve) in terms of reconciling theory, concepts, and data, and how their work with concepts and data informed the eventual substance and shape of the theory proposed.

Books about communication theory abound. Such books can be classified into at least four distinct types. One is a book that sets out an original theory of communication, such as the important statements by Ruesch and Bateson (1951, 1968), Cherry (1957, 1966), Watzlavick, Beavin, and Jackson (1967), Pearce and Cronen (1980), Berger and Bradac (1982), Sanders (1984), and Cushman and Cahn (1985). A second is a book that contains a collection of theoretical readings by a variety of authors, such as the influential volumes edited by Barnlund (1968) or Dance (1982). A third is a textbook survey of communication theory and communication theories, such as Bormann (1980,

1989), Fiske (1982), Trenholm (1986, 1991), and Littlejohn (1989). A fourth is the encyclopedia or handbook of communication theory, such as Arnold and Bowers (1984) and Berger and Chaffee (1987).

Developing Communication Theories is unique among the various kinds of books about communication theory. It presents a variety of authors who not only present their own theories, but who in the process describe, from their own vantage points, the processes by which they construct their theories. Thus, *Developing Communication Theories* provides a glimpse into not only what is made but into the making as well. Why is such an emphasis important? We believe there are two reasons. First, theories are humanly constructed products. They come from the efforts of one or more people actively to make something. As such, an understanding of the theories themselves is enhanced by learning about the making itself. In this volume, the authors reveal something about how it is they came to pose the questions they have posed, what led them to a particular formulation of those questions, and how early experiences at observing the empirical world shaped the making of their product. Studying a communication theory as a construction by a human agent provides a perspective on the product which could not as easily be gleaned without the author's self-reflective commentary.

A second reason for examining theories as human constructions is the instructional value provided to students of communication who themselves are engaged in the study of communication, not as mere passive receivers of information, but as active interpreters of arguments and proposals. By following five theorists, and one commentator on their efforts, through a narrative about their research, those of us who read these stories are provided the opportunity to share, even if partially, in the intricate and difficult process by which these products were made. Such a sharing provides us as readers with models and moves to employ in our own search for understanding, whether it is a search for understanding the arguments made by others or an effort ourselves to contribute to the ongoing conversation about communication. Certainly, a volume such as this helps any of us who desire to move from the former role, a relatively passive receiver, to the latter, an active user and interpreter of the riches of the lode of communication theory.

The occasion for assembling such a body of work and for assembling this particular body of work was a particular set of circumstances at the University of Washington in the Department of Speech Communication. We had the opportunity to invite to the department several prominent scholars who had distinguished themselves in efforts to construct communication theories (Albrecht was then on the Washington faculty). Given the opportunity to schedule these visits during the span of about a year, we decided to ask each of these scholars to address the theme of developing communication theories, with explicit attention to their own processes of theoretical development.

These visits included appearances by Jan Bavelas, Charles Berger, Joseph Cappella, Barbara O'Keefe, Edna Rogers, and John Wilson. Berger, Cappella, and O'Keefe have each contributed a chapter to this volume, which grew out of that series of oral presentations. As the compilers of the volume, Albrecht and Philipsen each contributed a chapter reporting the respective stories of their own research efforts over a sustained period of time.

One important part of the series of presentations from which the present volume grew was that they were situated within a scholarly community. Faculty members and students from the department attended the presentations, raised questions, and then, in subsequent days and months, drew from the presentations in the ongoing conversation of the departmental community. Albrecht and Philipsen, as well as Susan Kline, then a member of the department's faculty (now at The Ohio State University), and John Stewart, a member of the faculty, participated in all the sessions. Because of his active role in responding to the oral presentations, and his long-standing interest in the philosophy of communication and communication theories (Stewart, in press), we asked Stewart to write a comparative and integrative commentary on the various presentations. Thus, the volume we have presented simulates in part the social context in which it took its initial shape: a departmental colloquium series, with a focused invitation to diverse scholars, and with an active response by an interpreting audience. Thus, this collection of essays about communication itself remains at least partially true to the particular form and fora of communication from which it grew.

These are diverse essays in substance and method, a fact discussed in detail by Stewart in his final chapter. As to substance, the themes include:

1. the intersection of the structure of interpersonal ties that people establish in their lives and how those ties and the shape of those ties influence perceptions and processes of human activity (Albrecht);

2. the kinds of messages that communicators produce when they must face uncertainty in relationships and situations (Berger);

3. psychological forces that explain the intricate ways that humans construct interpersonal relationships in and through details of interactional behavior (Cappella);

4. the logics revealed in differences in the ways people formulae strategic messages (O'Keefe);

5. cultural codes that interlocutors deploy in the distinctive times and places in which spoken life is constructed and enacted (Philipsen);

But for all the diversity in their particulars, these chapters share a common substantive focus and a common spirit, and it is useful to set these out prior to the papers themselves. They have in common a concern with the theory and practice of the use of language and other means of communicative conduct in the living of social life. Their concern with language and other codes is not, primarily, with their structure or ecology or history, but with their use—with the practices they serve and which, in part, constitute them. That is, each of these chapters is concerned, broadly, with the pragmatics of human communication—with describing and/or explaining how people do things in and through communication as a structured human activity. They also have in common what could be called an empirical spirit. Although they differ in the particular research methods and styles employed, each of these chapters manifests a concern with grounding generalizations in some experience of the world. Each of the authors has built up a theory out of observations and experiences and has tested incrementally generalizations against the lessons of experience.

Much of the vitality of this volume derives from the commonality of focus on communication, studied systematically and with a recourse to some kind of data. Much of its vitality also derives from the substantive, stylistic, and methodological differences of the papers. Taken together they represent a diverse sample of the vitality of communication studies in these times.

1

Patterns of Sociation and Cognitive Structure

TERRANCE L. ALBRECHT

> *"The Herbens, Willi and Liza and dozens of other displaced lawyers, diplomats, businessmen, writers and artists strolled through the state parks around New York City in the fifties and early sixties, a hermetic society, a secret one, set entirely apart from the world I was taught about in either public or Sunday school. There my father became eloquent in his own language and my mother seemed to blossom, throwing off the wariness that marked her relations with people in the city. There, our family seemed normal and connected to other people. There was community, an interweaving of lives that went back in time, that formed frail bridges over the great gap that was the war.*
>
> *That gap was always there, a great dark pit into which, sooner or later, the conversation would inevitably fall. All of the people my parents knew had been part of it and it had become the ultimate standard by which they judged and were judged."*
>
> —Children of the Holocaust: Conversations with Sons and Daughters of Survivors

Theories about human communication, like humans themselves, pass through cycles of development. Seldom does a given theoretical project arrive at a fixed plateau of explanation. Rather, in such a project, what one seeks to explain and how one seeks to explain it are, like the subjects of study, continually in motion, in process.

The initial premise shared by the contributors to this volume is that theories about human communication derive from the interplay of conceptual frames and data. From this view, efforts to explore and understand communicative behavior consist of posing a series of research questions and of predictions made and tested, and fulfilled, unfulfilled, and/or modulated. Taken together, such an exploration makes the entire quest for knowledge a story.

The story revealed in this chapter is about the experience of undertaking the logical and empirical challenges posed by the system theory approach to communication. This theoretical position rests on the nature of part—whole linkages: that through interaction, individuals are inextricably enmeshed in a larger social order. In particular, the work that I had and my associates have done over the past fifteen years concerns how the individual's position within a social network reinforces and is reinforced by that individual's cognitive and communicative dispositions.

Our research program on structure and cognition is discussed in this chapter in the following sections: (1) how the original research question was generated; (2) the progress of our effort to operationally engage the idea; and (3) a review of the yield of the empirical work—the main findings, conclusions, successes, and failures we have encountered in this long-term research program.

EARLY FORMULATION

The term "sociation," as it is used in early writings by Georg Simmel (Wolff, 1950), refers to the spectrum of interactions that link people together throughout a society. In Simmel's terms, society is not a "substance" but the frequent occasions of mutual influence that occur when people interact (1950, 11). He argues that the texture and experience of social life includes the full range of interactions among people; that "Sociation continuously emerges and ceases and emerges again" (1950, 10). He asserts that society merely refers to a number of individuals; they are connected because they interact.

Such structures as envisioned by Simmel are the foundation for current conceptualizations of communication *networks*, or sets of overlapping dyadic links (e.g., Farace, Monge, and Russell 1977; Monge and Eisenberg 1987) formed through interaction, occurring among people existing within an arbitrary boundary. Network methodology involves measurement of the structural properties of sociometric positions of individual nodes, (e.g., liaison/nonlinker, integrativeness), links (e.g., reciprocity, multiplexity) and cliques (e.g., clustering, density). Apparent in these structures are patterns of integration and differentiation in a social system, whether the system is an organization, a nuclear or extended family, a society, or other social grouping.

Our research has been devoted to exploring ways that patterns of sociation (in our case, social networks) are systematically related to the attitudes and cognitions of individuals. Viewed systematically, this is a concern with ways in which the organism and the social environment interact (Fox 1989).[1] The network approach we have taken is therefore important for understanding how micro and macro levels of a system interrelate. Network structures (at the macro level) are thus treated as manifestations of individual and dyadic actions (at the micro level) (Mehan 1978). The reverse hypothesis is also empirically verifiable. Relationships can emerge as a function of the pattern of the larger social networks of two individuals (cf., Ridley and Avery 1979). For example, Salzinger (1982) found that relationships within clusters were perceived to be more important and multifunctional than those occurring outside of the same cluster contexts. Parks and Adelman (1983) showed that social network involvement with a romantic partner's network (kin and friends) was a key factor in predicting the stability and duration of a personal relationship. In addition, researchers investigating the "small world phenomenon" have demonstrated the existence of a larger frame of ties among total strangers crossing geographic boundaries. The estimate is that any two strangers in the United States are connected through an average of five links or "steps" (see Bernard and Killworth 1978, and Rogers and Kincaid 1981, for reviews). In effect, while a dyadic connection between two persons implies a pattern in the macro network, the relationship can be reinforced as well as induced by features of the larger structure.

The question turns to the nature of the process of communication occurring within the macro and micro level structures of interaction. A consistent argument has been that communication behavior has several key functions in formal and informal collectivities. Among the most important is the reduction of uncertainty and equivocality (Farace, Monge, and Russell 1977; Farace, Taylor, and Stewart 1978; Weick 1979). Uncertainty has been variously defined. Definitions range from the information-theory-based definition of a lack of discernible pattern among multiple alternatives (Farace, Monge, and Russell 1977), to the absence of requisite information (Weick 1979), to the lack of attributional confidence about cause-effect relationships (Berger and Calabrese 1975). Equivocality refers to the existence of multiple interpretations for a given symbolic set (Weick 1979).

It should be noted that the setting for our studies on communication has been the organization. Organizations are particularly fruitful sites for studying networks, individual cognitions, and communicative behaviors because people in modern institutional settings are frequently confronted with high rates of global economic and environmental change and rapidly developing technologies. Communication has differing impacts on people as they engage in transactions to reduce uncertainties and render their private and public spheres more predictable in the face of change (Miller and Monge 1985). Such transactions typically involve a process of mutual influence in order to negotiate shared meanings for complex environments. The definitions of how we think of ourselves as individuals are inextricably bound to the ways we are connected to others, particularly in the bureaucratic institutions that embed us for large amounts of our lives. Differences in our communicative ties to others have consequences for the form and content of meaning that we negotiate in our transactions with others. These, in turn, shape the form and character of our cognitive structures and, simply, how we think.

Initial studies

The early research we conducted was an effort to establish a focused explanation for the connection between communication network positioning and patterns of cognitive structure. In general, studies have shown a correlation between levels of network integration and attitudes and motivation (cf., Albrecht, Irey, and Mundy 1982; Moch 1980; Roberts and O'Reilly 1978). Parallel work by Walker (1985) provided evidence that network position (as determined by the extent to which individuals have direct communication ties with highly similar sets of network contacts) is a more powerful predictor of cognitive differences than either functional specialty or product type assignment. Individuals' general social interaction patterns were a stronger determinant of the nature of their attitudes than either their formal job position or their designated computer product group. Hence, one's routine communicative behavior in the system was found to have a greater effect on cognition than did the work specialty for which one was formally prepared and trained. This was further evidence that the influence of such behavior should not be underestimated.

The studies just cited provide general evidence of a relationship between one's communication network position in an organization and one's attitudes and beliefs about the work environment. An early study in our program (Albrecht 1979) shows the beginning of an effort to explain theoretically such relationships. This study was driven by a more uncertainty-based theoretic frame, that of Force Aggregation Theory (Gillham and Woelfel 1977; Woelfel 1972; Woelfel and Fink 1980). We investigated how differences among individuals' perceptions of the self and other salient objects in organizational contexts were related to various role positions in communication networks. The relationship was found to be a function of the structures of respondents' communication contacts throughout the organization.

Theorists advocating the Force Aggregation position in the 1970s argued that attitudes are based on the amount of weighted information organization members receive about objects they perceive as salient in the system. The absolute value of the information contained in each message is weighted by the number of messages received, whether a positive or negative valence is asserted, and the significance of the source. For example, a given incoming message (as the unit of analysis) about a topic would be coded for the volume of messages previously received about the topic, whether the message asserts a positive or negative view, and the extent to which the source of the message is perceived to be significant and/or credible regarding the topic.

The symbolic interaction roots of the theory are evident in the assumption that as members accrue messages and information about salient objects in their environment, those objects come to develop meaning for them within the context of the situation. Meanings for objects can be represented symbolically and then potentially shared or at least expressed. The theory is also rooted in classical conditioning (stimulus–response) models, in that the strength of an attitude is presumed to be a function of the strength of the reinforcement process accruing through the value of messages received over time. Thus, the implication of Force Aggregation Theory for our question—whether and how one's network position is related to one's work attitudes and motivation—should be obvious. One's location in the information network is an essential causal factor for the variety and amount of messages one is likely to encounter in the system.

The accumulated weight of our network findings and the theoretical implications of Force Aggregation Theory led to a theoretically driven prediction about individuals' networks and their cognitive maps of the workplace. Specifically, we predicted that communication linkers (versus nonlinkers, those with more restricted, homogeneous ties primarily embedded in relatively dense social clusters) would have differing attitude sets or "cognitive maps" of the workplace. As hypothesized, communication linkers in the organization tended to see themselves as more central in multidimensional cognitive space in the system, and the variability of their collective responses was lower. They also perceived a stronger association between their concepts of "self" and "job" and viewed concepts such as "management" and "the union" to be relatively closer together in psychological distance than did nonlinkers. The differences in the range of communication network contacts among managers and employees was strongly related to the ways people reduce their uncertainty about themselves and aspects of their organizations. This resulted in some highly disparate meanings and perceptions of self as associated with salient aspects of the workplace. The findings were important because the use of advanced computer programs[2] enabled us to verify empirically (in modern social contexts) the classic notions of Simmel and Durkheim, that individual cognitive processes are directly linked to patterns of personal communication contacts.

This work was extended and further supported in a subsequent longitudinal study (Albrecht 1984), where differences in the network ties among managers were related to their personal definitions of the self, job, perceptions of relationships to others, and selected motivational factors. We also found that those differences in cognitive structures held across three points in time. Figures 1 and 2 show how linkers (defined as network bridges and liaisons) differed in their cognitive perceptions from nonlinkers. Figure 1 is based on the ways linkers versus nonlinkers perceived that the concept of "my job" related to other key concepts in the workplace; figure 2 shows how these associations varied when the key concepts were related to the self concept (i.e., "me").

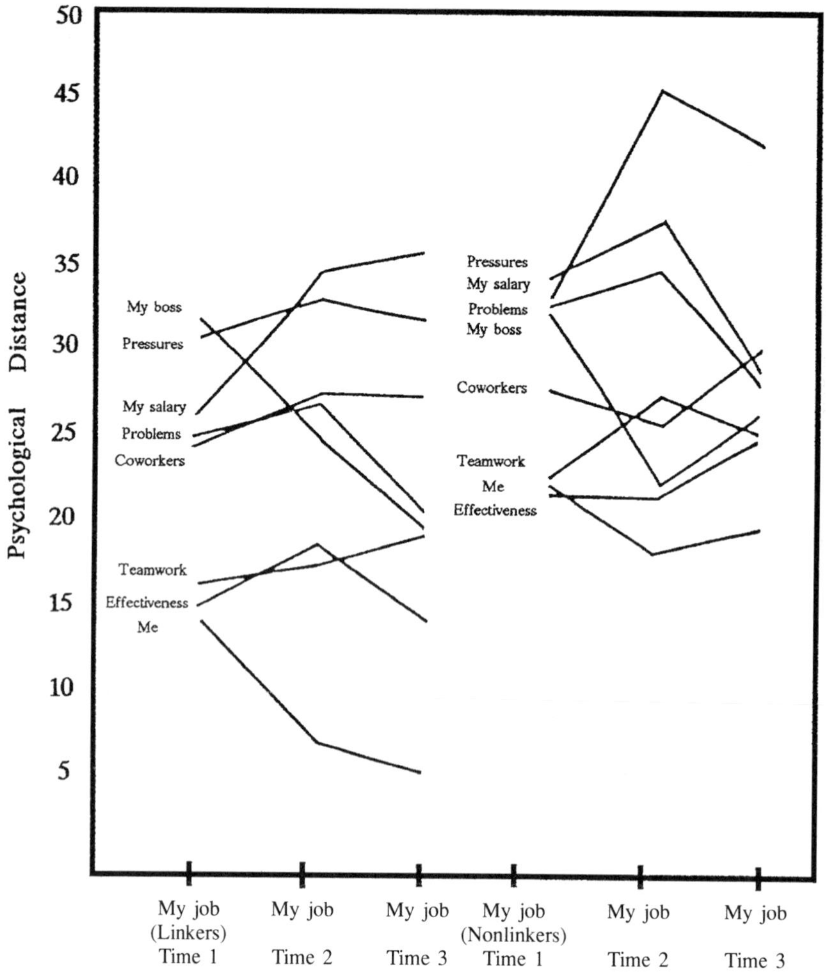

Fig. 1.1. Differences in job perceptions between linkers and nonlinkers across three points in time (Albrecht, 1984, p. 548)

Having established the general association between patterns of social structure and patterns of cognition, we moved to investigate how such patterns are related to interactions in which cognitive uncertainty was more directly relevant to the content of discussion. We explored how emergent relational patterns among organization members functioned to balance and hence help to manage the level of uncertainty associated with some types of interaction.

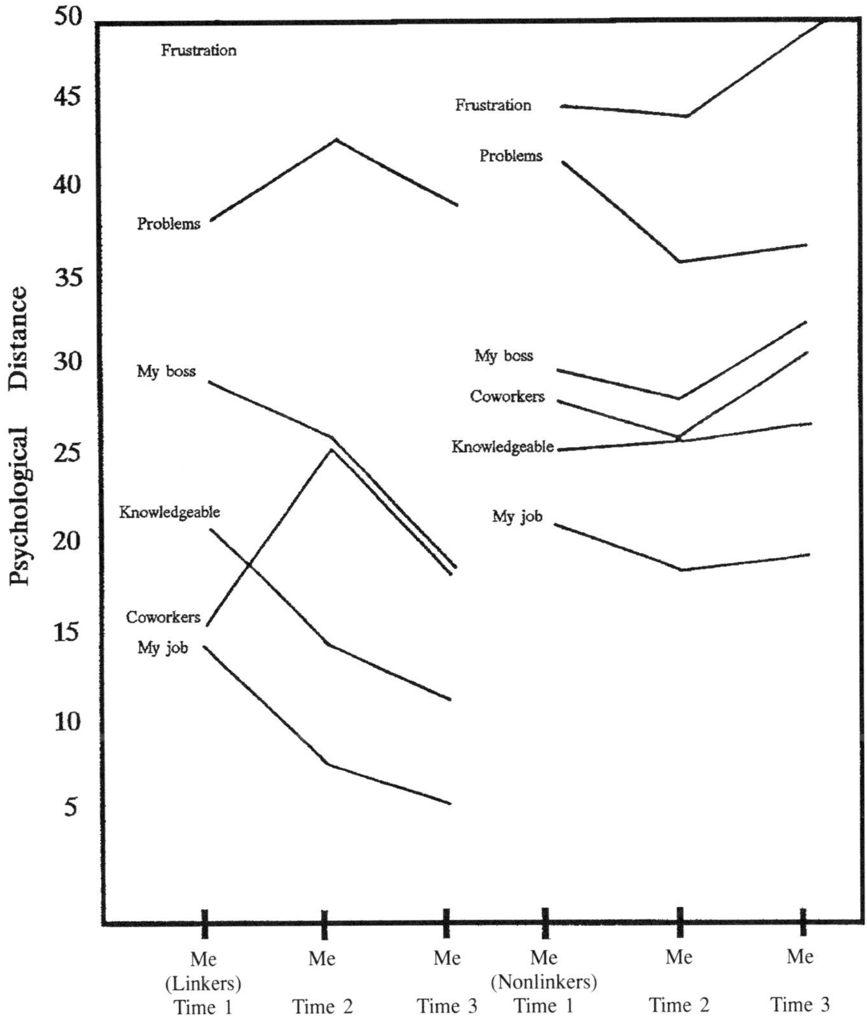

Fig. 1.2. Differences in self perceptions between linkers and nonlinkers across three points in time (Albrecht, 1984, p. 549)

COMMUNICATION STRUCTURES OF INNOVATION AND UNCERTAINTY

The genesis of this phrase of the research program dated to the early network studies we conducted in pursuit of other types of empirical and theoretic questions. These earlier studies centered principally on investigating the nature of job networks and the density/connectivity levels among individuals for efficient task accomplishment. Most communication network studies in the 1970s tended to follow the operational form of asking respondents to estimate the number of times they had interacted with each named contact in the system regarding each of three categories of content: work, social/maintenance, and innovation (see, for example, Farace, Monge, and Russell 1977). The assumption was that each category of general message content represents a different network structure. Thus, organizational members may be connected together in at least three different network patterns based on their types of talk (i.e., about job/task, social/maintenance, and innovation). A typical network data set for members of most organizations we studied tended to show relatively higher rates of interaction in both the job and social networks (though often dissimilar sociograms for the two) than in the innovation network. Close examination of the data also tended to reveal that the pattern of talk about innovation was much more restricted. A link reported by a respondent to a given contact in the innovation network tended to be one that also occurred in both the job and social nets. It is not surprising that an innovation tie between two individuals would overlap with a work tie. What was interesting to us was the consistent overlap with the social/maintenance category as well. It was this apparent *social* influence involved in the process, the role of perceived, social/personal communication, that captured our empirical attention. We began to ask whether social/personal talk serves as a kind of relational "fuel" for the kind of communication that carries a clear professional and/or personal element of risk.

The initial hypothesis for this type of communication pattern was the notion that new ideas are inherently uncertainty-producing. This would be particularly true in turbulent, competitive, low trust organizational settings. We argued that innovation-related topics are discussed in close, well-developed relationships, ones in which there is lower uncertainty toward the other party. Such ties would be well-developed at a social cognitive level (and hence carry greater interpersonal knowledge/certainty) because other types of information contents were also exchanged.

This also suggested that perhaps a paradox existed regarding communication about innovation (or other uncertainty-producing types of messages). An essential tension is inherent in the fact that much of communication occurs between people who have close network relationships (and thus probably have come to share similar perspectives) and the fact that in such relationships the potential dangers exist of pressures for groupthink and conformity. For people to discuss innovation, a reduction of interpersonal uncertainty is necessary (often expeditiously accomplished through the exchange of information about other topics). But an optimal level of psychological distance and uncertainty is necessary for the ideas to be promising and creative.

Our first empirical study to address this question was Albrecht and Ropp (1984). The main operational indicator of level of relationship was content multiplexity (again, defined as the extent to which two people in a relation-

Table 1.1. Comparison of innovation ties and average link strength with other types of network links (time 1 data)

	Electronics plant (n = 57)		Engineering firm (n = 113)		Social services department (n = 95)	
	Links n	Link Strength $\bar{x}$	Links n	Link Strength $\bar{x}$	Links n	Link Strength $\bar{x}$
Work ties only	571	5.06	1420	4.01	1080	3.37
Social ties only	144	2.13	962	4.26	72	2.28
Innovation ties only	26	2.08	17	3.44	6	1.30
Work and social ties only	306	9.26	887	13.40	274	9.21
Social and innovation ties only	36	2.67	15	2.54	1	1.00
Work, social, and innovation ties	289	5.16	514	8.46	188	3.89
Total	1508		4030		1694	

Note. Link strength equals the total number of conversations. Link strengths for all mixed-innovation ties represent only the number of interactions about innovation-related content.

Source: Albrecht & Ropp, 1984, p. 84.

ship talk about multiple topics such as work, social activities, new ideas, etc.). The more varied the information content perceived to flow in a link between two individuals, the more shared knowledge we hypothesized that each party had about the other and the nature of their relationship. We collected data in three organizations: an electronics plant and a social welfare department in the Southwest and an engineering firm in the Pacific Northwest. Tables 1 and 2 are displays of the findings on the distribution of link types in those data. The result was clear: talk about innovation was most likely to appear in multiplex innovation links and it was in these links that such talk occurred most often.

In addition, we found that same-status persons in multiplex links reported they discussed new ideas more frequently than did those in mixed status links. This evidence further added to our argument that relational uncertainty (more likely in superior-subordinate ties) is a factor in the types of relationships that can best (or least) tolerate the communication of potentially uncertainty-laden messages. Talk about innovation was also significantly less voluminous than talk about work and social topics. For example, in the three wave panel study of the electronics plant, the frequency of interaction involving new ideas was stable at only about thirteen percent of the volume of all reported talk. New ideas comprised approximately seventeen percent of all

Table 1.2. Chi-square analyses of differences in distributions of link types (time 1 data)

	Electronics plant (n = 57) Links		Engineering firm (n = 113) Links		Social services department (n = 95) Links	
	n	%	n	%	n	%
High multiplexity						
Work, social, and innovation ties	289	59	514	69	188	70
Low multiplexity						
Work and innovation ties	136	28	215	29	73	27
Social and innovation ties	36	7	15	2	1	1
Uniplex links	26	5	17	2	6	2
Innovation ties only	487	100	747	100	268	100
	$x^2 = 367.12$, df = 3, $p < .001$		$x^2 = 873.35$, df = 3, $p < .001$		$x^2 = 339.6$, df = 3, $p < .001$	

Source: Albrecht & Ropp, 1984, p. 85.

forms of interaction in the engineering firm, and only about seven percent of all the talk reported in the social welfare department was about innovation. Thus, talk about work and social topics dominated interaction, comprising approximately 83–93 percent of the total reported communication.

Having discovered this prominent pattern, we sought a fuller explanation of the findings in the multidisciplinary organizational literature. However, we found little of a social structural or a social cognitive nature to assist us with our theoretical understanding of the phenomenon. For example, the diffusion studies of Rogers (see Rogers 1983; Rogers and Shoemaker 1971) showed that successful dissemination of new products and ideas was dependent on reaching the target group through appropriate channels and on persuasive messages tailored to the existing beliefs, cognitions, and needs of the group. In a study of five companies, Kanter (1982; 1983) found that the most innovative companies were those that encouraged collaboration and allowed varied types of information to flow freely. These companies featured coalitions built of supporters of ideas, particularly middle managers, who collaboratively engineered ideas into action. However, the descriptive nature of Kanter's research still did not adequately explain for theory-building purposes why highly multiplex ties are the most probable pathways for talk about innovation.

Perhaps the closest theoretic perspective on the shapes and textures of social structures most likely to foster such talk is the well-known *strength of weak ties hypothesis* (Granovetter 1973, 1982; see also Adelman, Parks, and Albrecht 1987; Parks 1982; Rogers and Kincaid 1982). Basing their arguments principally on data from community network studies, proponents of this hypothesis assert that most new information is diffused, not through strong ties, but rather through secondary (though perhaps demographically homophilous) relationships outside the individual's primary group of dense network ties. According to Granovetter, strong ties are those relationships a focal individual has with significant family members, friends, work associates, etc., who also have ties to one another (hence the "density" of such clusters). A "weak-tie" is a relationship the focal individual has with someone who is outside of this cluster (one who is not tied to anyone else in the primary group).

A particular "strength" of a weak tie for the focal individual is the potential benefit that can come from the types of people with whom the weak tie is linked. Studies of weak ties have shown that it is through these so-called second order connections that focal individuals are most likely to gain information and referrals to find a job or health care resources in the community, be introduced to a new romantic partner, or gain new ideas for enhancing role and life transitions (Adelman et al. 1987; Hirsch 1980; McKinlay 1973). Weak ties may often be uniplex in character (meaning the content of messages exchanged is highly limited to only one or two topics). (Indeed, the actual contact that occurred may not even be remembered by the focal individual.) However, the idea that was communicated generally remains salient to the focal individual long after experiencing interaction with weak tie contacts.

The strength of weak ties hypothesis provided us with a contrasting perspective to frame our views on perceived uncertainty in message content and relationships. We did not reject the logical and empirical legitimacy of the hypothesis in general. However, the initial findings on multiplexity and innovation, together with the uncertainty-based explanation we had developed earlier, formed the basis for our argument that the weak ties position is curbed in the politically charged context of a formal or informal organization. Revolutionary ideas may enter an organization through weak external links. But once inside, the webs of multiplex relations that exist are likely the central, though restricted, pathways for the innovation process to take shape.

Addressing the weak ties hypothesis as an extant competing perspective was our first task. The question persisted as to why multiplexity was such a prominent factor. The extent to which persons were closely associated in the network seemed to be the common characteristic of the kinds of links that individuals reported in the innovation network. Our reasoning for this phenomenon developed based on certain assumptions about the communication of risk and an extension of the original thinking about relational uncertainty. As valuable as talk about new ideas is to an organization's viability in adapting and coping with turbulent environmental conditions, such talk is also potentially costly. New ideas represent risk because (1) these interactions can convey images of disruption to familiar routines, network relationships, power balances, and job security; and (2) proposing a new idea invites evaluation from others who are co-members of the same organizational network. One's self-concept is thus precariously exposed to others in the same political arena. It is not surprising, then, that our early studies found this type of talk to be relatively rare.

These data served as license for us to develop our theoretic assumptions regarding the quality of cognitive attributions individuals make about the relationships in which they discuss their ideas. We extended our conceptual frame to the practical force that face (Goffman, 1967) has in affecting decisions about the types of interactions an individual engages in, and how this process intertwines with the notion of cognitive uncertainty.

Goffman argued that individuals will seek to protect their own demeanor and the other's deference or face wants. Face is, of course, the public self-image that an individual wants to claim for him or herself. Obviously, talk about new ideas is potentially face-threatening given tacit cultural expectations that evaluative comments will likely follow disclosure of an idea.[3] Impending evaluations of one's ideas produce uncertainty regarding the valence of the other's evaluation as well as the possible use the other will make of the idea (i.e., theft for furthering one's own self-interests).

Scheff (1990) recently developed Goffman's perspective in asserting that the experience of shame is the principal social emotion operant in a social system (as is the experience of pride). Shame signals to the self and to the other an emotional state of the relationship and indicators of the presence of shame reflects a broken or endangered tie. Multiplexity in a relationship is therefore relevant, given that it can be a signal of the level of trust, certainty, and stability between two people. An individual would be unlikely to maintain a highly multiplex tie without some requisite certainty and trust, necessary for offsetting the potential risk of experiencing shame in interactions within the relationship and in the network as a whole. In effect, greater uncertainty and risk existing at the level of topic or content is at least partially balanced by the certainty felt toward the partner at the relational and network level.

The next two studies in our research program were attempts to empirically support this framework (both reported in Albrecht and Hall 1991b). First, using the link as the level of analysis, we sought to extend our findings on multiplexity by evaluating the affective nature and relational certainty associated with strong links. We conducted interviews and administered network surveys to members of a radiation oncology department in a major Northwest medical center. The unit had tripled in size in the previous seven years and the respondents represented a heterogeneous mix of research scientists, medical and human service professionals, and administrative support staff from around the world. We selected this setting because it was a highly differentiated system where new ideas and change were expected to be omnipresent in routine discourse among departmental members. Our task was to replicate the finding that highly multiplex channels would be the likely structures for talk about innovation. We also sought to explain the nature of these multiplex ties. We expected, based on the deference and demeanor conceptualization, that relationships in which people talked about innovation would also be higher in credibility, influence, trust, support, importance, and perceived receptivity to new ideas. We also hypothesized that the frequency of innovation talk would positively correlate with certainty toward the partner, perceived work compatibility, and aspects of satisfaction with the relationship overall.

We used the roster method to collect the network data. For each contact, respondents indicated whether they discussed any of six different topic areas and rated the relationship on such characteristics as trust, credibility, supportiveness, and importance. Respondents also filled out a separate form for each link regarding frequency of talk about innovation, satisfaction with communication about innovation, work compatibility, relationship uncertainty, and overall relationship satisfaction. As expected, we found that talk about innovation occurred in only about twenty-five percent of the links reported at Time 1. Of these links, two-thirds were highly multiplex and characterized as significantly more important, supportive, and credible.

Aggregated, Unaggregated, and De-meaned Data

A pivotal aspect of the interplay of concept-data-method in handling sociometric data is the question of the level of analysis to be used and implications for the types of statistical tests that can be applied. This was a challenge for us: the multiplexity hypothesis for talk about uncertainty is a statement about the type of relationship that exists. The conceptual unit of analysis is the dyad. However, the number of relationships (that form the total number of cases in the sample) are produced by a much smaller number of individuals.[4] One cannot assume that the cases reported are independent from one another (a single individual may produce up to n–1 cases). That is, judgments that a respondent makes regarding any one relationship may be affected in some way by the kinds of judgments made of one or more of the other relationships. This is methodologically problematic because many statistical tests (i.e., analysis of variance, correlation) assume clear independence of cases because nonindependence of data tend to yield biased, inflated statistical coefficients as results. There are at least two possible corrections for the problem. The first is simply to aggregate the judgments made by each individual by averaging the scores on trust, credibility, and other variables across the spectrum of links reported. However, this procedure was unsatisfactory for us because information is lost in the averaging process and more

Table 1.3. Correlations between communication frequency about innovation and perceptions of relationship uncertainty, satisfaction and compatibility

Relationship variables (Composite & individual items)	$r(n = 500)$ $p < .001$
Satisfaction with Innovation Communication	.61
—discussion about innovations are/could be rewarding	.51
—will want to talk about innovation in the future with contact	.66
—feel comfortable talking with contact about my ideas	.38
—talk/brainstorming about new ideas with contact has or could improve work relationship overall	.51
Work Compatibility	.57
—contact understands work I do	.52
—kind of work I do similar to contact	.49
Relationship Certainty	.55
—know contact well	.54
—can predict how contact will react to my ideas	.48
Relationship Dissatisfaction	.18
—dissatisfied with work relationship	.17
—fear contact will ridicule my ideas	.15

$p < .001$
Source: Albrecht & Hall, 1991b, p. 281.

important, reducing the relational data to the individual level is inconsistent with the dyad as the conceptual and therefore operational unit of analysis.

Another correlation (the one we adopted) is a process of "demeaning" the data.[5] The average reported judgments on a given variable (such as "trust") across an individual's set of links is subtracted from each score on that variable for each relationship reported. The resulting de-meaned or residualized score for the trust level of a given relationship is assumed to contain information unique to the judgment of that link, minus the average influence of judgments of all other links.

We correlated the residualized scores with frequency of talk about innovation and found positive associations with satisfaction with innovation communication, work compatibility, and relationship certainty (see table 3).

Our objective in the second study was to refine our measures and examine not only content but also relationship multiplexity. We wanted to demonstrate that a "quality" of network access could be found through the types of relational labels respondents used to characterize their work links. This could be another indicator of how people manage cognitive risk-uncertainty. We selected teachers and administrators from three buildings in an affluent suburban school district. The district was undergoing a number of changes due

Table 1.4. Frequency distribution for multiplexity categories and mean differences for amount of innovation talk

Content Multiplexity Level	*N*	%[a]	%[b]	*M*(s)
(1) Innov. only (uniplex)	50	3.3	7.2	2.22(1.73)
(2) Innov. + one other topic	185	12.2	26.8	2.01(2.03)
(3) Innov. + two other topics	185	12.2	26.8	2.07(1.97)
(4) Innov. + three other topics	271	17.9	39.2	3.83(5.89)
Total	691	45.6	100.0	

[a]percentages are based on all links (innovation and non-innovation ties)
[b]percentages are based on innovation links only
Source: Albrecht & Hall, 1991b, p. 283.

to multiple administrative and curricular shifts, and staff members had experienced considerable anxiety and uncertainty due to budget cutbacks and dismal long-range enrollment projections. We targeted public school educators for the societal importance of their occupations and their critical need for innovation and adaptation, particularly in periods of economic downturn.[6]

Relationship multiplexity is the extent to which two people are connected by multiple role requirements such as being friends, coworkers, as well as possibly golf partners (Tichy, Tushman, and Fombrun 1979). This allows system members to develop different kinds of relationships, with each shared event and setting affording an opportunity to glean more data on the other's behavior (further reducing uncertainty and increasing attributional confidence). Another example of the benefits of role multiplexity is illustrated in the work of Kanter (1982), who found that innovative middle managers were those who had opportunities to meet a variety of others in the organization often, under differing circumstances, and were thus able to form different types of work and social relationships with these people. This fostered the exchange of ideas and more expedient resources to implement proposals. Role multiplexity in our study was measured by having respondents report as many hierarchical, work, and social/personal relationships as they had with each contact.

Once again, we found in this study that content multiplexity was related to talk about new ideas (see the percentage breakdowns in table 4). Forty percent of the links where innovation was discussed were highly multiplex ties; such talk occurred in only forty-five percent of all reported communication links.

Relationship multiplexity did emerge as a factor in how people gauged their talk. Talk about ideas was reported by superiors, coworkers, and subordinates almost twice as much in ties where a type of relationship beyond just a status link was reported and almost three times as much in links where the contact was also perceived as a close friend. The greatest amount of interaction

Table 1.5. Correlations and partial correlations for frequency of talk about innovation and content variables 1555)[a]

Content Variables	*r*	partial corr
Work	.73*	.59*
Social/personal	.68*	.44*
gossip/griping	.64*	–.23**

[a]*Note.* Data represent de-meaned, residualized scores.
* p < .001
** p < .01

regarding innovation occurred in close friend ties across mixed-status and same-status links, but these were comparatively the fewest types of relationships reported. Given that relationship multiplexity and content multiplexity were unrelated (r = .02 n.s.), it remains a testable hypothesis as to whether these types of perceived connections among members of a system operate on differing dimensions of relational uncertainty and face threat.

Finally, again using residualized scores, we determined that talk about new ideas was positively related to different content areas. As shown in table 5, the simple bivariate correlations were strong, as were the partial correlation coefficients when each type of content was controlled. That is, the correlation between talk about new ideas and talk about work is $r = .59$, $p < .001$; the correlation for talk about new ideas and social/personal communication content was also strong ($r = .44$, $p < .001$). Talk about new ideas and gossip/griping behavior was correlated at r = –.23, $p < .01$. From this finding, we conclude that interactions based on gossip and griping tended to impede productive talk about innovation.

In conducting subsequent clique-detecting network analyses of the data from the three sites in the school district (Albrecht and Hall 1991a), we originally expected to ascertain cognitive and communicative differences between linkers and nonlinkers in the innovation networks. These would have been similar to the distinctions we discovered in our initial studies (Albrecht 1979, 1984). However, even using the most stringent parameter settings for Richards's PCNEGOPY (1986) program, we were unable to break down the network structures into multiple cliques with linkers and nonlinkers. The output continued to display an apparent core inner group and extended outliers.

Further, as we studied the results, we discovered a pattern that more nearly reflected our original conceptual framework. The pattern was a classic insider/outsider schism that paralleled the research literature on elites and outsiders in social systems.

Our argument for the conceptualization and findings on insider cliques in innovation networks was based on the following reasoning: insiders or *elites* are the privileged members of any stratum whose connections are visible signs of their control of resources, information, and decision making. Outsiders do not normally benefit from informal power and are often outside of information circles and prime resource allocation.

The clustering patterns of elites as well as their influence may be in part explained from the uncertainty reduction framework. Individuals who are reacting to uncertainty-producing events are more likely to choose relationships that provide face support in political settings. It is clear why an elite group would emerge as the centroid of the network, as opposed to individual linkers. The elite group is a stronger unit, less precarious or vulnerable than an individual person. A coalition of elites has more mass in driving the scope of influence of ideas in the system.

We analyzed relational attributions and content data in a 2 x 2 table of elite and outsider sources rating their elite and outsider contacts (see Albrecht and Hall 1991b). Multivariate analysis of variance results showed a significant association between the source of the judgment and the dependent variables (lambda (5, 68) = .69, $p < .001$, $eta^2 = .31$) and between the type of target and the dependent variables (lambda (5, 68) = .77; $p < .005$) with a more modest shared variance of $eta^2 = .23$).

In short, elites in organizational innovation networks are perceived more positively than any other group in the system, even as attributed by non-elite outsiders. These perceptions appear to be self-reinforcing. Apparently, elites dominate interaction across a variety of topics, buttressing their ability to manipulate and manage uncertainty in the organization. The interpersonal behavior of elites, as well as their innovation behavior, thus creates an intriguing stronghold for sustained power and influence in the organization. Elite members monopolize an invaluable but fragile aspect of organizational life, the collective talk about new ideas for renewal. In doing so, they effectively reinforce their own positions of privilege, power, and influence.

Ultimately, the empirical support for cognition and communicative structure lies in the interface of the individual with the system. How does the individual correspond with the spectrum of his or her perceived ties? How does the individual's perception of his or her array of contacts compare with the independent perceptions that the contacts have of the individual? Our most recent investigation was an effort to examine the individual-network connection as it related to key factors of organizational identification and personal control, innovativeness, and support (Johnson, Albrecht, and Hall 1990).

We first assessed contacts as seen by the focal individual, and second, the focal individual as seen by his or her contacts. Once again, we moved back and forth between the individual and the network level of analysis to determine whether there were systematic patterns associated with these arrays of contacts (what we termed a "relational horizon"). Results generally showed that respondents' average ratings of their contacts' influence, trustworthiness, supportiveness, credibility, and receptivity to new ideas was related to respondents' perceptions of how well they identified with the organization. We then averaged the ratings the contacts made of their perceptions of the individual's influence, trustworthiness, supportiveness, credibility, and receptiveness to new ideas. We found that the average of these ratings that contacts made of the individual were correlated with the individual's own perceived organizational identification and innovativeness. The results are summarized below:

- Respondents who were rated by their contacts as more supportive, receptive, and trustworthy tended to report the higher identification with the organization.
- Respondents with a relatively higher level of perceived personal control were rated by their contacts as more influential.
- Personal control was associated with beliefs that one's network contacts provided more credible information, were more supportive, and were generally more receptive to new ideas.
- Persons with high personal control were rated by their network contacts as more innovative. Their contacts also reported a higher frequency of interaction about a greater variety of topics (i.e., contacts reported greater multiplexity with those who perceived themselves to have higher personal control).

In short, perceptions of control are likely more linked to what others think about the individual (and the ways they grant the individual control) than to the individual's perceptions of his/her ties.

CONCLUSION

Understanding the relationship between individual cognition and social structure has been a process of posing related questions and incrementally working toward answers. We began with the meta-theoretic principles of system theory to warrant the investigation of the individual-network interface. We then moved to a more focused framing of cognition and interaction based on the uncertainty-face threat framework. This has served as a flexible and integral base of sufficient conceptual scope to drive and sustain our research program based on individuals, relationships, and social clusters. We have been guided by multi-level theory and have employed the use of multi-level analysis. This theory-data symbiosis has enabled us to find that one's cognitive dispositions are a function of one's sociation patterns, that multiplex, personal network relationships are the natural contexts used for managing cognitive uncertainty, and that the individual's self-perception is tied more to how the individual's aggregated system (network structure) views him/her than to the individual's own myriad of network perceptions.

We began this chapter with a quote from Epstein (1979) on the social system enacted by survivors of the Holocaust in New York. The poignancy of that passage rests on how perceptions of a young girl's feelings of protection and "normalcy" were enmeshed in the sense of a shared speech community, however displaced the interwoven lives, in a network that had history and roots. Theories and data about individuals and their communication networks are remarkable vehicles for revealing to us the essential stores of personal identity, institutional development, sheer survival, and life.

NOTES

*The author would like to thank Brad Hall, Gerry Philipsen, Robert Ivie and Geriane Johnson for helpful comments and discussions.

1. The tie of "sociation" and "network" to the individual can be viewed in an evolutionary sense, what Fox (1989) calls an "ethosystem." He argues that organisms and social environments interact, such that biological states and individual traits are distributed across the macro system, based on shifting arrangements and combinations. Hence, the individual-social distinction is not "absolute; it is relative. . . . For most purposes the distinction is not useful" (121).

2. These include data analysis programs such as GALILEO (Gillham and Woelfel 1977; Woelfel and Fink 1980) and PCNEGOPY (Richards 1986).

3. I am especially grateful to Brad Hall for crafting this argument, which appeared in our earlier coauthored work.

4. For example, the 60 respondents in our study produced a relational data set of n cases = 1515. (The maximum n of relationships that could have been derived with 60 respondents can be calculated as $n(n - 1)$, where n = the number of individual respondents.)

5. We acknowledge Judee Burgoon for this suggestion.

6. The motivation for innovation was at a challenge point; there was a felt need for change yet resistance was rampant, along with a type of sluggish homeostasis in the bureaucratic system. Many of the teachers were unable (and some even unwilling) to move to building-based models of school management and administrative downsizing.

REFERENCES

Adelman, M. B., Parks, M. R., & Albrecht, T. L. (1987). Beyond close relationships: Support in weak ties. In T. L. Albrecht & M. B. Adelman & Assoc., *Communicating social support* (pp. 126–147). Newbury Park: Sage.

Albrecht, T. L. (1979). The role of communication in perceptions of organizational climate. In D. Nimmo (Ed.), *Communication yearbook 3* (pp. 343–357). New Brunswick: Transaction Books.

Albrecht, T. L. (1984). Managerial communication and work perception. In R. Bostrom (Ed.), *Communication yearbook 8* (pp. 538–557). Newbury Park: Sage.

Albrecht, T. L., & Hall, B. J. (1991a). Relational and content differences between elites and outsiders in innovation networks. *Human Communication Research 17*, 535–561.

Albrecht, T. L., & Hall, B. J. (1991b). Facilitating talk about new ideas: The role of personal relationships in organizational innovation. *Communication Monographs 58*, 273–288.

Albrecht, T. L., & Ropp, V. A. (1984). Communicating about innovation in networks of three U.S. organizations. *Journal of Communication 34*, 78–91.

Albrecht, T. L., Irey, K. V., & Mundy, A. (1982). Integration in communication networks as a mediator of stress. *Social Work 27*, 229–234.

Berger, C. R., & Calabrese, R. J. (1975). Some explorations in initial interaction and beyond: Toward a developmental theory of interpersonal communication. *Human Communication Research* 1, 99–112.

Bernard, H. R., & Killworth, P. D. (1978). A review of the small world literature. *Connections* 2, 15–24.

Epstein, H. (1979). *Children of the holocaust: Conversations with sons and daughters of survivors.* New York: G. P. Putnam & Sons.

Farace, R. V., Monge, P. R., Russell, H. (1977). *Communicating and organizing.* Reading, Mass.: Addison-Wesley.

Farace, R. V., Taylor, J. A., & Stewart, J. (1978). Criteria for evaluation of organizational communication effectiveness: Review and synthesis. In B. Ruben (Ed.), *Communication yearbook 2* (pp. 271–292). New Brunswick, N.J.: Transaction.

Fox, R. (1989). The search for society: *Quest for a biosocial science and morality.* New Brunswick: Rutgers University Press.

Gillham, J., & Woelfel, J. (1977). The Galileo system of measurement; Preliminary evidence for precision, stability, and equivalence to traditional measures. *Human Communication Research 3*, 222–234.

Goffman, E. (1967). *Interaction ritual.* Garden City, N.Y.: Anchor Books.

Granovetter, M. (1973). The strength of weak ties. *American Journal of Sociology 78*, 1361–1380.

Granovetter, M. (1982). The strength of weak ties: A network theory revisited. In P. V. Marsden & N. Lin (Eds.), *Social structure and network analysis* (pp. 105–130). Beverly Hills, Cal.: Sage.

Hirsch, B. J. (1980). Natural support systems and coping with major life changes. *American Journal of Community Psychology 7*, 263–277.

Johnson, G., Albrecht, T. L., & Hall, B. J. (1990, November). *In the eye of the beholder: Organizational identification and personal control in innovation networks.* Paper presented at the annual meeting of the Speech Communication Association, Chicago.

Johnson, J. C. (1986). Social networks and innovation adoption: A look at Burt's use of structural equivalence. *Social Networks 8*, 343–364.

Johnson, J. C., & Miller, M. L. (1986). Behavioral and cognitive data: A note on the multiplexity of network subgroups. *Social Networks 8*, 65–77.

Kanter, R. M. (1982). The middle manager as innovator. *Harvard Business Review 60*, 95–105.

Kanter, R. M. (1983). *The changemasters: Innovation and entrepreneurship in the American corporation.* New York: Simon & Schuster.

McGrath, B. B. (1986). The social networks of terminally ill skid road residents: An analysis. *Public Health Nursing 3*, 192–205.

McKinlay, J. B. (1973). Social networks, lay consultation and help seeking behavior. *Social Forces 51*, 275–292.

Mehan, H. (1978). Structuring school structure. *Harvard Educational Review 48*, 32–64.

Miller, K. I., & Monge, P. R. (1985). Social information and employee anxiety about organizational change. *Human Communication Research 11*, 365–386.

Moch, M. (1980). Job involvement, internal motivation, and employees' integration into networks of work relationships. *Organizational Behavior and Human Performance 25*, 15–31.

Monge, P. R., & Eisenberg, E. (1987). Emergent communication networks. In F. Jablin, L. Putnam, K. Roberts, & L. Porter (Eds.), *Handbook of organizational communication* (pp. 304–342). Newbury Park, Cal.: Sage.

Parks, M. R. (1982). Ideology in interpersonal communication: Off the couch and into the world. In M. Burgoon (Ed.), *Communication yearbook 5* (pp. 79–107). New Brunswick, N.J.: Transaction Books.

Parks, M. P., & Adelman, M. B. (1983). Communication networks and the development of romantic relationships: An expansion of uncertainty reduction theory. *Human Communication Research 10*, 55–79.

Peters, T. (1988). *Thriving on chaos.* New York: Alfred A. Knopf.

Richards, W. R. (1986). *The NEGOPY network analysis program.* Burnaby, B. C.: Simon Fraser University, Department of Communication, Laboratory for Computer and Communication Research.

Roberts, K. H., & O'Reilly, C. A. (1978). Organizations as communication structures: An empirical approach. *Human Communication Research 4*, 283–293.

Rogers, E. M. (1983). *Diffusion of innovations.* New York: The Free Press.

Rogers, E. M., & Kincaid, L. (1981). *Communication networks: Toward a new paradigm for research.* New York: The Free Press.

Rogers, E. M., & Shoemaker, F. L. (1971). *Communication of innovations: A cross-cultural approach.* New York: The Free Press.

Rolland, I., & Jansen, R. (1981). Total involvement as a productivity strategy. *California Management Review 24*, 40–48.

Salzinger, L. L. (1982). The ties that bind: The effect of clustering on dyadic relationships. *Social Networks 4*, 117–145.

Scheff, T. J. (1990). *Microsociology: Discourse, emotion and social structure.* Chicago: University of Chicago Press.

Tichy, N. M., Tushman, M., & Fombrun, C. (1979). Social network analysis for organizations. *Academy of Management Review 4*, 507–519.

Truex, G. F. (1981). Kinship and network: A cognitive model of interaction. *Social Networks 3*, 53–70.

Walker, G. (1985). Network position and cognition in a computer software firm. *Administrative Science Quarterly 30*, 103–130.

Weick, K. (1979). *The social psychology of organizing.* Reading Mass.: Addison-Wesley.

Woelfel, J., & Fink, E. L. (1980). *The measurement of communication processes: Galileo theory and method.* New York: Academic Press.

Wolff, K. H. trans. (1950). *The sociology of Georg Simmel.* New York: The Free Press.

2

Message Production under Uncertainty

CHARLES R. BERGER

Uncertainty is a key ingredient of social interactions occurring in virtually all communication contexts, whether these interactions involve complete strangers or individuals who share a lengthy relationship history. Even those who believe that they "know each other well" may find that their ability to predict and explain each others' beliefs and actions is impaired in particular encounters, thus making interaction both awkward and difficult to accomplish (Planalp & Honeycutt 1985; Planalp, Rutherford, & Honeycutt 1988). Since physical and social-psychological change is constant, the multitude of explicit and implicit choices that interlocutors must make concerning what they will say to one another and how they will say it necessarily involves considerable decision making under uncertainty. Words that may offend on one occasion may become the object of humor on another. The same smile displayed at two different times may be subject to diametrically opposed interpretations by the same person. Such uncertainties may make the task of individual message creators and interpreters, who may be attempting to reach particular instrumental and discourse goals, particularly difficult.

These uncertainties are even more pronounced for those communicating through the mass media. In these mediated communication venues, individuals must formulate and disseminate their messages without the benefit of direct feedback from those who are destined to receive them. In short, the acts of opening one's mouth to speak or putting pen to paper are inherently risky, whether one is involved in ongoing face-to-face interactions or creating mass media messages. In all of these communication contexts intentions may be misconstrued, producing potential negative consequences ranging from mid-air collisions between aircraft, through ruined reputations of highly visible public figures, to the hurt feelings of family members, friends, and lovers.

This chapter will explore the myriad of relationships between uncertainty and social interaction processes. In the first section, an account of the development of Uncertainty Reduction Theory or URT will be presented (Berger 1979, 1987, 1988a; Berger & Bradac 1982; Berger & Calabrese 1975; Berger & Gudykunst 1991). As this narrative will demonstrate, much of the research spawned by URT has focused on the strategies that individuals use to reduce their uncertainties about others, and the influence uncertainty exerts on behavior during initial encounters between strangers. Since this research has been reviewed in detail elsewhere (Berger & Gudykunst 1991), only a brief outline of this work will be provided. In the second section of this chapter, attention will be directed toward a phenomenon that research driven by URT has yet to address. This issue concerns the strategies that individuals use when they are forced, as they inevitably are, to generate and deliver messages under uncertainty. A significant postulate undergirding this discussion is that in all social interactions some measure of uncertainty exists and that the potentially negative effects of this uncertainty must be hedged against in order to avoid such undesirable interaction outcomes as failing to reach instrumental goals, being misunderstood, or angering, hurting, or embarrassing others.

Of course, on occasion, individuals may have as their primary goal the induction of such negative emotional states in others (Petronio, Snyder, & Bradford 1992). Moreover, under certain conditions, individuals might, with malice or forethought, render their intentions ambiguous through strategic control of their verbal and nonverbal actions (Goffman 1969). Nevertheless, like Goffman (1959) and Brown and Levinson (1978, 1987), I assume that in the great majority of social encounters, individuals have an implicit social contract stipulating that they will endeavor to save each others' faces as well as their own as they pursue other goals. Furthermore, consistent with Grice's (1975) conversational maxims, it is plausible to assume that in a large majority of their conversations participants are bound by convention to be as truthful and unambiguous as possible in expressing their intentions and as relevant as possible in responding to their partners. These notions follow directly from Grice's (1975) quantity, quality, relation, and manner maxims. Consequently, although intended ambiguity is more the exception than the rule in daily interactions, even under the full force of conversational maxims, residual uncertainties remain and must be taken into account.

WHY UNCERTAINTY REDUCTION THEORY (URT)?

Although readers already familiar with URT would very likely answer this question by referencing the formal axiomatic presentation of the theory (Berger & Calabrese 1975), URT had its origins in even hoarier texts than this one and in heretofore unstated premises. Of course, any attempt to provide a complete and fully accurate account of the development of URT at this point in time would be futile; however, there are a number of obvious influences that shaped the theory's development.

"The Acquaintance Process Revisited"

An unpublished paper by this title reported the results of systematic observations of unobtrusively tape recorded initial conversations between college students who were complete strangers to each other (Berger 1973). There were several motivations for this investigation. One of these stemmed from deficiencies of previous research investigating the friendship formation among students living in a special research house. Newcomb (1961) reported, in his book *The Acquaintance Process*, that students who shared similar attitudes and values were more likely to become friends with each other than students who displayed dissimilar attitudes and values. However, although Newcomb's study involved systematic interviews and observations of the students, there was no attempt to examine their interactions with each other in any detail; that is, while students were interviewed intensively over the course of the research project, there was virtually no direct analysis of their conversations. Thus, this study was undertaken to fill in this gap left by Newcomb.

As the tapes of these initial conversations between strangers were transcribed, it became apparent that the first few minutes of the conversations involved content and floor exchange patterns that were extremely similar across nearly all of them. There was so much similarity among the conversations that it became an exercise in boredom to transcribe them; they were, in large part, extremely predictable. Such questions as "Where are you from?," "What's your major?," and "What dorm do you live in?" were asked with great regularity. Moreover, such other potentially relevant questions as "What is your grade point average?" or "Are you liberal or conservative?" never were asked during the conversations. In addition to these highly predictable content features, there was an equally highly predictable question-answer exchange structure in these conversations. When individuals provided a piece of information about themselves in answer to their partner's request for the information, they subsequently requested the same type of information from their partner. This pattern of question-asking and question-answering was taken as evidence for the operation of the norm of reciprocity during initial interactions between strangers (Gouldner 1960).

In an action pattern as predictable as the ones just described, skeptics responded to the findings reported in the paper with the "college sophomores as subjects" canard. These critics asserted that the patterns of content and structure observed in these initial interactions were simply unique to college students and were not typical of the initial interaction patterns that might be observed in other subject populations. However, our subsequent informal observations of initial interactions between non-college student strangers meeting at cocktail parties suggested interaction patterns similar to those observed among the students. While it is true that non-students would be unlikely to ask for each other's major, they would very frequently ask the functionally equivalent question: What do you do (for a living)? Moreover, the question-answer format observed in the student interactions also was apparent in these non-student interactions. Additional triangulating evidence concerning the nature of these initial interactions was provided by Altman and Taylor (1973), who described initial conversations between strangers in manner similar to the characterization presented in the paper. Moreover, a large-scale study of a random sample of adults living in a Chicago suburb (N = 204) revealed patterns of information sequencing in initial interactions similar to those observed in actual interactions between strangers (Berger, Gardner, Clatterbuck, & Schulman 1976). Contrary to the skeptics' claims, then, the patterns reported by Berger (1973) appear to be quite robust across a variety of subject populations (see Kellermann 1991; Kellermann, Broetzmann, Lim, & Kitao 1989; Kellermann & Lim 1990).

Why These Patterns?

Just as the sun rises in the East and sets in the West, predictable patterns of social interaction, like those observed when strangers meet, beg for explanation. One non-explanation-explanation for such patterns is to label them "communication rituals" and to pretend that the act of labeling the pattern serves to explain it. However, this exercise in hypostatization does little, if anything, to explain why such predictable interaction patterns occur during initial encounters between total strangers. As a result, Berger and Calabrese (1975) devised a formal, axiomatic theory, which has come to be called Uncertainty Reduction Theory (URT), consisting of seven axioms and twenty-one derived theorems, to explain patterns of verbal and non-verbal behavior observed during initial encounters between strangers. The theory argued that strangers have little basis for predicting each other's beliefs and attitudes, so that these conversational topics are avoided in favor of the exchange of more neutral biographical and demographic information.

While Altman and Taylor (1973) argued that such biographic and demographic information is "superficial," Berger (1975) demonstrated how perceptions of increased similarity along demographic lines could produce increased estimates of belief and attitude similarity. The initial interaction "ritual," then, serves as a convenient way of dealing with the high levels of uncertainty inherent in encounters between strangers. Berger and Calabrese (1975) also observed that one could not only experience uncertainty regarding the beliefs and potential actions of one's interaction partner, one could also encounter considerable uncertainty concerning the actions, including verbal and nonverbal communicative acts, that one might deploy to achieve one's goals in the interaction. In general, uncertainty reduction was seen as a prerequisite for achieving the level of control necessary to achieve one's instrumental and interaction goals.

One early objection to this theoretical account asserted that individuals might not wish to expend the time and energy necessary to reduce their uncertainties about a stranger. In response to this possibility, Berger (1979) stipulated the conditions that give rise to increased motivation to reduce uncertainty. Specifically, he argued that when co-interactants (1) have the ability to mete out rewards and/or punishments, (2) are likely to be encountered in subsequent interactions, and (3) act in unpredictable ways, individuals are more likely to be motivated to reduce their uncertainties about their partners, although the viability of the third antecedent was later questioned, because individuals might be "put off" by another's deviant behavior (Berger 1987). While some evidence supported the prediction that both outcome dependence and anticipated initial interaction led individuals to gather more information about a potential partner (Berscheid, Graziano, Monson, & Dermer 1976; Calabrese 1975; Harvey, Yarkin, Lightner, & Town 1980), other evidence suggested that after an initial interaction, individuals anticipating a second interaction did not necessarily increase their information-gathering efforts when their outcomes were dependent on their partner and when their partner behaved in a deviant manner (Douglas 1987; Kellermann & Reynolds 1990); however, in this latter study subjects were asked to respond to hypothetical scenarios, thus raising the usual questions concerning the external validity of the study's findings. Moreover, in a study in which strangers engaged in initial interactions, Douglas (1993) reported that individuals anticipating future interaction demonstrated more information-seeking behavior during their conversations than did their counterparts who did not anticipate future interaction. Berger and Douglas (1981) also found that, in contrast to people not anticipating interaction with a specific target stranger, those anticipating interaction tended to judge slides picturing the target stranger in informal social situations to be more informative than did the individuals who did not anticipate interaction. This finding was interpreted as support for the notion that those anticipating interaction experienced greater motivation to reduce their uncertainty and did so by being more attentive to slides depicting the target stranger to informal social situations, situations that provide observers with more uncertainty-reducing information than do formal ones.

The original version of URT implied that uncertainty would be reduced over time, as individuals interacted with each other. Indeed, considerable evidence has supported this claim (Clatterbuck 1979; Douglas 1990; VanLear & Trujillo 1986). This general trend was questioned, however, in two studies that suggested that even in established relationships, vents might occur that undermine the beliefs interaction partners hold about each other, thus raising their uncertainty levels (Planalp & Honeycutt 1985; Planalp, Rutherford, & Honeycutt 1988). These studies demonstrated that such events as finding out that one's relational partner is cheating or that one's partner is spreading negative information about one to others were the kinds of revelations that increased uncertainties in established relationships. The great majority of these uncertainty-increasing events reported by respondents were negative in tone, even though in the abstract one could experience pleasant surprises from a relationship partner. These negative events not only increased uncertainty, they served to reduce satisfaction with the relationship.

Finally, it has been suggested that URT is not an adequate theory of relationship development. Sunnafrank's (1986) reincarnation of URT labeled Predicted Outcome Value (POV) theory asserts that individuals in relationships are preoccupied with maximizing rewards from relationships and minimizing costs (Adams 1965; Homans 1961, 1974; Roloff 1981; Thibaut & Kelley 1959). Given this preoccupation, he argues, individuals will not attempt to reduce their uncertainties about each other unless they feel that their relationships are likely to yield a favorable reward-cost ratio. As the careful reader will notice, however, this postulate is identical to the first antecedent condition to uncertainty reduction specified by Berger (1979) and discussed above; that is, individuals will increase their uncertainty reduction efforts when they believe others can control the outcomes they will experience.

Unfortunately, Sunnafrank (1986) missed a critical point concerning the relationship between uncertainty reduction and the reward-cost calculations he and equity theorists allege those involved in relationships make. Specifically, assuming that such calculations are made, it must be assumed further that, in the context of developing relationships, arriving at these estimates is itself an exercise in uncertainty reduction (Berger 1986). Such estimates, if they exist, are not givens at the onset of an initial encounter between strangers; rather, they are developed based on information gleaned during initial and ensuing encounters, and these estimates are constantly modified over time. Thus, to claim that predicted outcome values somehow supersede uncertainty reduction efforts is misguided, because the predictions of outcome values are arrived at through the acquisition of information about one's interaction partner, information that reduces uncertainty.

Although the status of URT as a theory of relationship development can be questioned, the assertion that individuals involved in social interactions and in relationships must reduce their uncertainties about each other so that they can engage in adaptive behavior seems unassailable (Berger 1987, 1988a). Part of this adaptive exercise involves making inferences about the outcomes that the relationship is likely to produce. Moreover, studies of developing relationships have demonstrated that individuals' uncertainty levels may mediate relationship outcomes, suggesting that uncertainty reduction processes may play a significant role in determining relationship outcomes. In support of this expectation, Parks and Adelman (1983) reported that relationships between romantically involved couples showed longer survival rates when those involved in them evidenced lower uncertainty levels concerning each other. Similarly, Cate (1991) found evidence supporting the proposition that decreased uncertainty levels promote higher levels of relational satisfaction; a similar finding was reported by Surra and Bohman (1991). Consistent with these findings, additional studies generally have reported inverse relationships between uncertainty and interpersonal attraction, that is, high levels of uncertainty associated with low attraction levels (Clatterbuck 1979; Van Lear & Trujillo 1986). Given this relatively high level of consistency across studies, it would seem premature to dismiss uncertainty as a potentially important correlate of relationship outcomes.

HEDGING AGAINST UNCERTAINTY

As the preceding discussion indicates, URT has been invoked to explain a variety of relationship development processes; however, to date little work has been done to explicate in detail the role uncertainty plays in the context of ongoing interaction episodes. As argued previously, when individuals are engaged in interactions with others, the messages they exchange are constructed and deployed under conditions of uncertainty. In even the most routine communication episodes, co-interactants have some measure of uncertainty about each other's beliefs, affective states, goals, and plans for reaching these goals, as they converse with each other. Of course, some of this uncertainty is dealt with by making inferences about these beliefs, affective states, goals, and plans; in fact, students of discourse comprehension have argued that inferences concerning the goals and plans of fellow interactants are critical for understanding their discourse (Bruce 1980; Bruce & Newman 1978; Carberry 1990; Cohen, Morgan, & Pollack 1990; Green 1989; Hobbs & Evans 1980). As Green (1989) put it:

> Understanding a speaker's intention in saying what she said the way she said it amounts to inferring the speaker's plan, in all of its hierarchical glory, although there is room for considerable latitude regarding the details. (1989, 14)

While inferences concerning goals and plans may be accurate enough to sustain discourse, these inferences themselves may be shrouded in uncertainty, although individuals may act routinely as if their inferences are facts and the words they utter to others "carry meaning." Perhaps the pervasiveness of this "conduit metaphor" in individuals' thinking and talk about communication, a world in which words are vessels of meaning (Reddy 1979), is itself a strategy for glossing the potentially high levels of uncertainty that may accompany the production of both spoken and written discourse. For even when verbal and nonverbal messages are sent to those whom we think we know well, it is possible that their beliefs, affective states, goals, and plans have changed significantly since our last encounter with them, or that these attributes are in the process of changing while we interact with them, even though we are wont to believe in the stability of such attributes.

In spite of tendencies for assuming higher levels of stability than may be the case, individuals both perceive and take into account changes in their fellow interlocutors' beliefs, intentions, and affective states. In addition, individuals may recognize, either explicitly or implicitly, the necessity for hedging against potential unanticipated side-effects their messages may produce; that is, individuals may employ strategies for coping with the uncertainties inherent in message generation and dissemination. These strategies may be applied consciously both before and during the communication episode, and they may be applied at a non-conscious level as well. It is to these strategies that the focus now turns.

Information Acquisition

One obvious way to cope with the uncertainties inherent in the production of messages is to acquire information about the individuals who will be the targets of one's messages, as well as the social context within which these messages are likely to be received. Such information may be obtained in advance of the communication episode and used to guide message generation; however, in the case of face-to-face interactions this information also can be acquired on-line, as interaction episodes unfold. It has been suggested that information can be acquired using *passive, active, and interactive strategies* (Berger 1979, 1987, 1988a; Berger & Bradac 1982; Berger & Kellermann, in press). In using *passive* strategies individuals obtain information about others by observing them unobtrusively. A distinct advantage of employing these strategies is that observers do not have to allocate scarce cognitive resources to managing conversations with targets or to manipulating impressions they are making on targets. Indeed, from the perspective of the information gatherer, acquiring information unobtrusively obviates the possibility that targets can proffer social selves that are intended to create certain beliefs and judgments in observers (James 1950; Schlenker 1980). Several investigations of passive strategies have revealed that unobtrusive observers find informal social situations in which targets are actively interacting with others to be more informative than formal social contexts, social contexts in which the target is not involved in social interaction with the others present, or solitary contexts (Berger & Perkins 1978, 1979; Berger & Douglas 1981). This preference probably stems from the fact that in informal social situations individuals' actions are less constrained and thus potentially more informative than actions displayed in the other contexts (Jones & Davis 1965).

Active information acquisition strategies do not involve direct interaction between the observer and the target. Rather, the information seeker acquires information about the target by asking others for their judgments of the target. Evidence suggests that individuals acquire a considerable amount of their information about others through these third-party sources (Hewes, Graham, Doelger, & Pavitt 1985). Moreover, individuals are sensitive to the possibility that information acquired from such sources may be biased, and they believe that they can correct for these biases using "second-guessing" techniques. Considerable work has been done to explore the cues that prompt second-guessing and the strategies individuals use to ferret out bias and correct for it (Doelger, Hewes, & Graham 1986; Hewes & Graham 1989; Hewes, Graham, Doelger, & Pavitt 1985; Hewes, Graham, Monsour, & Doelger 1989).

Another, as yet unexplored set of active strategies involve a form of naive social experimentation (Berger 1988a). It seems reasonable to suppose that on occasion information seekers may not only unobtrusively observe targets but set up situations in which they can observe targets respond to a set of conditions the observers have created *a priori*. For example, observers using such strategies might arrange for a friend to meet the target and then observe the friend and target interact to see how the target responds to a "known other." Thus, if the target appears to respond positively to the friend, the observer might conclude there is a good possibility that she too will get along with the target if they meet. Of course, in this example the observer could also interrogate the friend after the conversation to glean the friend's impressions of the target.

Finally, *interactive* strategies involve face-to-face interaction between information seekers and targets. Although these strategies are most demanding of scarce cognitive resources for their implementation, since the information seeker must not only gather information but simultaneously attend to impression and conversation management concerns, a distinct advantage of these strategies is that they enable information seekers to enact behaviors calculated to elicit specific information from targets. Moreover, if targets are perceived not to be forthcoming with the desired information, seekers can alter their strategies in order to surmount these counteractions.

Several studies (Berger & Kellermann 1983, 1986, in press; Kellermann & Berger 1984) suggest that those acquiring information during interactions employ strategies that vary in intrusiveness from direct interrogation, through strategic disclosure of information with the hope that targets will reciprocate the disclosure (e.g., I'll tell you my yearly income, you tell me yours), to the least intrusive strategy of relaxing targets with the intention of encouraging them to talk about themselves, an approach akin to non-directive psychotherapy (Rogers 1951). These three strategy types also vary with respect to the degree of control the information seeker has over the responses of targets.

Asking questions to acquire specific pieces of information is potentially the most efficient of the three strategies since there are no guarantees that targets will reciprocate disclosures or spontaneously reveal a desired datum. However, while interrogation potentially is the most efficient strategy of the three, it might be most likely judged to be the least socially appropriate by targets, especially if many different questions are asked (Berger & Kellermann 1983; Kellermann 1988; Kellermann & Berger 1984). Consequently, information seekers using interactive strategies must weigh the trade-offs between efficiency and social appropriateness before strategies are instantiated in social action. Kellermann (1988) has employed these two meta-goals as bases for predicting strategy choice for a number of different interaction goals.

In an investigation related to this body of research, Baxter and Wilmot (1984) asked individuals involved in romantic relationships how they assessed their partners' levels of commitment to their relationships. They discovered a number of strategies they labeled "secret tests." These tests included asking third parties for their opinions, direct questioning, jealousy tests, hinting, physical separation, and testing limits. Baxter and Wilmot were able to fit most of the secret tests they uncovered into the tripartite passive, active, and interactive information acquisition strategies typology outlined above. While this typology hardly constitutes an explanatory theory of information acquisition, it appears to serve a useful heuristic function in thinking about information acquisition strategies. Future research should determine whether the three information acquisition categories hold in social contexts other than those already studied, and whether the three categories are represented when goals other than information acquisition are pursued. Furthermore, work should be done to determine the conditions under which the various types of strategies are deployed; that is, in some situations, passive strategies may be more efficient than interactive and active strategies, while in other situations, the relative efficiency of the strategy types may differ.

Although this discussion of information acquisition strategies has focused on the means by which social actors obtain information, it would be an oversight not to recognize that individuals in social situations may wish to remain opaque to inquisitive others by instantiating strategies that counter others' information-seeking attempts. Employing an intelligence-gathering metaphor, Goffman (1969) discussed a few ways people might employ to mask their true intent in social situations, and the moves that might be employed to counter the information-gathering efforts of others. Berger and Kellermann (1989) studied directly strategies that individuals used to avoid revealing information about themselves to their inquisitive conversational partners. This study demonstrated that those instructed to thwart the information-gathering attempts of their partners, who had been instructed to acquire as much information as possible about their partners during the conversation, did so by: (1) directing the conversation toward aspects of their partner's self, (2) providing vague answers to questions, (3) encouraging their partners to speak, (4) introducing more frequent and longer pauses in their speech in order to slow down the conversation, and (5) presenting themselves in a less relaxed and cooperative manner to reduce their own attractiveness. In addition to using these strategies, a few of these low revealers assumed the role of a high seeker by asking numerous questions to their partners about themselves, thus deflecting their partner's information-seeking attempts by requiring them to answer questions about themselves. An important implication of this research is that even when individuals attempt to cope with the uncertainties inherent in any social interaction by acquiring uncertainty-reducing information, targets of their uncertainty reduction efforts may undermine their goal by deploying their own counter-strategies for a variety of reasons. Consequently, attempts to acquire information may not lead message producers down the royal road to uncertainty reduction, and apparent "information" that is acquired from others may not reduce uncertainty but increase it. Given this possibility, then, additional means for hedging against uncertainty must be available to enable message producers to ply their trade with some degree of effectiveness.

Plans and Planning

Interpersonal communication researchers and others interested in the study of social interaction have found it useful to view social interaction as a goal-directed activity (Read & Miller 1989; Tracy & Coupland 1990). While there has been a virtual avalanche of research describing the multitude of strategies individuals employ to reach a number of specific goals, from compliance-gaining to comforting, there has been a decided dearth of theory aimed at explaining such goal-directed social action (Berger, in press a). Among interpersonal communication researchers there are a few notable exceptions to this trend (Dillard 1990a,b; Greene 1990). In addition to these initial theoretical forays, Berger (in press a) has advocated a plan-based approach to the study of strategic communication.

Within this perspective, goals are viewed as desired end-states toward which social actors strive, while plans are cognitive representations of action sequences designed to produce these desired end-states (Berger, in press a). Plans are viewed as guides to social action rather than entities that energize action (Berger, in press a; Brand 1984; Kreitler & Kreitler 1987; Levelt 1989; Lichtenstein & Brewer 1980; Miller, Galanter, & Pribram 1960; Sacerdoti 1978; Schank & Abelson 1977; Srull & Wyer 1986; Wilensky 1983). It is assumed that plans are hierarchically organized with abstract action representations at the top of the hierarchy and progressively more concrete representations toward the bottom. Considerable evidence supports this claim (see Lichtenstein & Brewer 1980).

New plans may be devised in advance of a particular interaction, but old plans may also be retrieved from memory as interactions unfold. In fact, Waldron (1990) found that of some 2,273 thoughts generated by subjects during reviews of videotapes of their just completed interactions, 27 percent had to do with planned actions for reaching interaction goals; an additional 17 percent were concerned with progress toward reaching interaction goals. Thus, 44 percent of the thoughts that persons reported having while trying to reach interaction goals were focused on their goals and their plans for reaching them. These figures may underestimate the amount of planning activity that takes place while interactions are in progress because not all of this activity necessarily occurs at the level of conscious awareness where it can be assessed verbally. The instantiation of frequently-used old plans may take place in a highly automatic fashion (Hammond 1989a,b; Kellermann 1992); in fact, in order for individuals involved in conversations to maintain the flow of interaction, these automatic processes must be prepotent over more cognitively demanding conscious processes (Green 1989). Nevertheless, Waldron's data provide ample evidence that social interactants may use their capacity for engaging in forethought to aid them in their quest to achieve their goals as they interact. In addition, individuals may devise message plans for reaching their goals before participating in a specific communication episode, as textbooks on job interviewing and public speaking advise, and there is evidence that when anticipating interactions in social contexts more informal than these, individuals may imagine interactions with others before they actually occur (Honeycutt 1991; Honeycutt, Zagacki, & Edwards 1989).

Planning activity, whether it occurs in advance of interaction or on-line as interactions unfold, is certainly a way to hedge against uncertainty. As part of the planning process, individuals may not only devise new plans or retrieve old ones for attaining their goals, they may also simulate mentally their plans before enacting them to determine whether the plan, as currently formulated, contains any potential "bugs." The process of "de-bugging" message plans in view of projected responses by those who will receive messages not only may aid message planners in hedging against uncertainty, it may increase the degree of flexibility social actors can achieve when they realize their interaction plans in action. However, planning may not be successful in coping with uncertainty since the activity of planning itself can produce plans with varying levels of sophistication and potential effectiveness. When it comes to planning, not all planners are created equal. This specific issue is taken up in the following section.

Plan Complexity

Intuitively, one might suppose that an optimal way to approach planning under conditions of uncertainty would be to develop highly detailed plans or multiple, alternative plans; plans that would specify in detail the actions, both general and specific, that might be used to attain the focal goal or goals. This approach to pursuing goals seems more rational and potentially effective than one in which social actors approach their goals spontaneously. While not germane directly to the issue of plan effectiveness, evidence suggests that children who hold general beliefs supporting the efficacy of planning as an activity are more likely than their more spontaneous counterparts to develop plans that contain greater detail when asked to devise plans for reaching specific goals (Kreitler & Kreitler 1987). Moreover, other research has demonstrated that planners asked to specify the kinds of information they would like to have about target individuals, as well as the information they would like to have about the social context within which the interaction with the target will take place, are more likely to devise plans containing more actions and more diverse actions than individuals who are not asked for their information preferences in advance of their planning (Berger & diBattista 1992a). Interestingly, in this experiment, in spite of the fact that those who requested specific items of information about targets and situations did not receive the information they requested, their plans were more elaborate than those who did not make pre-planning requests. Apparently, the act of requesting person and situation information itself encourages more complex planning.

While the potential advantages of complex plans for dealing with the uncertainties surrounding social interaction seem transparent, at least one study suggests that devising complex messages in advance of pursuing a communication goal may actually debilitate verbal fluency (Berger, Karol, & Jordan 1989). This study found that individuals who devised persuasion plans containing larger numbers of specific arguments to support their position were significantly less verbally fluent than their counterparts whose persuasion plans included fewer specific arguments. This inverse relationship between the number of arguments and verbal fluency was most pronounced ($r = -.62$) in a condition in which individuals' planned actions were questioned prior to entering the persuasive encounter. In this condition, participants were asked to indicate what they would do in the event that four different actions contained in their plans failed to bring about the desired result. Overall, individuals in this condition were less fluent verbally than their counterparts in a condition in which participants developed persuasion plans that were not questioned and a condition in which participants engaged in no planning before the persuasion task. Another experiment included in this study demonstrated that questioning the potential effectiveness of planned actions had the effect of encouraging individuals, so questioned, to devise alternative actions, thus increasing the complexity of their plans. Since there is ample evidence that the verbal disfluency created by increased rates of vocalized and non-vocalized pausing can undermine auditor's judgments of message producers' credibility (Berger 1985, in press b; Miller & Hewgill 1964; Newton & Burgoon 1990), it may be that actions guided by highly complex plans may undermine the ultimate communicative effectiveness of those who use them because of the verbal disfluencies that may accompany their deployment.

Contingent Planning

In addition to coping with uncertainty by developing more detailed message plans, individuals may be able to anticipate targets' actions that might thwart their plans and to generate contingent actions to deal with these potential blocks. Intuitively, although contingent planning would seem to be a very rational and desirable way with which to deal with uncertainty, there is evidence that in a number of different domains, individuals do not think contingently when developing their plans. In two studies which college students were asked how they would go about getting a new roommate to like them, only a very small percentage of participants included any contingent actions in their plans (Berger & Bell 1988; Berger & diBattista 1992a), and in the former study no participants included contingent actions in their plans. While it is true that in both of these investigations participants did include more contingent actions in their plans to ask someone out for a date, the rates were still relatively low.

While one might be tempted to dismiss these findings on the grounds that participants in these studies may not have been highly involved in pursuing the goals given them in the hypothetical situations, thus suppressing high levels of contingent planning, evidence from the domain of urban and transportation planning suggests that individuals pursuing goals in these planning arenas, where the stakes are considerably higher, do not anticipate relatively obvious threats to the successful realization of their plans. For example, those who developed the Bay Area Rapid Transit (BART) system underestimated significantly the amount of time and money it would take to make the system fully operational (Hall 1982). These gross underestimates were predicated on the faulty assumption that new and untried transportation technologies would work from the beginning with minimal start-up problems. Of course, because new technologies were employed, it took a long time period and considerable money to correct the inevitable glitches that arise in newly deployed technologies. A similar gross underestimate of the costs involved in developing and implementing a new technology occurred in the case of the Super Sonic Transport (SST). Thus, even when the financial stakes are high, contingent planning appears to be underutilized by those whose business it is to plan (Hall 1982).

There are at least two related explanations for this aversion to contingent planning activity. First, when individuals set goals and devise plans for reaching them, they may be overcome by the feeling that because they now have a plan that appears to lead to the desired end-state, the plan will be successful automatically. This explanation is encapsulated by the aphorism "Thinking makes it so," or, perhaps more appropriately, "Saying makes it so," both of which are, of course, of dubious validity. Nevertheless, the euphoria created by arriving at a possible route to a goal may induce planners to suspend further consideration of either potential blocks to the plan they have devised or alternative, potentially more efficient plans for reaching the goal. Second, since contingent planning requires additional time and effort and is demanding of scarce cognitive resources, the prerequisites for contingent planning fly in the face of the miserly tendencies of information processors (Fiske & Taylor 1984). Even in the more mundane area of introductory public speaking courses, instructors often complain that students do not like to take the time to construct outlines for speeches, let alone alternative outlines or outlines that incorporate contingencies predicated on audience members' responses.

Contingent planning requires that individuals be willing to entertain the possibility that the plans they have formulated, no matter how complex and potentially sophisticated, may fail when implemented. The tendencies to avoid anticipating failure once plans are made may be especially acute when planning is done in groups. Group pressures brought to bear on individual members in the name of being "good team players" may silence dissenting voices that could raise questions about the likelihood of failure of the plan as a whole or various sub-parts of the plan. Not allowing these skeptics to express themselves in group planning contexts may create conditions antithetical to the initiation of contingent planning activity. One of the more vivid demonstrations of this lack of critical questioning occurred during the planning of the ill-fated Bay of Pigs invasion during the Kennedy Administration (Janis & Mann 1977), and similar processes may have been at work during the increasing escalation of the Vietnam War during the Johnson Administration, even in the face of mounting anti-war sentiment in many sectors of the general public. The notion promulgated by several Johnson administration figures during 1967 that there was "light at the end of the tunnel," when referring to ultimate victory in the Vietnam war (Berman 1989), could well be symptomatic of a severe case of success bias.

While the potential hedge against uncertainty offered by contingent planning is potentially powerful, efficient and effective plans to achieve goals may require a minimum of contingent planning. In planning to walk to the corner newsstand to purchase a newspaper, it would be foolish to plan for the possibility that one's walk might be interrupted by a falling aircraft. Such an event is possible, however, the probability that one will have to confront such a contingency is so low, even when one lives in a location where air traffic is heavy, that it is unreasonable to develop actions for dealing with it. Given that contingency planning is a resource intensive activity, it is critical that planners allocate these resources wisely. Some goals simply may not demand elaborate contingency planning for their successful achievement.

When Plans Fail: The Hierarchy Hypothesis

Even though individuals may devise elaborate plans that anticipate multiple sources of failure by including contingent actions, their plan-guided actions may fail to bring about desired end-states. One response to this failure is to abandon the goal; however, for purposes of the present discussion, it will be assumed that individuals who experience such failure are sufficiently motivated to continue pursuing their goals. When unanticipated contingencies appear, plans must be modified on-line as they are being enacted (Waldron 1990). An important question is how individuals go about altering plans when their plans fail to bring about desired end-states.

A program of research designed specifically to shed light on this issue has explored how individuals alter their message plans in response to not being understood by their conversational partners (Berger 1993; Berger & Abrahams 1993; Berger & diBattista 1992b, in press). The theoretical grounding for these experiments is embodied in the *hierarchy hypothesis.* This hypothesis asserts that when individuals are thwarted in their attempts to achieve goals, their first tendency is to alter lower level elements of their message plans. Low level, more concrete elements of message plans include the vocal intensity and speech rate at which the message is delivered, while higher level message units are concerned with the structure and the sequencing of message content. The propensity to alter lower level units first is predicated on the assumptions that: (1) higher level message plan alterations require more cognitive resources for their implementation, and (2) individuals are "cognitive misers" who resist expending large amounts of effort to perform cognitive operations (Fiske & Taylor 1984).

Several experiments have provided support for the hierarchy hypothesis. Two studies have shown that geographic direction-givers, who were requested to provide their directions a second time but to use an alternative walk route required significantly more time to begin the second rendition of their directions than did individuals who were asked to provide their directions a second time but at a slower speech rate (Berger 1993; Berger & Abrahams 1993). Those asked to provide more landmarks in the second rendition of their directions demonstrated average response latencies that were between these two extremes (Berger 1993). In these studies it was assumed that asking for a new route constituted a high level message plan alteration, while requesting that the direction-giver speak more slowly demanded a low level alteration. It was further assumed that altering landmarks would be intermediate between these extremes. In both of these studies, response onset latency was used to index the amount of cognitive load experienced by the research participants.

In additional research, Berger and diBattista (1992b, in press) found that regardless of the locus of communication failure, individuals showed higher levels of vocal intensity, a low level alteration, while providing the second rendition of their directions than they did when they gave the first rendition of their directions. Moreover, in both of these studies only 4–5 percent of direction-givers spontaneously changed the walk route of their directions, when those receiving the directions indicated that they were having difficulty following the directions but did not specify the walk route itself as the locus of the communication failure. These findings support the view that when given the choice, individuals prefer to make low level message plan alterations in response to goal failure because these alterations require fewer cognitive resources for their implementation. The hierarchy hypothesis and its postulates also provide an explanation for the often observed tendency of individuals interacting with others who do not understand their language to repeat what they have said previously but to say it in a louder voice. This strategy for overcoming non-acoustic-based communication failures is clearly dysfunctional.

Just as planners may be insensitive to the necessity for anticipating potential blocks to their planned actions through contingent planning, the research germane to the hierarchy hypothesis suggests that when goal failures occur, communicators may not necessarily make optimal adaptations for surmounting the barriers that may be placed in the path of their goal-directed actions. In the context of social influence episodes, for example, this latter tendency is no more apparent than in the behavior of parents toward their non-compliant children. It is commonplace to observe parents who, having failed to secure compliance from their children in an initial influence attempt, simply repeat the content of their first compliance-gaining message but do so in a louder voice during the second rendition, as if increasing vocal intensity is likely to be the most efficient or effective way to secure the child's compliance. This strategy may require considerably less effort than one requiring the reformulation of arguments and appeals used in the message; however, this savings in effort may not match the potential loss of efficiency and effectiveness. Furthermore, increased vocal intensity not only may be ineffective in securing compliance *per se*, it may promote angry and hostile responses from those subjected to the intense voice, thus lowering further the likelihood of compliance and raising the probability of long-term relationship deterioration between the influence agent and the target.

Although we have done no research on this issue to date, an important theoretical and practical question is how to encourage those who experience goal failure to: (1) take time to diagnose the source of the failure, (2) take time to alter their plans, and (3) alter their plans at the appropriate levels of the message plan hierarchy. Clearly, some failures may require only low level alterations, for example, speaking louder to someone who is hearing impaired or speaking more slowly to a non-native speaker of one's language; however, many if not most goal failures are ones that demand higher level, more cognitively demanding modifications for their successful repair. Finding ways to encourage communicators to acquire the skills and the levels of motivation necessary for making these high level alterations to message plan hierarchies is an important theoretical and research challenge.

When Plans Fail: Accretive Planning

The discussion of the hierarchy hypothesis suggested that it is neither necessary nor desirable to abandon completely a particular message plan when it fails to bring about desired end-states. Even high level alterations to message plan hierarchies may require only minor modifications to render them more successful. The addition of a few facts, statistics, or a new argument may transform an ineffective plan into one that is quite successful. Consequently, major investments of scarce cognitive resources may be wasted if an entire message plan is abandoned when it fails, although, as has been noted, planners need to be prepared to make such investments when necessary.

There is some evidence that individuals may make adaptations to goal failures that tend to be relatively conservative. Berger and Kellermann (1986) reported that individuals whose goal it was to find out as much as possible about their conversational partners (High Seekers) whom they just met asked no more or fewer questions of their partners when the partners were instructed to provide as little information about themselves as possible (Low Revealers) or when they were instructed to reveal as much information about themselves as possible (High Revealers). High Seekers did not vary the number of questions they asked of their partners in response to goal failure. Rather, the High Seekers paired with Low Revealers tended to ask more questions concerned with their partners' goals and plans than did their non-thwarted counterparts. In addition, the thwarted High Seekers provided more verbal backchannel responses like "Oh, really?" or "is that so?" to encourage their low-revealing partners to disclose more information about themselves, and the High Seekers asked a greater proportion of questions directed toward the self of the Low Revealers.

In general, the High Seekers whose information acquisition goal was blocked did some of the same things they would do in normal circumstances, that is, ask the same number of questions, but vary other aspects of their message plans such as backchannel responses and the types of questions they asked. These patterns of message plan alterations suggest an accretive planning strategy in which the planner continues to do what normally works at some message plan levels but adds variations at other levels. Presumably, if the High Seekers found evidence that their increased backchanneling brought about more personal revelations from their formerly reticent partners, they would continue to elevate their backchanneling levels, although this possibility was not assessed directly in this study. The findings of this study also suggest the possibility that incremental, trial-and-error approaches to message plan alterations may be used when goal failures occur. How *a priori* contingency planning affects these patterns of message plan alteration is an issue worthy of further research attention.

When Plans Fail: Framing and Reframing

Messages designed to reach a variety of instrumental and communication goals not only may fail to bring about desired goal-states, they also may cause individuals to lose face (Brown & Levinson 1978, 1987; Goffman 1959, 1969). Consider the potential threats to face present when, for example, an individual asks another out for a date, a situation in which a refusal might be read as personal rejection. When such requests are made, it is rare for requesters to be perfectly certain that targets will accede to their requests; as a consequence, people may frame their requests in such a way that any refusal's threat to their face is nullified. Humor is clearly one such framing device. If a date-request, for example, is delivered in a humorous context and is turned down, the individual making the request can claim that it was just a "joke" and direct the conversation to more innocuous topics. In fact, Berger (1988b) found that males, who were more likely to request dates in the population studied, used this humorous frame more frequently in their date-request plans than did females. Apparently, then, this kind of framing device can be used when potential threats to face are considerable, as they are for the date-requester.

In the date-request example, the individual making the request attempts to structure the encounter such that when the request is made, there is the possibility of redefining the authenticity of the request. However, it may happen that unanticipated contingencies may arise during the interaction that require a reframing of the encounter in order to save face. A similar "just kidding" or "lighten up" frame may be used to defuse potentially angry responses to comments, when those making the comments sense that their conversational partners are becoming miffed at what they have said to them. Again, in this latter case no attempt is made to build a humorous context before the comment is delivered, as in the date-request situation. The "just kidding" or "lighten up" frame is an *ex post facto* attempt to undo unanticipated negative side effects produced by one's messages.

In general, both of these cases illustrate attempts to cope with the inevitable uncertainties that accompany the dissemination of messages in face-to-face encounters. Message producers can seek information about their targets, have their goals in sharp focus, devise plans that contain numerous contingencies, alter plans that fail at various levels of abstraction, and vary some message attributes while holding others constant. In spite of these efforts to cope with uncertainty, messages may still fail to bring about desired goals, and, what is worse, may precipitate such unanticipated negative consequences as loss of face. Consequently, given the vagaries inherent in all communication situations, it behooves message planners to activate these framing strategies to hedge against potential worst-case scenarios. In such a scenario, individuals would fail to gain compliance from a given target and lose face in the process. This kind of outcome would probably make future attempts to gain compliance from the same target that much less likely to succeed, since one's credibility has been compromised. Thus, a fundamental planning objective for those engaging in message construction and dissemination should involve face preservation, especially if a long-term relationship with the target of one's goal-directed actions is anticipated.

CONCLUSION

In this chapter, I have attempted to demonstrate that uncertainty is a fundamental feature of communicative activity, whether that activity takes place in face-to-face interaction contexts or mass-mediated venues. In all of these contexts, message producers are faced not only with the problem of understanding their message targets to the degree that they can devise potentially effective messages for achieving their goals, producers must also choose from the myriad of possible combinations of verbal and nonverbal actions those that are most likely to bring about desired outcomes. A primary difficulty is that because message targets are not stationary, since social-psychological change is constant, message producers can never reduce fully their uncertainties about their targets or their own message choices, and once messages are disseminated, message producers must face the possibility that they could have "said it a better way."

Given the uncertainties intrinsic to the message production process, it is natural to assume that adaptive beings would devise a variety of strategies for hedging against the potential deleterious effects of these uncertainties. These negative effects could range from failure to reach the primary goals of the communication episode, e.g., comforting or compliance-gaining, to loss of face. An obvious way these uncertainties can be reduced is through the acquisition of information, although, for a variety of reasons, message producers might not be able to secure the information they require. Since information gathering is not a sure route to uncertainty reduction, other strategies, those directly related to message planning, must be used to hedge against uncertainty. These hedges include the development of complex message plans that contain numerous contingencies, and the alteration of plans when goal failures occur during communication episodes. Finally, message producers can attempt to frame *a priori* communication episodes that allow them to reinterpret the intent of the episode if goal failure occurs. Similarly, episodes may be reframed *ex post facto* when goal failures occur in order to avoid unanticipated negative consequences.

Throughout this presentation, pains have been taken to note that each of the strategies for hedging against the potential negative consequences of uncertainty has limitations, and the immediate demands of face-to-face interaction might make it difficult for individuals to employ these strategies, at least in a highly conscious way. Nevertheless, the deployment of these strategies is vital for the accomplishment of instrumental and communication goals. Since many, if not most, face-to-face encounters seem to be carried off with little or no difficulty, it might be surmised that uncertainty discussed in this chapter constitutes, at most, a minor irritant to message producers and to those who consume their messages. Perhaps it is because message producers employ these hedging strategies both explicitly and implicitly that most interactions progress in what appears to be a relatively orderly way; however, when message producers wish they were able to "take back" what they have said to others, uncertainty has not been effectively hedged.

REFERENCES

Adams, J. S. (1965). Inequity in social exchange. In L. Berkowitz (Ed.), *Advances in experimental social psychology* (Vol. 2) (pp. 267–300). New York: Academic Press.

Altman, D. A., & Taylor, D. (1973). *Social penetration: The development of interpersonal relationships.* New York: Holt, Rinehart, & Winston.

Baxter, L. A., & Wilmot, W. W. (1984). Secret tests: Social strategies for acquiring information about the state of the relationship. *Human Communication Research 11,* 171–201.

Berger, C. R. (1973, December). *The acquaintance process revisited: Explorations in initial interaction.* Paper presented at the annual convention of the Speech Communication Association, New York.

Berger, C. R. (1975). Proactive and retroactive attribution processes in interpersonal communication. *Human Communication Research 2,* 33–50.

Berger, C. R. (1979). Beyond initial interaction: Uncertainty, understanding, and the development of interpersonal relationships. In H. Giles & R. St. Clair (Eds.), *Language and social psychology* (pp. 122–144). Oxford: Basil Blackwell.

Berger, C. R. (1985). Social power and interpersonal communication. In M. L. Knapp & G. R. Miller (Eds.), *Handbook of interpersonal communication* (pp. 439–499). Newbury Park, Cal.: Sage Publications.

Berger, C. R. (1986). Uncertain outcome values in predicted relationships: Uncertainty reduction theory then and now. *Human Communication Research* 13, 34–38.

Berger, C. R. (1987). Communicating under uncertainty. In M. E. Roloff & G. R. Miller (Eds.), *Interpersonal processes: New directions in communication research* (pp. 39–62). Newbury Park, Cal.: Sage Publications.

Berger, C. R. (1988a). Uncertainty and information exchange in developing relationships. In S. W. Duck (Ed.), *Handbook of personal relationships* (pp. 239–255). Chichester: John Wiley & Sons.

Berger, C. R. (1988b). Planning, affect, and social action generation. In L. Donohew, H. E. Sypher, & E. T. Higgins (Eds.), *Communication, social cognition, and affect* (pp. 93–116). Hillsdale, N.J.: Lawrence Erlbaum.

Berger, C. R. (1993, November). *Planning, plan adaptation and cognitive load: An assessment of the hierarchy hypothesis.* Paper presented at the annual convention of the Speech Communication Association, Miami.

Berger, C. R. (in press a). A plan-based approach to strategic communication. In D. E. Hewes (Ed.), *The cognitive bases of interpersonal communication.* Hillsdale, N.J.: Lawrence Erlbaum.

Berger, C. R. (in press b). Power, dominance, and social interaction. In M. L. Knapp & G. R. Miller (Eds.), *Handbook of interpersonal communication (2nd ed.).* Newbury Park, Cal.: Sage Publications.

Berger, C. R., & Abrahams, M. F. (1993, May). *Altering communication plans in response to goal failure.* Paper presented at the annual convention of the International Communication Association, Washington, D.C.

Berger, C. R., & Bell, R. A. (1988). Plans and the initiation of social relationships. *Human Communication Research 15*, 217–235.

Berger C. R., & Bradac, J. J. (1982). *Language and social knowledge: Uncertainty in interpersonal relations.* London: Edward Arnold.

Berger, C. R. & Calabrese, R. J. (1975). Some explorations in initial interaction and beyond: Toward a developmental theory of interpersonal communication. *Human Communication Research 1*, 99–112.

Berger, C. R., & diBattista, P. (1992a). Information seeking and plan elaboration: What do you need to know to know what to do? *Communication Monographs 59*, 368–387.

Berger, C. R., & diBattista, P. (1992b, October). *Adapting plans to failed communication goals.* Paper presented at the annual convention of the Speech Communication Association, Chicago.

Berger, C. R., & diBattista, P. (in press). Communication failure and plan adaptation: If at first you don't succeed, say it louder and slower. *Communication Monographs.*

Berger, C. R., & Douglas, W. (1981). Studies in interpersonal epistemology III: Anticipated interaction, self-monitoring, and observational context selection. *Communication Monographs 48*, 183–196.

Berger, C. R., Gardner, R. R., Clatterbuck, G. W., & Schulman, L. S. (1976). Perceptions of information sequencing in relationship development. *Human Communication Research 3*, 29–46.

Berger, C. R., & Gudykunst, W. B. (1991). Uncertainty and communication. In B. Dervin (Ed.), *Progress in communication sciences*, Vol. X, (pp. 21–66). Norwood, N.J.: Ablex.

Berger, C. R., Karol, S. H., & Jordan, J. M. (1989). When a lot of knowledge is a dangerous thing: The debilitating effects of plan complexity on verbal fluency. *Human Communication Research 16*, 91–119.

Berger, C. R., & Kellermann, K. A. (1983). To ask or not to ask: Is that a question? In R. N. Bostrom (Ed.), *Communication yearbook 7* (pp. 342–368). Newbury Park, Cal.: Sage Publications.

Berger, C. R., & Kellermann, K. (1986, May). *Goal incompatibility and social action: The best laid plans of mice and men often go astray.* Paper presented at the annual convention of the International Communication Association, Chicago.

Berger, C. R., & Kellerman, K. (1989). Personal opacity and social information gathering: Explorations in strategic communication. *Communication Research 16*, 314–351.

Berger, C. R., & Kellermann, K. (in press). Acquiring social information. In J. A. Daly & J. M. Wiemann (Eds.), *Communicating strategically.* Hillsdale, N.J.: Lawrence Erlbaum.

Berger, C. R., & Perkins, J. W. (1978). Studies in interpersonal epistemology I: Situational attributes in observational context selection. In B. D. Ruben (Ed.), *Communication yearbook 2* (pp. 171–184). New Brunswick, N.J.: Transaction Press.

Berger, C. R., & Perkins, J. W. (1979, November). *Studies in interpersonal epistemology II: Self-monitoring, involvement, facial affect, similarity and observational context selection.* Paper presented at the annual convention of the Speech Communication Association, San Antonio.

Berman, L. (1989). *Lyndon Johnson's war: The road to stalemate in Vietnam.* New York: W. W. Norton.

Berscheid, E., Graziano, W., Monson, T., & Dermer, M. (1976). Outcome dependency: Attention, attribution, and attraction. *Journal of Personality and Social Psychology 34*, 978–989.

Brand, M. (1984). *Intending and acting: Toward a naturalized theory of action.* Cambridge: MIT Press.

Brown, P., & Levinson, S. C. (1978). Universals in language usage: Politeness phenomena. In E. N. Goody (Ed.), *Questions and politeness* (pp. 56–289). Cambridge: Cambridge University Press.

Brown, P., & Levinson, S. C. (1987). *Politeness: Some universals in language usage.* New York: Cambridge University Press.

Bruce, B. C. (1980). Plans and social actions. In R. J. Spiro, B. C. Bruce, & W. F. Brewer (Eds.), *Theoretical issues in reading comprehension* (pp. 367–384). Hillsdale, N.J.: Lawrence Erlbaum.

Bruce, B., & Newman, D. (1978). Interacting plans. *Cognitive Science 2*, 195–233.

Calabrese, R. J. (1975). *The effects of privacy and probability of future interaction on initial interaction patterns.* Unpublished doctoral dissertation, Department of Communication Studies, Northwestern University, Evanston, Ill.

Carberry, S. (1990). *Plan recognition in natural language dialogue.* Cambridge: MIT Press.

Cate, R. M. (1991, May). *Relationship thinking: A measure and some initial studies.* Paper presented at the Third International Network Conference on Personal Relationships, Normal, Ill.

Clatterbuck, G. W. (1979). Attributional confidence and uncertainty in initial interaction. *Human Communication Research 5*, 147–157.

Cohen, P. R., Morgan, J., & Pollack, M. E. (1990). *Intentions in communication.* Cambridge: MIT Press.

Dillard, J. P. (Ed.) (1990a). *Seeking compliance, the production of interpersonal influence messages.* Scottsdale: Gorsuch Scarisbrick.

Dillard, J. P. (1990b). The nature and substance of goals in tactical communication. In M. J. Cody & M. L. McLaughlin (Eds.), *The psychology of tactical communication* (pp. 70–90). Clevedon, England: Multilingual Matters.

Doelger, J. A., Hewes, D. E., & Graham, M. L. (1986). Knowing when to "second guess": The mindful analysis of messages. *Human Communication Research 12*, 301–338.

Douglas, W. (1987). Question-asking in same- and opposite-sex initial interactions: The effects of anticipated future interaction. *Human Communication Research 14*, 230–245.

Douglas, W. (1990). Uncertainty, information seeking, and liking during initial interaction. *Western Journal of Speech Communication 54*, 66–81.

Douglas, W. (1993). *Uncertainty reduction during acquaintanceship: A reexamination of the anticipated future interaction hypothesis.* Unpublished manuscript, School of Communication, University of Houston, Houston.

Fiske, S. T., and Taylor, S. E. (1984). *Social cognition.* New York: Random House.

Goffman, E. (1959). *The presentation of self in everyday lie.* Garden City, N.Y.: Doubleday Anchor.

Goffman, E. (1969). *Strategic interaction.* Philadelphia: University of Pennsylvania Press.

Gouldner, A. (1960). The norm of reciprocity: A preliminary statement. *American Sociological Review 25*, 161–178.

Green, G. M. (1989). *Pragmatics and natural language understanding.* Hillsdale, N.J.: Lawrence Erlbaum.

Greene, J. O. (1990). Tactical social actions: Towards some strategies for theory. In M. J. Cody & M. L. McLaughlin (Eds.), *The psychology of tactical communication* (pp. 31–47). Clevedon, England: Multilingual Matters.

Grice, H. P. (1975). Logic and conversation. In P. Cole & J. L. Morgan (Eds.), *Syntax and semantics: Vol. 3. Speech acts* (pp. 41–58). New York: Seminar Press.

Hall, P. (1982). *Great planning disasters.* Berkeley: University of California Press.

Hammond, K. J. (1989a). *Case-based planning: Viewing planning as a memory task.* New York: Academic Press.

Hammond, K. J. (1989b). *Chef.* In C. K. Riesbeck & R. C. Schank (Eds.), *Inside case-based reasoning* (pp. 165–212). Hillsdale, N.J.: Lawrence Erlbaum.

Harvey, J. H., Yarkin, K. L., Lightner, J. M., & Town, J. P. (1980). Unsolicited interpretation and recall of interpersonal events. *Journal of Personality and Social Psychology 38*, 551–568.

Hewes, D. E., & Graham, M. L. (1989). Second-guessing theory: Review and extension. In J. A. Anderson (Ed.), *Communication yearbook/12* (pp. 213–248). Newbury Park, Cal.: Sage Publications.

Hewes, D. E., Graham, M. K., Doelger, J., & Pavitt, C. (1985). "Second guessing": Message interpretation in social networks. *Human Communication Research 11*, 299–334.

Hewes, D. E., Graham, M. L., Monsour, M., & Doelger, J. A. (1989). Cognition and social information gathering strategies: Reinterpretation assessment in second-guessing. *Human Communication Research 16*, 297–320.

Hobbs, J. R., & Evans, D. A. (1980). Conversation as planned behavior. *Cognitive Science 4*, 349–377.

Homans, G. C. (1961). *Social behavior: Its elementary forms.* New York: Harcourt Brace Jovanovich.

Homans, G. C. (1974). *Social behavior: Its elementary forms* (Revised Edition). New York: Harcourt Brace Jovanovich.

Honeycutt, J. M. (1991). Imagined interactions, imagery and mindfulness/mindlessness: In R. Kunzendorf (Ed.), *Mental imagery* (pp. 121–128). New York: Plenum.

Honeycutt, J. M., Zagacki, K. S., & Edwards, R. (1989). Intrapersonal communication and imagined interactions. In C. Roberts & K. Watson (Eds.), *Readings in intrapersonal communication* (pp. 167–184). Scottsdale: Gorsuch Scarisbrick.

James, W. (1950). *The principles of psychology.* New York: Holt.

Janis, I. L., & Mann, L. (1977). *Decision making: A psychological analysis of conflict, choice, and commitment.* New York: Free Press.

Jones, E. E., & Davis, K. E. (1965). From acts to dispositions: The attribution process in person perception. In L. Berkowitz (Ed.), *Advances in experimental social psychology* (pp. 219–266). New York: Academic Press.

Kellermann, K. (1988, March). *Understanding tactical choice: Metagoals in conversation.* Paper presented at the Temple University conference on goals in discourse. Philadelphia.

Kellermann, K. (1991). The conversation MOP II: Progression through scenes in discourse. *Human Communication Research 17*, 385–414.

Kellermann, K. (1992). Communication: Inherently strategic and primarily automatic. *Communication Monographs 59*, 288–300.

Kellermann, K., & Berger, C. R. (1984). Affect and the acquisition of social information: Sit back, relax, and tell me about yourself. In R. Bostrom (Ed.), *Communication yearbook 8* (pp. 412–445). Newbury Park, Cal.: Sage Publications.

Kellermann, K., Broetzmann, S. Lim, T., & Kitao, K. (1989). The conversation MOP: Scenes in the stream of discourse. *Discourse Processes 12*, 27–62.

Kellermann, K., & Lim, T. (1990). The conversation MOP: III. Timing scenes in discourse. *Journal of Personality and Social Psychology 59*, 1163–1179.

Kellermann, K., & Reynolds, R. (1990). When ignorance is bliss: The role of motivation to reduce uncertainty in uncertainty reduction theory. *Human Communication Research 17*, 5–75.

Kreitler, S., & Kreitler, H. (1987). Plans and planning: Their motivational and cognitive antecedents. In S. L. Friedman, E. K. Skolnick, & R. R. Cocking (Eds.), *Blueprints for thinking: The role of planning in cognitive development* (pp. 110–178). New York: Cambridge University Press.

Levelt, W. J. M. (1989). *Speaking: From intention to articulation.* Cambridge: MIT Press.

Lichtenstein, E. H., & Brewer, W. F. (1980). Memory for goal directed events. *Cognitive Psychology 12*, 412–445.

Miller, G. A., Galanter, E., & Pribram, K. H. (1960). *Plans and the structure of behavior.* New York: Holt, Rinehart, & Winston.

Miller, G. R., & Hewgill, M. A. (1964). The effect of variations in nonfluency on audience ratings of source credibility. *Quarterly Journal of Speech 50*, 36–44.

Newcomb, T. M. (1961). *The acquaintance process*. New York: Holt, Rinehart & Winston.

Newton, D. A., & Burgoon, J. K. (1990). The use and consequences of verbal influence strategies during interpersonal disagreements. *Human Communication Research* 16, 477–518.

Parks, M. R., & Adelman, M. B. (1983). Communication networks and the development of romantic relationships: An expansion of uncertainty reduction theory. *Human Communication Research 10*, 55-79.

Petronio, S., Snyder, E., & Bradford, L. (1992, October). *Planning strategy for the embarrassment of friends: An application and test of Berger's planning theory.* Paper presented at the annual convention of the Speech Communication Association, Chicago.

Planalp, S., & Honeycutt, J. M. (1985). Events that increase uncertainty in personal relationships. *Human Communication Research 11*, 593–604.

Planalp, S., Rutherford, D. K., & Honeycutt, J. M. (1988). Events that increase uncertainty in personal relationships II: Replication and Extension. *Human Communication Research 14*, 516–547.

Read, S. J., & Miller, L. C. (1989). Inter-personalism: Toward a goal-based theory of persons in relationships. In L. A. Pervin (Ed.), *Goal concepts in personality and social psychology* (pp. 413–472). Hillsdale, N.J.: Lawrence Erlbaum.

Reddy, M. J. (1979). The conduit metaphor—A case of frame conflict in our language about language. In A. Ortony (Ed.), *Metaphor and thought* (pp. 284–324). New York: Cambridge University Press.

Rogers, C. R. (1951). *Client-centered therapy, its current practice, implications, and theory.* Boston: Houghton Mifflin.

Roloff, M. E. (1981). *Interpersonal communication: The social exchange approach.* Newbury Park, Cal.: Sage Publications.

Sacerdoti, E. D. (1977). *A structure for plans and behavior.* New York: Elsevier.

Schank, R. C., & Abelson, R. P. (1977). *Scripts, plans, goals and understanding.* Hillsdale, N.J.: Lawrence Erlbaum.

Schlenker, B. (1980). *Impression management: The self-concept, social identity, and interpersonal relations.* Monterey: Brooks-Cole.

Srull, T. K., & Wyer, R. S. (1986). The role of chronic and temporary goals in social information processing. In R. Sorrentino & E. T. Higgins (Eds.), *Handbook of motivation and cognition* (pp. 503–549). New York: Guilford Press.

Sunnafrank, M. (1986). Predicted outcome value during initial interactions: A reformulation of uncertainty reduction theory. *Human Communication Research 13*, 3–33.

Surra, C. A., & Bohman, T. (1991). The development of close relationships: A cognitive perspective. In G. J. O. Fletcher & F. D. Fincham (Eds.), *Cognition in close relationships* (pp. 281–306). Hillsdale, N.J.: Lawrence Erlbaum.

Thibaut, J. W., & Kelley, H. H. (1959). *The social psychology of groups.* New York: John Wiley.

Tracy, K., & Coupland, N. (Eds.) (1990). *Multiple goals in discourse.* Philadelphia: Multilingual Matters.

VanLear, C. A., & Trujillo, N. (1986). On becoming acquainted: A longitudinal study of social judgments. *Journal of Social and Personal Relationships 3*, 375–392.

Waldron, V. R. (1990). Constrained rationality: Situational influences on information acquisition plans and tactics. *Communication Monographs 57*, 184–201.

Wilensky, R. (1983). *Planning and understanding: A computational approach to human reasoning*. Reading, Mass.: Addison-Wesley.

3

The Development of Theory about Automated Patterns of Face-to-Face Human Interaction

JOSEPH N. CAPPELLA

This is a book about substantive theory in communication. In crafting my contribution to this endeavor, I take it that two goals are paramount: to provide some insight of a general sort into the theory-making process and to offer a case study of theory development in a particular substantive domain. I will try to reward the reader's time spent with approaches to both questions.

SOME COMMENTS ON DEVELOPING THEORY

Courses in methodology and statistics give the impression that scientific practices are formulaic. Long lists of do's and don'ts, appropriate and inappropriate technique, make up the central material of such courses. Creativity seems to take second place to technique, mere cookery as Socrates might say. In fairness, there is some truth to these observations about scientific method, procedure, and analysis (although the cunning sometimes required in good experimental design contradicts the apparent formulaic nature of research).

However, the construction of good theory is anything but formulaic. Although philosophers of science (Nagel 1961) and social science (Kaplan 1964; Kerlinger 1973) have written extensively about the nature of theory and criteria for evaluating theory, little of value can be said in general about how to construct subtle, testable, and useful theories. Those of us who, for good or ill, have been engaged in the development of theory can reflect on our experiences but the reader should be warned not to expect guidelines for theory development like those Campbell and Stanley (1966) have provided for experimental design.

A Myth about Laws

One useful function that my comments about theory might be able to serve would be to debunk what I believe are some myths about the nature of social scientific theory. *The first myth is that good theories are sets of laws.* My reason for arguing that this is a myth is not that it is not believed by many practitioners. In fact, in several articles about communication theory the trichotomy among "laws, rules, and systems" suggests that one fundamental type of theory is built around laws of communicative behavior (Berger 1977; Cushman 1977). The view that theories are sets of laws is misleading because, I believe, theories must fundamentally be explanations and laws do not necessarily explain.

Consider the following simple counter-example. Every time I enter my office, if I flip the light switch upward, the overhead light goes on; if I flip the switch downward, the light goes off. This regularity is certainly like a law. Its conditions of application are narrow but can be extended to other contexts with some success. The problem with laws like this one is that it does not explain why the movement of the switch position is followed by the lights going on or off. It does not explain because it does not give a causal account of the linkage between the switch and the lighting or dimming of the bulbs. Laws can be crafted to be causal laws but, in general, laws are not necessarily causal. When laws do not explain, they are in my opinion useless in meeting the primary goal of theory, which is explanation.

Implicit in my argument is the supposition that causal accounts are explanatory and that mere covariation even with time sequencing (i.e., law) is radically insufficient for explanation. Why are causal accounts privileged? First, causal accounts make explicit the nature of the linkage between antecedent and consequent. In the light switch example, the absence of further causal linkages makes it possible to deal with a break in the wiring between the switch and the light box. No one would think to look for the hidden wires (and potential breaks, shorts, loose connections) without some knowledge about the kind of linkage between switch and light and knowledge about the necessity for continuous electron flow. The first reason, then, for privileging causal accounts is that, at least in principle, they suggest the interventions necessary to fix breakdowns in a system.

Second, causal accounts are privileged for psychological reasons related to comprehension and understanding. One of the most important ways that humans achieve what Bransford and McCarrell (1974) call the "click of comprehension" is by grasping the causal relationships that exist among a set of events, items, ideas, words, and so on. For example, to understand the important role of a carburetor in a standard combustion engine, it is necessary to explain the causal relationships among gasoline injection, sparking, timing, pistons, and their connections to the drive train. What determines an acceptable causal explanation (that is, one which needs no further elaboration) depends on the knowledge that the individual already has and accepts as given. In the case of the engine's carburetor, some knowledge about combustion is necessary to understand that gasoline and air must be mixed in the presence of a spark to create an explosion.

The principle that I am trying to illustrate with this example is that causal explanation is central to theory building because causal explanation is central to ordinary human understanding. If, as I claim, the purpose of theory is to explain, then the nature of explanations in theories should dovetail with the human psychology of comprehension. A corollary conclusion is that what constitutes an acceptable explanation depends upon pre-existing knowledge which itself needs no further explanation. In scientific explanation, this prior knowledge exists not in individuals but in the community of scholars that constitutes the practitioners in a domain of study.[1]

The Myth of Causal Linkage

The centrality of causal knowledge to the development of theory leads to a *second myth: causal relationship can be established unequivocally.* Here I take the lead from Richard W. Miller (1987), who argues in his *Fact and Method* that "causation . . . has no informative and general analysis" (6). Miller's position is that no unassailable logical explication of the concept of causality is possible, whether one focuses on the human or physical and biological sciences. His view is based on a variety of condemnations of conceptions of causality but one of the central arguments is that all causal claims require an inferential leap. The presumed size of the leap is dependent upon reigning viewpoints about what is acceptable and what is unacceptable causal inference. For example, in the physical sciences before electromagnetic forces were accepted as forms of causal influence, force needed to be explained in terms of the very human "push-pull" types of effect. Invisible forces (such as electromagnetic) acting over a distance were not readily admitted as acceptable causal agents in part because the inferential leaps were too large to accept.

However, Miller is not a nihilist nor another member of the bandwagon of science bashers. Rather, he is a realist who recognizes both the importance and the limitations of causal thinking in the development of theory. But if causal explanation is central to theory and, at the same time, no general, informative conception of causality is possible, how can theorists proceed to confirm and disconfirm their causal accounts? Miller's answer, and one that I accept as both reasonable and congruent with practice, is that "confirmation . . . is the fair causal comparison of a hypothesis with its current rivals" (155). Basically, his answer is that confirmation is the attempt to build a coherent causal case for a position and to settle arguments about competing causal accounts of the phenomena. Before elaborating on Miller's position some, let us turn our attention to two other myths about confirmation and disconfirmation of theories through empirical means.

The Myth of Confirmation

The third myth about theories is that they can be confirmed empirically. On logical grounds, theories cannot be confirmed through empirical means alone (Giere, 1984). The confirmation of theories empirically occurs through its predictions, which take the form: if H is true, then P is true (where H is a hypothesis derived from the theory and P a prediction dependent upon the truth value of the hypothesis). But elementary courses in logic show us that the observation of the consequent, P, allows no conclusion about the existence or truth value of H. Thus, on logical grounds alone, affirming the consequent does not allow affirmation of the antecedent and so this means of empirical confirmation is shut off.

The alternative is to deny the consequent. Again elementary logic tells us that the absence of the consequent, not-P, entails the absence of the antecedent, not-H. Thus, it would seem that theories could acquire confirmatory empirical evidence by denying the consequent. Unfortunately, this method produces a paradoxical result in which all kinds of irrelevant evidence must be accepted as confirmatory. For example, the claim that all humans have DNA can, on logical (but unreasonable) grounds, be confirmed by observing things without DNA such as coffee cups, Toyota Corollas, antique washboards, spandex, and so on, all of which are nonhuman. The bottom line is that normal logical criteria of confirmation do not seem to be helpful in empirical justification of a theory's predictions.

The Myth of Disconfirmation

The fourth myth is derived from the third and holds that theories can be disconfirmed. The fallacies that lay behind the third myth were recognized long ago by philosophers of science and led some away from criteria for confirmation to criteria for disconfirmation (Popper 1959). After all, the reasoning goes, if denying the consequent is a logically acceptable basis for denying the antecedent, then, when not-P is observed in the context of H (rather than not-H), the hypothesis (if P, then H) derived from the theory is false and the theory too must be incorrect.

Although logically acceptable for the purposes of disconfirmation, Popper's procedures are useless in practice, especially in the social sciences (although also in the physical sciences). The reasons are twofold. First, most theories are a complex network of assumptions and propositions from which certain hypotheses are derived for testing (if H, then P). If a particular prediction is disconfirmed, is the entire theory disconfirmed or only that part of the theory involved in deriving the prediction? Even focusing on the part that is involved in the derived hypothesis, which proposition or assumption can be identified as the source of the erroneous conclusion? If the theory is successful in other ways, it would make little practical sense to scrap the whole because a single prediction is disconfirmed. The first problem with the disconfirmation criterion, then, is that it is based on a simplistic view of the theories from which the prediction is derived. Because theories are networks of associations, finding the problematic linkage in the face of disconfirmatory evidence is non-trivial.

The second problem is that predictive hypotheses (if H, then P) are conceptual rather than operational claims. Testing them requires operationalizing the constructs contained in H and in P. Except in the most extreme cases, operational definitions seldom exhaust the domain of meaning spanned by the conceptual terms they test. In the face of disconfirmation, then, there will typically be residual meaning in the prediction that has not been touched by the particular operational test. The fact that theoretical terms are broader in meaning than their operational counterparts adds to the difficulty of moving from disconfirmation in particular operational context to disconfirmation of the theory from which the tested hypothesis is derived.

Let me summarize what appears to be an unhappy state of affairs with regard to theories. I have maintained that theories are at heart general explanations. In turn, explanations should be causal for reasons of psychological utility (comprehension) and practical utility (intervention). But no general, logical account of causality is possible and the standard criteria for confirming or disconfirming competing causal accounts are found wanting. What, then, are the alternatives? Is confirmation of causal theory possible and, if so, how?

In building toward answers to these questions, Miller (1987) implicitly invites us to orient our thinking about theory differently. Theories are more like arguments, causal arguments, than like formal mathematical or logical systems. As such, evaluating them relative to their competitors is not a mechanical process dictated by well-defined rules and hierarchical decision points but rather depends upon the same criteria required by other forms of argument: substantive knowledge, pertinent and thorough evidence, warrantable reasoning, low inference causal linkages, and so on. Theories are confirmed to the extent that fair comparisons to rival theories are decided in terms of the focal rather than the rival theories. Of course, settling honest disagreements through rational argument is notorious for its imprecision and lack of closure. However, real debates over scientific theories are debates over incomplete, imprecise, and circumstantial accounts of phenomena just as is the case in legal, political, and public advocacy.

Miller would have been remiss, however, if he did not attempt to delineate some of the bases for "fair comparisons" of causal theory. Comparison depends upon the existence of rival, articulate, and competitive theories. "Fairness" suggests that some standards of comparison are possible. In comparing alternative causal accounts, Miller suggests that first the level of the comparison be taken into consideration. When the theories are at the same level (level I differences) both are operating with similar methods, principles, and operational techniques. Reminiscent of Kuhn (1962), the theories may be said to be operating within the same paradigm. At issue, then, is which causal account is to be preferred. Criteria for evaluation here will include a weighing of successful and unsuccessful empirical tests, favoring low as opposed to high inference linkages in the causal story, preferring deeper causal accounts (reductionistic) rather than shallower ones, searching for connections to other related theories, and so on (Miller 1987, 200–212).

Level II comparisons recognize that the theories being disputed are "competing for dominance of a major field" (Miller 1987, 212) and so the very process of what constitutes acceptable testing procedures is at issue. Controversies between Chomsky (1959) and Skinner (1957) in the explanation of the origins of verbal behavior and, more recently, in interaction analysis between conversation analysts and quantitatively based researchers (Sacks, Schegloff, & Jefferson 1974; Duncan & Fiske 1977) are representative of level II controversies. Miller believes that successful arguments are ones that not only account for more of the empirical anomalies than the competitors but argue against competing theories by employing principles accepted within the rival's framework. A third possibility for fair comparison is to search for contradictory evidence outside of either theoretic domain but whose implications favor one of the rivals. For example, Fiske's (1986) theories about oppositional readings of media texts have been criticized for the excessive cognitive demands placed on viewers under conditions that normally require only limited resources (Condit 1989). In this instance, the frequency of occurrence of oppositional readings is undermined on the basis of argument and evidence from human cognition. Although settling level II disputes is no small task, what is at issue is not merely a particular causal account of a set of phenomena but dominance of a field of inquiry.[2]

Let me summarize my position. Good theories are causal explanations of puzzling phenomena which craft precise and coherent arguments in support of the account offered and offer reasons for dismissing competing causal accounts. Good theories can be evaluated by assessing their ability to account for a broad range of puzzling facts, to offer successful arguments against competitors, and to provide deep causal explanations that connect without contradiction to bodies of accepted knowledge in other domains of inquiry. The adventure of theory construction does not admit a methodology independent of substantive knowledge. The evaluation of theory will never be driven by simplistic recipes. Good theories are good causal arguments.

A THEORY OF FACE-TO-FACE INTERACTION

Much of the research that I have conducted in the past twenty years has been directed at crafting causal accounts of the patterns of interaction in two-person conversations. These accounts have focused on three broad areas: (a) interspeaker influences on the durations and intensities of certain vocal and kinesic behaviors, what I have called mutual influence (Cappella 1981) or adaptation (Cappella, Palmer, & Donzella 1991); (b) turn-taking (Cappella 1985a; Duncan & Fiske 1977); (c) the biological and evolutionary bases for mutual adaptation and emotional signalling (Cappella 1991). Within these three areas, I have struggled to articulate causal accounts of the mechanisms that might lie behind the observed behavioral regularities. The remainder of this chapter will discuss the outlines of this struggle in explaining mutual influence and adaptation (I will not discuss turn-taking or the evolutionary model for reasons of space). In the process, perhaps certain of the skeletal abstractions of the earlier sections will take on flesh and bones.

Early Research

Our studies of dyadic interaction began with attempts to replicate the important work of Jaffe and Feldstein (1970) on the sequential structure of talk and silence sequences.

Their work was important to me for several reasons. First, much of the work in interpersonal communication at the time was influenced significantly by the work of Newcomb (1961) and Byrne (1971) on attitude similarity and attraction. Although this work was consequential in the study of attraction generally, some have argued that early relationship formation may depend more on information that people normally have at their disposal (for example, interactional styles) than is the case with the information provided by bogus (or real) attitude scales (Cappella 1984; Duck 1976). Thus, it might be more interesting, and certainly more realistic, to study the role of similarity in interactional styles as the basis for attraction. Jaffe and Feldstein's work provided the benchmark conceptualization for interactional style at least as applied to the vocal behaviors of talk and silence.

Second, Jaffe and Feldstein were actually studying the dynamics of interaction rather than making inferences about processes from static data. One of the basic distinctions in studying social interaction is that between similarity in aggregate behaviors (for example, mean rates of speech for two partners) and adjustments in manifested behavior by the partners in real time (for example, the correlation between two persons' rates of speech over forty thirty-second units of the interaction). The former is called mutual influence and the latter processes is called adaptation. Both are based on interaction and behavior but mutual influence is an aggregate and static measure requiring comparisons across pairs of individuals to assess statistical reliability while adaptation is a dynamic phenomenon that can be assessed on a single pair of persons (if the amount of observation time is long enough). From the outset, our work on social interaction was geared toward studying the actual dynamics of interaction at the level of the individual dyad.

The initial study conducted was a replication of a Jaffe and Feldstein (1970) design in which persons had three conversations but switched partners in the second and third conversations (Cappella 1980). Only talk and silence behaviors were coded. Our hope was that a certain class of models, called Markov models, would allow accurate prediction of the distribution of talk and silence sequences within a conversation and, more interestingly, would allow prediction of such sequences in conversations of persons who had not yet interacted. That is, using the definition of person A's style from a conversation with partner B (and C's with a partner D), could we predict the distribution of talk and silence behaviors when A is paired with person C? Although both within-conversation and between-conversation predictions were statistically significant, the predictions within the same conversation were stronger than those when persons switched to new partners.

What was obviously happening was that people were not maintaining their same talk and silence style as they switched partners. The style was not fixed but was adjusted somehow. That the adjustment existed was the first, unsurprising finding; Describing the process of adjustment and then trying to explain how the adjustment came about was trickier.

Both Eliot Chappel (1970) and Matarazzo and Wiens (1972) had reported correlations between activity levels for partners in interaction. For example, indicators of conversational tempo for partners (rates of speech and latency to respond) were positively related across pairs in many circumstances. Jaffe and Feldstein (1970) offered similar findings. The problem with these findings is that they are aggregate measures of similarity across pairs of partners and say nothing about the individual dynamics of adaptation. For example, a group of dyads may show no overall correlation in aggregate measures of pausing even though some pairs may actually be adapting toward one another while other pairs are adapting away from one another.

To get around this problem, each conversation was analyzed separately. For example, a thirty-minute interaction was divided into sixty thirty-second time periods and speech rate within each period calculated for each person.[3] produces two series of observations which can be assessed for the kind of correlation that exists between the series using the methods of time series analysis (Cappella 1980b; McCleary & Hay, 1980). Using this technique, a considerable amount of variation across dyads in the degree and kind of adaptation was found. Some partners adjusted toward one another, some away, and some showed no regular pattern of adjustment at all.

These findings did motivate some early thoughts about why these adjustments were occurring and what mechanisms might account for such processes. However, if only talk and silence behaviors exhibited these adjustments, then a theory about adaptation in talk and silence processes would be a narrow theory indeed. The effort required to build theory should first ensure that the ground for the structure is empirically quite solid. So, I explored a broader evidentiary base for our own findings about adaptation in vocal behaviors. I am trying to give the reader a bit of the history of our study of mutual influence because the exploration of a wider set of research was based on what was to us an anomaly: individual adjustment in style with new partners but variation across persons in how this adjustment took place.

Supporting evidence

Mutual adaptation is arguably the essential characteristic of every interpersonal interaction. The basis for this argument is fourfold.

Mutual adaptation is pervasive. A substantial body of research indicates that social ineractions are marked by processes of mutual influence (Cappella 1981, 1985b, 1991). In adult interactions, mutual adaptation has been observed among various speech behaviors including accents (Giles & Powesland 1975), speech rate (Street 1984; Webb 1972), pauses (Cappella & Planalp 1981; Feldstein & Welkowitz 1978), latency to respond (Cappella & Planalp 1981), vocal intensity (Natale 1975), fundamental vocal frequency (Buder 1991), and turn durations (Matarazzo & Wiens 1972). A range of kinesic behaviors exhibit adaptive patterns as well including postural and gestural behaviors (LaFrance 1982; Maurer & Tindall 1983), movement synchrony (Bernieri, Reznick, & Rosenthal 1988), gaze (Klienke, Staneski, & Berger 1975; Noller 1984), head nods and facial affect (Hale & Burgoon 1984), facial displays of emotion (Krause, Stemer, Sanger-Alt, & Wanger 1989), and more generalized hostile affect (Gottman 1979; Pike & Sillars 1985). More deliberate behaviors such as self-disclosures (Davis 1976, 1977), excuses (McLaughlin, Cody, & Rosenstein 1983), and stares (Greenbaum & Rosenfeld 1978) exhibit the patterns of contingent responsiveness characteristic of adaptation. The diversity of behaviors implicated in mutual adaptation is testimony to the centrality of this process, and the mechanisms behind it, in human interaction.

Mutual adaptation occurs in the earliest forms of human interaction. Although it may not be surprising to find that children with well-developed language capacity exhibit adaptation to adult partners in non-content speech behaviors (Street & Cappella 1989), similar findings with the linguistically less developed are striking. Jasnow and Feldstein (1987) found matching in latency of response for mothers and their nine-month-old infants. Bernieri,

Reznick, and Rosenthal (1988) observed greater synchrony in body movements during interactions between mothers and their 14–18-month-old infants than between mothers and a different infant. Adaptation of the infant to the mother has been observed even earlier with 3- and 4-month-olds (Symons & Moran 1987; Cohn & Tronick 1987). In a remarkable demonstration of synchrony in stimulation, Berghout-Austin and Peery (1983) conducted a statistically reliable test of movement synchrony between neonates 30–56 hours old and an experimenter. The experimenter simply talked to the neonate at a facial distance of nineteen centimeters. Movement synchrony was present in all five infants.

The effects of infant responsiveness to the mother are not simply a function of the mother's usually positive affect. Murray and Trevarthen (1985) had mothers adopt a blank face expression while interacting with their 6–12-week-old infants. In comparison to normal play situations the infants exhibited more signs of distress, less smiling and relaxation, and less gaze toward the mother during the blank-face sequence. In a variation of this theme, these same authors played back to the infant a videotape of the mother playing in a previous session with her infant. The mother was behaving normally but her behavior was "out of sync" with that of her infant. The infant responded in a parallel way to the "out of sync" mother and to the "blank faced mother" suggesting that synchrony rather than affect that was the regulative force.

Together with an array of other data (Cappella 1991; Field 1987), the above studies suggest that adaptation occurs not only in childhood and infancy but even very early in the life of the neonate. Such evidence can be interpreted, I think, as strong support for the claim that mutual adaptation is a fundamental process in human social relations.

Mutual adaptation is associated with important relational outcomes and individual differences. Positive social evaluations have been associated with certain types of mutual adaptation in interaction. Welkowitz and Kuc (1973) found that partners who were rated higher on warmth also exhibited greater similarity on speech latency. Street (1982) constructed audio tapes in which an interviewee's speech rate, latency, and duration converged, partially converged, or diverged with respect to that of an interviewer. The divergent speech was evaluated more negatively. Similar findings on rate, content, and pronunciation were obtained by Giles and Smith (1979). These findings have been replicated in naturalistic contexts as well (Street 1984).

It is not only vocal features of speech that are related to evaluative social judgments. Davis and Martin (1978) found that the percentage of responsive comments, independent of their frequency, was positively related to attraction. Davis and Perkowitz (1979) observed that the number of pleasurable shocks given depended on how responsive the recipient was and the level of appropriateness of the response. Recent work by Bernieri (1988) found that judges' ratings of movement synchrony between high school students in a teaching situation was positively associated with the students' self reports of rapport, a conclusion espoused by Tickle-Degnen and Rosenthal (1987) on the basis of their literature review. Even ratings of movement synchrony between infants and their mothers are positively associated with independent ratings of the child's positivity (Bernieri, Reznick, & Rosenthal 1988).

The research summarized above suggests that the presence of mutual influence in automatic behaviors may be associated with positive assessments of those interactions by observers of the interaction as well as participants. Accumulating evidence is beginning to suggest that deviation from normal mutual adaptation processes may be characteristic of certain at-risk populations. Fararone and Hurtig (1985) studied socially skilled and unskilled males in interaction finding that skilled conversationalists showed a greater degree of sequential patterning than did the less skilled. Feldstein, Konstantareas, Oxman, and Webster (1982) observed reciprocity in certain speech behaviors for counselors and parents of autistic children but not between the autistic children and their parents. Similar findings have been obtained with adult schizophrenics (Glaister, Feldstein, & Pollock 1980) and depressives (Jaffe & Anderson, in press).

At the relationship level, Gottman's (1979) widely cited findings are relevant. Although all of the couples he studied tended to show reciprocity in hostile affect in discussions about common problems in their marriages, the less well-adjusted couples showed greater hostile affect than the better adjusted couples. These findings have been replicated with other data by Gottman (1979 using the data of Rausch, Barry, Hertel, & Swain 1974) and in other contexts by Margolin and Wampold (1981) and Schapp (1982). Pike and Sillars (1985) also found greater reciprocity in negative vocal affect for dissatisfied as opposed to satisfied married couples. Using face-directed gaze rather than negative affect, Noller's (1984) satisfied couples exhibited greater correlation between partners than did the dissatisfied couples. Overall, partners in satisfying, established relationships appear to differ in the type of mutual influence their interaction shows relative to those in less satisfied relationships.

The pattern of covariation observed in adults between patterns of interactional adaptation and relational outcomes and individual competencies is no less true of the interactions between infants and their primary caretakers. Ainsworth (1978) reported some data indicating that infants who were responded to more sensitively by their mothers at three months also were more securely attached at twelve months. Isabella, Belsky, and van Eye (1989) provided a more direct test of the synchrony-attachment hypothesis. Mothers and their infants were observed interacting at one, three, and nine months of age and categorized as primarily synchronous or asynchronous during the observed interactional period. Pairs that were synchronous at ages one and three months tended to be securely attached at one year. Because secure attachment by the infant is central to exploration, cognitive growth, the development of later interactional ties, and the functioning of all primate species (Bowlby, 1969), these data are important indications of the potential significance of adaptation to the development of the organism.

Certain conditions may also interfere with the development of normal adaptive interchanges. For example, interactions between three- and five-month-old infants and their mothers were less synchronous when the infants were pre-term than when they were full-term (Lester, Hoffman, & Brazelton 1985). Mothers who were asked to "look depressed" seemed to induce by their observing infants greater facial distress, higher activity and heart rate, and more attempts to engage the mother in normal interaction (Cohn & Tronick 1983) than did mothers who displayed normal interactions. When mothers who were depressed were asked to "look depressed," their infants' responsiveness was no different from what it was when the mothers were asked to interact normally with their infants. These infants seemed less agitated and less active overall and also exhibited lower heart rates (Field 1984). Field et al. (1988) have also shown that the interactional patterns of 3–6-month-old infants with depressed mothers are maintained when the infant interacts with a stranger who is not herself depressed. A great deal more research is necessary in this area before we know whether these interaction patterns of depressed mothers with their infants have negative long-term consequences for the mother-infant bond and for individual development. Nevertheless, the results are certainly suggestive of the significance of mutual adaptation in infant development.

Implications for theory

The early studies and review of literature that we conducted provided the outlines for subsequent ventures into the domain of theory. What the evidence above suggests is that adaptation and mutual influence are regular occurrences in human social interactions, even in the earliest interactions of infant and mother. They also suggest that the degree and type of adaptation and mutual influence also distinguish satisfying from unsatisfying relationships and may also distinguish certain at-risk populations from their more competent counterparts.

The data do not suggest their own explanation; but they imply the kinds of constraints that must be satisfied by subsequent excursions into the nether world of causal explanation. Let me draw out some of the constraints. First, a good theory of adaptation must be broad enough to encompass the range of behaviors that seem to be governed by some form of rule of adaptation. A first cut would distinguish between relatively automatic and relatively deliberate behaviors. For example, explaining why speech tempo might be contagious may take quite a different form than explanations of reciprocity of self-disclosure. Most of my theoretical work has focused on the more automatic forms of adaptation, both because I was struck with the continuities across adult populations and infant populations and because the findings were more subtle (and less predictable) than those for the more deliberate behaviors.

The range of behaviors exhibiting some form of adaptation showed that the typical form of adaptation was not necessarily toward greater similarity (sometimes called reciprocity), nor necessarily toward greater difference (sometimes called compensation). Rather, the typical form of the adaptation depended on the behavior being studied. For example, speech tempo between partners is typically reciprocal, invasions of personal space typically produce strong compensatory reactions.

A third constraint was a direct result of the methodological decision to study individual dyads. As noted, our early studies showed that not all dyads followed the same patterns of adaptation even with the same behavior. Variation in adaptation could be a function of individual differences, relational differences, and social situational constraints (Cappella 1981). These complexities must be accounted for by a good theory of mutual influence.

The apparent continuity of adaptive processes for more automatic behaviors across the developmental spectrum from infancy to adulthood is both a puzzling conclusion and striking. Why should adaptation occur so early in the ontogeny of the organism? What function do such processes serve? How can we explain their existence and their purpose in the development of the species?

Two lines of explanation were developed. The first focused on a theory of adaptation between adult partners and also between infants and adult caretakers in relatively automatic behaviors manifested during social interaction. This was called discrepancy-arousal theory (Cappella & Greene 1982). A second, and quite different, tack explored the evolutionary and biological bases for the existence of adaptation processes in the human species (Cappella 1991). I will consider only the former theory in the sections below, leaving meta-theoretical comments on biological origins to another forum.

Discrepancy-Arousal (DA) Theory

Discrepancy-arousal theory was designed to account for the research findings in the literature on mutual influence. This chapter is not the place to enter the minutiae of the theory. It has been described thoroughly elsewhere (Cappella & Greene 1982; Cappella 1983) and debated (Street & Giles 1982; Burgoon & Hale 1988). A synopsis of the theory will identify its parts and their temporal relation.

Two persons in interaction assess each other's behavior relative to their own expectation about the other's behavior. This comparison is a kind of discrepancy wherein the expected behavior is determined by social situational factors, individual preferences, and experience with the partner (if any).

Discrepancy is assumed to produce arousal in the form of cognitive activation. Most theories of cognitive activation, alerting, and attention assume that discrepancy (or its variants in terms of interruption or unusualness) is a key causal force (Mandler 1975). In turn, cognitive activation is posited to determine affective response. These two components of the theory are nontrivial because the overall relationship between discrepancy and affect is nonlinear and varies as a function of individual differences as well as relational factors. Following Berlyne (1967), activation levels are presumed to influence affective responses so that excessive changes in activation are experienced as affectively negative and low to moderate changes are experienced as affectively neutral to positive. The affective changes, in turn, are paralleled by behavioral avoidance (for negative affect) and behavioral approach (with positive affect).

The theory explains the existence of both reciprocal and compensatory effects as a function of the overlap of regions of acceptance and rejection which, in turn, depend upon individual differences, prior experience with the partner, relationship stage, and situational norms. For example, in neutral to mildly positive social settings with acquaintances, severe violations of personal space should be very arousing, experienced as affectively negative, and result in avoidance responses and, hence, compensation. However, when the partners are intimates, the region of acceptance is widened and violations of personal space norms are experienced as affectively positive and approach results. With a different behavior like speech tempo, very high rates of speech might be arousing but would probably have to reach extreme rates before they were experienced as affectively negative with concomitant withdrawal.

The theory did not, of course, arise *ex nihilo* nor simply from the foundations of prior research findings. Other explanatory avenues were available but not chosen. In the spirit of Miller's "plausible causal alternatives" let us consider briefly other theories. Argyle and Dean's (1965) equilibrium theory and its extensions (Argyle & Cook 1976) were rejected almost immediately. Equilibrium theory grew from Argyle's early research on distance and gaze, which found that a strong compensatory relationship existed between these two behaviors. Equilibrium theory was constructed primarily to explain compensatory effects and, as a consequence, was not well suited to handle the reciprocal effects obtained in other behavioral domains (self-disclosure, speech tempo, and so on). Also, equilibrium theory offered an explanatory mechanism, namely approach and avoidance forces, which had no obvious measurable counterpart. The explanation would be extremely difficult to test without falling prey to tautology. Thus, equilibrium theory was rejected on grounds of breadth (failure to explain reciprocal effects) and testability (no independent measures of approach and avoidance forces).

Other theories were also rejected. Burgoon (Burgoon & Jones 1976; Burgoon 1978) had a theory of personal space violations that was not considered a competitor because it was too narrow in scope. Similarly, Stern's (1974) schema theory was too specific, applying to infants' responses to human facial displays (even though the discrepancy component of his theory was used centrally in DA theory). The chief causal competitors were Giles' Accommodation Theory (Giles & Powesland 1975) and Patterson's Arousal Labeling theory (Patterson 1976). Each of these was rejected for two reasons, the same in both cases. Both were excessively flexible, in my opinion. For example, the cognitive process of "labeling" in Patterson's theory could account for any outcome post hoc and could be used to predict any outcome. This ease in accounting for results makes it impossible ever to reject definitively either of these theories based on the prevailing results.

The second problem is more substantive. Both Patterson's and Giles's theories require a good deal of cognitive weighing of information (in the form of labeling in the former and attribution in the latter) that runs counter to the rather rapid adjustments that seem to be occurring in speech tempo, gesture, gaze, and so on. Although attribution and labeling certainly occur over the course of an interaction, explaining adjustments that occur in 1–2-second time frames would seem to require a more rapid and automatic mechanism. Thus, DA theory posited arousal change as the mediating mechanism between perception of the partner's behavior and response to it. This mechanism was thought to solve the "speed of response" problem by employing an automatic and relatively rapid mediating process.

These various accounts have been debated (Andersen 1985; Burgoon & Hale 1988; Street & Giles 1982), and newer competitors have arisen (Burgoon & Hale 1982; Giles, Mulac, Bradac, & Johnson 1987; Patterson 1982). A variety of tests of the predictions of the various theories have also been carried out but no crucial tests have been attempted, perhaps because such tests are almost impossible to design. The point is that, while the development of theory depends upon the pattern of findings that needs to be explained, the causal account chosen takes place in the context of prevailing causal accounts and offers an argument for preferring one account over another. Sometimes these arguments are meta-theoretical (breadth, simplicity, and so on) and sometimes substantive (for example, cognitive demands); occasionally, they are empirical. They are seldom definitive until all appeals to the various courts of scientific and scholarly discourse are heard.

Evidence for DA Theory

Three categories of evidence have been used to test DA theory: consistency with previous research, new research advancing the empirical evidence for processes of adaptation, and research testing predictions derived directly from

DA. Evidence showing that DA theory is consistent with previous evidence can be of two broad kinds. First, the theory must be consistent with and explain findings indicative of mutual influence and adaptation. The central goals of the theory are to offer an explanation of how adaptation occurs at all in social encounters and to account for the variation that occurs in adaptation as a function of individual, relational, and social variables. If the theory is unsuccessful in meeting either of these goals, then it must be judged a failure. These basics are reviewed in Cappella and Greene (1982), Cappella (1983), and Cappella and Greene (1984), and will not be repeated here.

A second kind of consistency with established findings considers indirect predictions from the theory and the empirical evidence in support of such inferences. For example, although the theory is about patterns of behavioral covariation, we would also expect patterns of covariation in arousal between partners under certain conditions, because arousal change is hypothesized to be a mediator of discrepancy and behavioral response. Such evidence exists and is reviewed in Cappella (1983, 127–128). Recent research by Levenson and Gottman (1983, 1985) corroborates such covariation and its significance for the conduct of interaction. Such indirect predictions could be multiplied many times over. They represent the causal structure of the theory. In the absence of supporting evidence for such linkages, the theory must again be called into question.

What I hope to clear is that a theory has primary goals and secondary inferences. Evaluation of the theory's success begins with its ability to account for the primary fact pattern (in the case of DA the primary fact pattern is behavioral adaptation) and to adduce evidence to support the secondary inferences from the network of proposed causal linkages. Because many theories involve the construction of circumstantial cases, both direct and indirect evidence are important in building a strong causal argument.

Two tests of DA. Two indirect tests of the explanatory mechanisms posited by DA have been undertaken. Both employed personality differences as the basis for predictions and used an experimental paradigm that manipulated conversational distance using a confederate. Research on conversational distance shows that when distances that are close are compared to normal distances, people withdraw by reducing face-directed gaze, vocalization, latency to escape, and postural directness and orientation (Cappella 1981; Patterson 1973). This effect is very strong and easily produces compensatory reactions under conditions of neutral to positive attraction and in the absence of significant cultural differences in norms for personal space.

If DA theory is correct, then this compensatory reaction ought to be able to be modified by factors that would widen the acceptance region for behaviors that are discrepant from expectation. By widening the acceptance region, what would be too much arousal change would be experienced as an acceptable amount of arousal change. Compensatory reactions should become reciprocal under such conditions.

Self monitoring is a personality variable introduced by Snyder (1974, 1979) which posited that persons high in this characteristic (a) would be concerned with appropriateness of their actions, (b) would be attentive to situational cues for how to act, (c) would be capable of controlling their actions, (d) would use this ability, and (e) would be less consistent in their behavior across situations than would their low self-monitoring counterparts. It appears that high self monitors should behave as if what is socially discrepant or unusual behavior would depend upon the cues given by the partner rather than looking inward to their own standards. If the partner adopts a close distance for conversation, the high self monitors might in turn define the conversation as a personal and intimate one, and reciprocate rather than compensate (or withdraw) from the interaction. This is equivalent to the highs having a wider acceptance region than the lows.

In a study testing this hypothesis (Cappella 1985c), high and low self monitors interacted in an interview setting with a confederate of the same sex who randomly took a close seated position (about twelve inches knee to knee) or a normal position (about twenty-four inches). The interactions were videotaped and later coded for a variety of vocal and kinesic behaviors. The ones of primary interest here are an index of affiliation (a sum of gaze and posture and orientation) and smiles and laughter. Both the low and high self-monitoring subjects compensated for the close distances of the confederate but the high self monitors, particularly those who scored highly on the acting subscales of the self monitoring scale, compensated significantly less than the lows. Thus, while the fully crossed interaction between distance and self monitoring did not obtain, the expected interaction did obtain with the highs compensating less, presumably because they were operating with a wider acceptance region.

The second study in this series focused on individuals who were high and low in sensation seeking (Zuckerman 1979). High sensation seekers should also have a wider acceptance region because it is more difficult to arouse them than the low sensation seekers exploded to the same level of stimulation. Also, when they do become aroused, the highs treat the arousal as positive, whereas the lows tend to treat the arousal as negative. Using sensation seeking as a possible mediator directly implicates the arousal change-affect complex central to the mechanisms of DA theory. The prediction was similar to that of the study with self monitors: the high sensation seekers should compensate less than the lows to a manipulation of close (as opposed to normal) interpersonal distance.

The experimental situation was the same as that described in the study of self monitors, as was the coding of behaviors. The desired interaction between sensation seeking and distance on nonverbal affiliative response did not materialize, although the means were in the correct directions. When a measure sensitive to the person's experience of arousal in the situation was employed as a state measure of sensation seeking (Zuckerman 1976), the desired interaction effect did result. Thus, people who experienced the interaction as arousing and as affectively positive tended to compensate less than those who experienced it as arousing and affectively negative. If DA theory's account is correct, the width of acceptance regions would be cited as the explanatory mechanism for the observed effect.

The tests of DA conducted so far are rather indirect. That is, there are several inferential steps between the manipulation and the prediction. Even if the predictions had been overturned by the results, the theory could not be immediately cast aside, because the reasoning linking personality differences to differences in widths of acceptance regions must itself be assumed to be correct. Since this reasoning is not a component of DA theory, studies using a network of personality reasoning and DA assumptions can only test the combined network (reasoning plus assumptions) and not the theoretical assumptions alone.

The point that I would like to emphasize, though, is that it is common practice throughout the sciences to test networks of propositions. Some of the propositions will be provided by the theory under investigation (in this case DA theory), some will come from experimental procedures (e.g., acceptable manipulations of personal space), and some will come from outside the domain of the theory proper (e.g., characteristics of high sensation seekers). Any given test, then, tests the network of propositions giving support to the network if successful and, if unsuccessful, disconfirming some component of the network but leaving open just what has been disconfirmed.

Recent studies of adaptation. Research related to DA theory has also focused on advancing the empirical base of studies of adaptation. The empirical work on interaction is biased overwhelmingly toward studies of aggregate similarity and difference between partners; far less attention has been given to the actual dynamics of adaptation. To redress this imbalance, work in our laboratory has been considered the dynamics of nonverbal exchange in 3- to 6-year-old children in interaction with an experimenter (Street & Cappella 1989), and in adults in free discussion situations (Cappella, Palmer, & Donzella 1991).

In the former study, children interacted with an experimenter in a play situation. Their voices were tape recorded and transcribed. The extent to which each child adapted the tempo of his or her voice (speech rate and latency to respond are the prime indicators of this construct) to that of the experimenter was assessed using cross correlational procedures common in time series analysis. The larger the correlation, the greater the adaptation of the child to the adult. The sign of the correlation indicates whether the adaptation is toward the experimenter (positive) or away (negative). On the basis of the transcript, we also coded the level of syntactic development and pragmatic development (via a judgment of topical responsiveness). A judge also evaluated the degree of involvement exhibited by the children. Thus, each child had a score for speech adaptation (the cross correlation) as well as several indicators of linguistic and social development.

The overall trend was for the children to show reciprocity (positive cross correlation) in speech tempo. However, they exhibited a considerable amount of variation in the magnitude and type of adaptation. None of the variation in this measure was explained by simple differences in age. Children who were more advanced in pragmatic development (that is, judged to be more topically responsive) also adapted more to the partner. This study shows that individual dyads can be evaluated for degree of adaptation and that these measures of behavioral responsiveness can also be accounted for by individual differences in development.

In a recent study with adult females, adaptive processes across a broader range of kinesic and vocal behaviors were the focus (Cappella, Palmer, & Donzella 1991). Two groups of four females interacted with all others in the group, two at a time. One group consisted of highly expressive individuals, while the other group members were low in expressiveness. The persons' behaviors were coded for vocal behavior as well as face-directed gaze, illustrators (speech-related gestures), adaptors (other gestures), smiles and laughter, and posture and orientation. Although several indices were developed and studied, one, dubbed "activity," deserves special mention. This index represents social stimulation present during interaction and is a sum of floor-holding, vocalization, illustrators, adaptors, and smiles.

Individual time series analysis for each dyad on the activity index showed that people tended to reciprocate one another's activity. None of the dyadic pairs (twelve in all) showed compensatory interaction patterns, although two dyads were not adaptive at all. Overall, the degree of adaptation of the high expressive pairs was no different from that of the low expressive pairs, even though the highs were on average more active than the lows. Importantly, individuals who were high adaptors in one dyad were not necessarily high adaptors in another; persons who elicited adaptation did not necessarily do so consistently. It appears that the degree of adaptation is negotiated uniquely for each dyad, even though the overall pattern is one of reciprocity in activity levels. A final result of consequence is the observed positive association between attraction to the partner and adaptation to the partner: people who adapted more to the partner were also more attracted to the partner.

Together, these two studies suggest that adaptation in vocal and kinesic behaviors is a robust phenomenon occurring both early in human development and later in adult life. Of consequence, in my opinion, is the fact that both studies employ measures of an individual's temporal adaptation to the partner which can be assessed for statistical reliability. I think it is fair to say that there is accumulating evidence that people adjust certain of their behaviors (the automatic ones) to those of their partners and that these adjustments are consequential to the individuals and their relationship. While DA theory and most of its competitors were built around a base of research that was primarily static, evidence now available indicates that dynamic processes are behind these static effects and that theory must catch up with these developments.

Whither DA Theory?

DA theory is still a viable causal account of the process of adaptation in interaction, especially involving those behaviors that are more automatic rather than deliberate. The theory is capable of explaining the existing results on mutual influence, and much evidence supports its indirect predictions as well. Challenges for DA theory include incorporating the accumulating evidence on the dynamic aspects of adaptation and dealing with the conflicting evidence on the role of arousal in interaction. Recent research by Sparks and Greene (1992) has questioned the relationship between certain forms of autonomic arousal and nonverbal, behavioral response. At the same time, other research by Levenson and Gottman (1983, 1985) shows that partners' covariation in arousal during interaction is predictive of marital satisfaction and stability several years later. The exact role of arousal change, the nature of the arousal being activated, and its relationship to affective response remain to be clarified, not only for DA theory but for the study of human interaction in general.

CONCLUSIONS

My goal in this chapter has been to show that theory construction is the construction of a causal argument that is superior to its competitors on empirical, substantive, and meta-theoretical grounds. Whether DA theory is a superior theory to its competitors is a judgment best left to others. At a minimum, it is a causal theory. DA does argue its plausibility through refutation of alternatives, the accumulation of evidence, both directly favoring its causal components and supporting its indirect linear and nonlinear correlations. The case for DA theory can be said to be circumstantial but I would hold that the case for all but the most highly advanced theories is circumstantial at some level.

As long as one is trying to build theory, here conceptualized as causal explanations of an extant fact pattern, one should expect to be operating in the realm of the circumstantial, the plausible, and the argumentative. What

I do not think that I have been able to show definitively is that the arguments that are made are successful or unsuccessful relative to the standards of accepted knowledge within the field of study. To show this, I think one must be an insider in the area under discussion. Despite the fact that this chapter has had to operate on the periphery of the substantive domain, I hope that its claims are nonetheless seen as plausible. It is up to the reader to carry these claims to his or her own areas of substantive research and test them there.

Theory construction is in my opinion much less driven by procedure than are activities like experimental design or construct validation. Successful theory is not merely general, logically consistent, definitionally precise, coherent, elegant, and so on. First and foremost, successful theory is substantively and predictively subtle, giving a deep understanding of the phenomena by uncovering the processes that lie behind the facts to be explained. Whether the uncovering is ultimately accepted or rejected will depend upon deliberations not unlike those carried out in legal conflict or in serious debates of public policy.

NOTES

1. As soon as a community of individuals is introduced as the arbiters of what is acceptable and unacceptable prior knowledge, then questions of the social distribution of power are raised as the possible basis for what is anointed and what condemned.

2. Miller (1987) also treats level III comparisons in which what counts as a legitimate perception is at issue. For example, extrasensory communication is not accepted as a legitimate form of information transfer by the vast majority of researchers and theorists practicing in the discipline. At issue is what counts as real information transfer and how can such transfers be perceived. The very bases of what is real are challenged in level II disputes. Obviously, they are far less common than comparisons at level I and II.

3. Actually, we have experimented with a variety of time units from turn (as defined by Jaffe and Feldstein [1970]) to real time units of 3 secs, 22 sec, 30 secs, and 1 minute. In Cappella, Palmer, and Donzella (1991) we argue that a time unit smaller than the average turn is a desirable time unit because it allows within-turn variation to be studied.

REFERENCES

Ainsworth, M. D. (1978). *Patterns of attachment: A psychological study of the strange situation.* Hillsdale, N.J.: Lawrence Erlbaum.

Andersen, P. A. (1985). Nonverbal immediacy in interpersonal communication. In A. W. Siegman & S. Feldstein (Eds.), *Multichannel integrations of nonverbal behavior* (pp. 1–36). Hillsdale, N.J.: Lawrence Erlbaum.

Argyle, M., & Dean, J. (1965). Eye contact, distance, and affiliation. *Sociometry 28,* 289–304.

Argyle, M., & Cook, M. (1976). *Gaze and mutual gaze.* Cambridge: Cambridge University Press.

Berger, C. R. (1977). The covering law perspective as a theoretical basis for the study of human communication. *Communication Quarterly 25*, 7–18.

Berghout-Austin, A. M., & Peery, J. Craig. (1983). Analysis of adult-neonate synchrony during speech and nonspeech. *Perceptual and Motor Skills 57,* 455–459.

Berlyne, D. E. (1967). Arousal and reinforcement. In D. Levine (Ed.), *Nebraska Symposium on Motivation* (pp. 1–110). Lincoln: University of Nebraska Press.

Bernieri, F. J. (1988). Coordinated movement and rapport in teacher-student interactions. *Journal of Nonverbal Behavior 12*, 120–138.

Bernieri, F. J., Resnick, J. S., & Rosenthal, R. (1988). Synchrony, pseudosynchrony, and dissynchrony: Measuring the entrainment process in mother-infant interactions. *Journal of Personality and Social Psychology 54,* 243–253.

Bowlby, J. (1969). *Attachment and loss: Vol. I. Attachment.* New York: Basic Books.

Bransford, J. D., & McCarrell, N. S. (1974). A sketch of a cognitive approach to comprehension. In W. B. Weimar & D. S. Palermo (Eds.), *Cognition and the symbolic processes* (pp. 189–229). Hillsdale, N.J.: Lawrence Erlbaum.

Buder, E. (1991). Vocal Synchrony in Conversations: Spectral analysis of fundamental voice frequency. Unpublished Doctoral Dissertation, Department of Communication Arts, University of Wisconsin-Madison.

Burgoon, J. K. (1978). A communication model of interpersonal space violations: Explication and initial test. *Human Communication Research 4*, 129–142.

Burgoon, J. K., & Hale, J. L. (1988). Nonverbal expectancy violations: Model elaboration and application to immediacy behaviors. *Communication Monographs 55*, 58–79.

Burgoon, J. K., & Jones, S. B. (1976). Toward a theory of personal space expectations and their violations. *Human Communication Research 2,* 131–146.

Byrne, D. (1971). *The attraction paradigm.* New York: Academic Press.

Campbell, D. T., & Stanley, J. C. (1966). *Experimental and quasi-experimental designs for research.* Chicago: Rand-McNally.

Cappella, J. N. (1980a). Talk and silence sequences in informal social conversations II. *Human Communication Research 6*, 130–145.

Cappella, J. N. (1980b). Structural equation modeling: An introduction. In P. R. Monge & J. N. Cappella (Eds.), *Multivariate Techniques in Communication Research* (pp. 57–109). New York: Academic Press.

Cappella, J. N. (1981). Mutual influence in expressive behavior: Adult-adult and infant-adult dyadic interaction. *Psychological Bulletin 89*, 101–132.

Cappella, J. N. (1983). Approaching and avoiding others: Involvement in dyadic interaction. In J. Wiemann and R. P. Harrison, *Nonverbal Interaction: Sage Annual Review of Communication Research* (pp. 113–148). Hillsdale, N.J.: Sage, 1983.

Cappella, J. N. (1984). The relevance of the microstructure of interaction to interpersonal relations. *Journal of Personal and Social Relationships 1*, 239–264.

Cappella, J. N. (1985a). Controlling the floor in conversation. In A. O. Siegman & S. Feldstein (Eds.), *Multichannel integrations of nonverbal behavior* (pp. 69–103). Hillsdale, N.J.: Lawrence Erlbaum.

Cappella, J. N. (1985b). The management of conversations. In M. L. Knapp & G. R. Miller (Eds.), *The handbook of interpersonal communication* (pp. 393–438). Beverly Hills: Sage.

Cappella, J. N. (1985c). Reciprocal and compensatory reactions to violations of distance norms for high and low self monitors. In M. L. McLaughlin (Ed.), *Communication Yearbook 9* (pp. 359–376). Beverly Hills: Sage.

Cappella, J. N. (1991). The biological origins of automated patterns of human interaction. *Communication Theory 1*, 4–35.

Cappella, J. N., & Greene, J. O. (1982). A discrepancy-arousal explanation of mutual influence in expressive behaviors for adult-adult and infant-adult interactions. *Communication Monographs 49*, 89–114.

Cappella, J. N., & Greene, J. O. (1984). The effects of distance and individual differences in arousability on nonverbal involvement: A test of discrepancy-arousal theory. *Journal of Nonverbal Behavior 8*, 259–286.

Cappella, J. N., & Planalp, S. (1981). Talk and silence sequences in informal conversations III. Interspeaker influence. *Human Communication Research 7*, 117–132.

Cappella, J. N., Palmer, M. T., & Donzella, B. (1991). Individual consistency in temporal adaptations in nonverbal behavior in dyadic conversations: High and low expressive groups. Unpublished paper presented at the International Communication Association Conference, Chicago, May 1991.

Chapple, E. D. (1970). *Culture and biological man.* New York: Holt, Rinehart, & Winston.

Chomsky, N. (1959). Review of *Verbal Behavior* by B. F. Skinner. *Language 35*, 26–58.

Cohn, J. F., & Tronick, E. Z. (1983). Three-month-old infants' reaction to simulated maternal depression. *Child Development 54*, 185–193.

Cohn, J. F., & Tronick, E. Z. (1987). Mother-infant face-to-face interaction: The sequence of dyadic states at 3, 6, and 9 months. *Developmental Psychology 23*, 68–77.

Condit, C. M. (1989). The rhetorical limits of polysemy. *Critical Studies in Mass Communication 6*, 103–122.

Cushman, D. P. (1977). The rules perspective as a theoretical basis for the study of human communication. *Communication Quarterly 25*, 30–45.

Davis, D., & Martin, H. J. (1978). When pleasure begets pleasure: Recipient responsiveness as a determinant of physical pleasuring between heterosexual dating couples and strangers. *Journal of Personality and Social Psychology 36*, 767–777.

Davis, D., & Perkowitz, W. T. (1979). Consequences of responsiveness in dyadic interaction: Effects of probability of response and proportion of content-related responses on interpersonal attraction. *Journal of Personality and Social Psychology 37*, 534–550.

Davis, J. D. (1976). Self-disclosure in an acquaintance exercise: Responsibility for level of intimacy. *Journal of Personality and Social Psychology 33*, 787–792.

Davis, J. D. (1977). Effects of communication about interpersonal process on the evolution of self-disclosure in dyads. *Journal of Personality and Social Psychology 35*, 31–37.

Duck, S. (1976). Interpersonal communication in developing acquaintance. In G. R. Miller (Ed.), *Explorations in interpersonal communication* (pp. 127–147). Beverly Hills: Sage.

Duncan, S., & Fiske, D. W. (1977). *Face-to-face interaction*. Hillsdale, N.J.: Lawrence Erlbaum.

Fararone, S. V., & Hurtig, R. R. (1985). An examination of social skill, verbal productivity, and Gottman's model of interaction using observational methods and sequential analysis. *Behavioral Assessment 7*, 349–366.

Feldstein, S., Konstantareas, M., Oxman, J., & Webster, C. D. (1982). The chronography of interaction with autistic speakers: An initial report. *Journal of Communicative Disorders 15*, 451–460.

Feldstein, S., & Welkowitz, J. (1978). A chronography of conversation: In defense of an objective approach. In A. W. Siegman and S. Feldstein (Eds.), *Nonverbal behavior and communication* (pp. 329–378). Hillsdale, N.J.: Lawrence Erlbaum.

Field, T. (1984). Early interactions between infants and their postpartum depressed mothers. *Infant Behavior and Development 7*, 527–532.

Field, T. (1987). Affective and interactive disturbances in infants. In J. D. Osofsky (Ed.), *Handbook of infant development*. 2nd ed. (pp. 972–1007). New York: John Wiley.

Field, T., Healy, B., Goldstein, S., Perry, S., Bendel, D., Schanberg, S., Zimmerman, E. A., & Kuhn, C. (1988). Infants of depressed mothers show "depressed" behavior even with nondepressed adults. *Child Development 59*, 1569–1579.

Fiske, J. (1986). Television: Polysemy and popularity. *Critical Studies in Mass Communication 3*, 391–408.

Giere, R. N. (1984). *Understanding scientific reasoning*. New York: Holt, Rinehart, & Winston.

Giles, H., & Powesland, P. F. (1975). *Speech style and social evaluation*. London: Academic Press.

Giles, H., & Smith, P. M. (1979). Accommodation theory: Optimal levels of convergence. In H. Giles & R. N. St. Clair (Eds.), *Language and social psychology* (pp. 45–65). Oxford: Blackwell.

Giles, H., Mulac, A., Bradac, J. J., & Johnson, P. (1987). Speech accommodation theory: The first decade and beyond. In M. L. McLaughlin (Ed.), *Communication Yearbook 10* (pp. 13–48). Newbury Hills, Cal: Sage.

Glaister, J., Feldstein, S., & Pollock, H. (1980). Chronographic speech patterns of acutely psychotic patients. *The Journal of Nervous and Mental Disease 168* (#4).

Gottman, J. M. (1979). *Marital interaction*. New York: Academic Press.

Greenbaum, P., & Rosenfeld, H. M. (1978). Patterns of avoidance in response to interpersonal staring and proximity: Effects of bystanders on drivers at a traffic intersection. *Journal of Personality and Social Psychology 36*, 575–587.

Hale, J. L., & Burgoon, J. K. (1984). Models of reactions to changes in nonverbal immediacy. *Journal of Nonverbal Behavior 8*, 287–314.

Isabella, R. A., Belsky, J., & van Eye, A. (1989). Origins of mother-infant attachment: An examination of interactional synchrony during the infant's first year. *Developmental Psychology 25*, 12–21.

Jaffe, J., & Anderson, S. (in press). Speech rate study in major depressive disorders: Degree of response to medication. In S. Feldstein, C. Crown, & J. Welkowitz (Eds.), *Speech sounds and silences: A social psychological approach to clinical concerns*. Hillsdale, N.J.: Lawrence Erlbaum.

Jaffe, J., & Feldstein, S. (1970). *Rhythms of dialogue*. New York: Academic Press.

Jasnow, M., & Feldstein, S. (1987). Adult-like temporal characteristics of mother-infant vocal interactions. *Child Development 57*, 754–761.

Kaplan, A. (1964). *The conduct of inquiry*. San Francisco: Chandler.

Kerlinger, F. N. (1973). *Foundations of behavioral research* (2nd edition). New York: Holt, Rinehart, & Winston.

Kleinke, C. L., Staneski, R. A., & Berger, D. E. (1975). Evaluation of an interviewer as a function of interviewer gaze, reinforcement of subject gaze, and interviewer attractiveness. *Journal of Personality and Social Psychology 31*, 115–122.

Krause, R., Steimer, E., Sanger-Alt, C., & Wanger, G. (1989). Facial expression of schizophrenic patients and their interaction partners. *Psychiatry 52*, 1–12.

Kuhn, T. S. (1962). *The structure of scientific revolutions*. Chicago: University of Chicago Press.

LaFrance, M. (1982). Posture mirroring and rapport. In M. Davis (Ed.), *Interaction rhythms: Periodicity in communicative behavior* (pp. 279–298). New York: Human Sciences Press.

Lester, B. M., Hoffman, J., & Brazelton, T. B. (1985). The rhythmic structure of mother-infant interaction in term and pre-term infants. *Child Development 56*, 15–27.

Levenson, R. W., & Gottman, J. M. (1983). Marital interaction: Physiological linkage and affective exchange. *Journal of Personality and Social Psychology 45*, 587–597.

Levenson, R. W., & Gottman, J. M. (1985). Physiological and affective predictors of change in relationship satisfaction. *Journal of Personality and Social Psychology 49*, 85–94.

Mandler, G. M. (1975). *Mind and emotion*. New York: Wiley.

Margolin, G., & Wampold, B. E. (1981). Sequential analysis of conflict and accord in distressed and nondistressed marital partners. *Journal of Consulting and Clinical Psychology 49*, 554–567.

Matarazzo, J. D., & Wiens, A. N. (1972). *The interview: Research on its anatomy and structure*. Chicago: Aldine.

Maurer, R. E., & Tindall, J. H. (1983). Effects of postural congruence on clients' perception of counselor empathy. *Journal of Counseling Psychology 30*, 158–163.

McLaughlin, M. L., Cody, M. J., & Rosenstein, N. E. (1983). Account sequences in conversations between strangers. *Communication Monographs 50*, 102–125.

McCleary, R,. & Hay, R. A. (1980). *Applied time series analysis for the social sciences*. Beverly Hills: Sage.

Miller, R. W. (1987). *Fact and method*. Princeton: Princeton University Press.

Murray, L., & Trevarthen, C. (1985). Emotional regulation of interactions between two-month-olds and their mothers. In T. M. Field & N. A. Fox (Eds.), *Social perception in infants* (pp. 177–198). Norwood, N.J.: Ablex.

Nagel, E. (1961). *The structure of science*. New York: Harcourt, Brace.

Natale, M. (1975). Convergence of mean vocal intensity in dyadic communication as a function of social desirability. *Journal of Personality and Social Psychology 32*, 790–804.

Newcomb, T. M. (1961). *The acquaintance process*. New York: Holt, Rinehart, and Winston.

Noller, P. (1984). *Nonverbal communication and marital interaction.* Oxford: Pergamon Press.

Patterson, M. L. (1973). Compensation in nonverbal immediacy behaviors. *Sociometry 36*, 237–252.

Patterson, M. L. (1976). An arousal model of interpersonal intimacy. *Psychological Review 83*, 235–245.

Patterson, M. L. (1982). A sequential functional model of nonverbal exchange. *Psychological Review 89*, 231–249.

Pike, G. R., & Sillars, A. L. (1985). Reciprocity and marital communication. *Journal of Personal and Social Relationships 2*, 303–324.

Popper, K. R. (1959). *The logic of scientific discovery.* New York: Basic Books.

Rausch, H. L., Barry, W. A., Hertel, R. K., & Swain, M. A. (1974). *Communication, conflict, and marriage.* San Francisco: Jossey-Bass.

Sacks, H., Schegloff, E. A., & Jefferson, G. (1974). A simplest systematics for the organization of turn taking for conversation. *Language 50*, 697–735.

Schaap, C. (1982). *Communication and adjustment.* Lisse, Netherlands: Swets & Zeitlinger.

Skinner, B. F. (1957). *Verbal behavior.* New York: Appleton-Century-Crofts.

Snyder, M. (1974). The self monitoring of expressive behavior. *Journal of Personality and Social Psychology 30*, 526–537.

Snyder, M. (1979). Self-monitoring processes. In L. Berkowitz (Ed.), *Advances in experimental social psychology* (Vol. 12, pp. 85–128). New York: Academic Press.

Sparks, G. G., & Greene, J. O. (1992). On the validity of nonverbal indicators as measures of physiological arousal. *Human Communication Research 18*, 445–471.

Stern, D. N. (1974). Mother and infant at play: The dyadic interaction involving facial, vocal, and gaze behavior. In M. Lewis & L. A. Rosenblum (Eds.), *The effect of the infant on its caregiver* (pp. 187–213). New York: Wiley.

Street, R. L., Jr. (1982). Evaluation of noncontent speech accommodation. *Language and Communication 2*, 13–31.

Street, R. L., Jr. (1984). Speech convergence and speech evaluation in fact-finding interviews. *Human Communication Research 11*, 139–169.

Street, R. L., & Cappella, J. N. (1989). Social and linguistic factors influencing adaptation in children's speech. *Journal of Psycholinguistic Research 18*, 497–519.

Street, R. L., & Giles, H. (1982). Speech accommodation theory: A social cognitive approach to language and speech behavior. In M. Roloff & C. Berger (Eds.), *Social cognition and communication* (pp. 193–226). Newbury Hills, Cal.: Sage.

Symons, D. K., & Moran, G. (1987). The behavioral dynamics of mutual responsiveness in early face-to-face mother-infant interactions. *Child Development 58*, 1488–1495.

Tickle-Degnen, L., & Rosenthal, R. (1987). Group rapport and nonverbal behavior. *Review of Personality and Social Psychology 9*, 113–136.

Webb, J. T. (1972). Interview synchrony: An investigation of two speech rate measures. In A. W. Siegman & B. Pope (Eds.), *Studies in dyadic communication* (pp. 115–133). New York: Pergamon.

Welkowitz, J., & Kuc, M. (1973). Interrelationships among warmth, genuineness, empathy and temporal speech patterns in interpersonal interaction. *Journal of Consulting and Clinical Psychology 41*, 472–473.

Zuckerman, M. (1976). General and specific traits and states: New approaches to assessment. In M. Zuckerman & C. D. Spielberger (Eds.), *Emotion and anxiety: New concepts, methods, and applications* (vol. 3). Hillsdale, N.J.: Lawrence Erlbaum.

Zuckerman, M. (1979). *Sensation seeking: Beyond the optimal level of arousal.* Hillsdale, N.J.: Lawrence Erlbaum.

4

Variation, Adaptation, and Functional Explanation in the Study of Message Design

BARBARA J. O'KEEFE

One central set of questions addressed in research on interpersonal communication concerns the nature, causes, and effects of variation in interpersonal messages. Most of the research stimulated by these questions can be seen as addressing the problem of adaptation, that is, how messages are shaped to fit their functions. Recent commentaries on this research have noted that the adaptation problem has most often been approached by positing that individuals have a repertoire of strategies and, in a given situation, select a strategy that best meets their objectives (O'Keefe 1990; Seibold, Cantrill, & Meyers 1985). This view of message adaptation has been termed the "Strategy Choice Model" of message design (Seibold et al. 1985).

However, with the development of Brown and Levinson's (1978) analysis of politeness, a new kind of functional explanation has appeared. This alternative, which has been variously called a "Rational Goals Model" (O'Keefe & Shepherd 1987) or a "Strategic Inference Model" (Jacobs 1985), treats message production as rational and coordinated deployment of functionally significant message features such as indirectness, mitigations, hedges, contextualizing phrases, and the like. A more descriptive label for this sort of view would seem to be "Message Design Model," since on this view messages are seen as assemblies of features that have complex relationships to multiple message functions.

The development of my own theoretical perspective can be seen as movement away from one specific Strategy Choice theory, constructivism, toward a specific Message Design Model, the theory of message design logic. This chapter summarizes the conceptual and empirical issues that have influenced the direction my work on message adaptation has taken. The first section discusses the general problem of explaining message diversity. The second section contrasts the Strategy Choice and Message Design Models as accounts of message structure and effects. The third section of the paper discusses the development of the theory of message design logic as an extension and generalization of Brown and Levinson's message design model.

However, while my research program can be reconstructed as reflecting a move from a Strategic Choice Model to a Message Design Model, such a reconstruction is both historically selective and overly deterministic. As a corrective, the concluding section of this chapter discusses the complex interplay of theory, data, and method in the development of the theory of message design logic.

THE NATURE OF MESSAGE VARIATION

In studies of communication, as in studies of biological evolution, the concepts of adaptation and variation tend to be linked. Much of the advice given to students of communication equates adaptation with variation: since early times, speakers have been advised to vary their messages to fit the character of their audiences. Researchers attempting to study processes of listener adaptation have most often operationalized adaptation as varying the message in response to different situational conditions (see, for example, Alvy 1973; Flavell, Botkin, Fry, Wright, & Jarvis 1968; Higgins 1981).

Message Variation as a Focal Problem in Communication Research

Although there has been a great deal of interest in the nature, causes, and effects of message variation, the phenomenon of variation itself has received little explicit attention. Even so, the fact that a given communicative task can often be addressed in a variety of ways has served as the point of departure for a great deal of research in communication. If, for every communication task, there were essentially one message (or message format) employed to perform that task, then there would be little need to address such classic questions as (a) what different kinds of messages are employed to persuade, comfort, resist compliance, etc.; (b) why some messages are more effective than others in persuading, comforting, teaching, etc.; (c) how skill and personality variations (e.g., cognitive complexity, shyness) influence the kinds of messages people produce, and so on. Hence, before discussing alternative accounts of message variation, it is useful to consider the nature of message variation itself.

It is generally taken for granted in communication research that—at least for the most interesting communication tasks—there are alternative messages that might be employed, and, moreover, the alternative messages differ in effectiveness. This assumption, while fundamental to research on message adaptation, is not universally held. Linde and Labov (1975), for instance, attribute message variation to the method employed in eliciting messages:

variations in messages arise from the use of unusual tasks, differences in world knowledge, and the like. As they note, "the systematic character of language emerges most clearly when speakers are dealing with familiar topics, following intricate but well-practiced routines" (926).

In general, though, communication scholars make the contrary presumption, that communicative tasks will elicit significant functional variation in messages. This presumption could derive from either of two sources. The first is direct observation of variation in communication skill: In our roles as teachers and researchers of communication processes, we have many opportunities to observe multiple individuals attempting the same communication task, producing different messages with differential success. Anyone who has taught interpersonal, public speaking, or writing skills courses has observed this fact of communication. Similarly, in more formal investigations of communication behavior, individuals have been asked how they would handle an assigned communication task; quite variable messages are generally elicited even when subjects all address the same communication task (for reviews of such research, see Burleson 1989; O'Keefe & Delia 1988; Seibold et al. 1985).

A second source of the presumption that messages vary in form and effectiveness may be rhetorical theory, with its view of discourse as shaped to fit the requirements of situations and analyzable as displaying either good or poor fit to the task at hand. Both the possibility of adaptation and the relevance of functional evaluation derive from the rhetorical view that in any situation, a rhetor has many options and rhetorical success is a function of the choices made.

Regardless of the reason, however, the assumption that messages display functional variation is commonly held by communication researchers. Indeed, the methods employed most often in studying message design guarantee that it will appear that, for a given task, there are diverse message designs that might be employed; tasks that fail to elicit significant variation across situational conditions or speakers are generally thought not to be terribly interesting communication tasks.

This focus on diversity creates a misleading picture of message design. Many (perhaps the great majority of) communication tasks elicit fairly uniform performance from different individuals. One clear example of this is Linde and Labov's (1975) study of apartment descriptions. Subjects were asked to produce descriptions of their place of residence; Linde and Labov found that the overwhelming majority of these descriptions appeared to follow a uniform formula, in which not only the general strategy for describing (a "tour" of the apartment) but also the kinds of descriptive detail included and omitted were consistent across describers.

Kellermann and her associates (Kellermann, Broetzmann, Lim, & Kitao 1989; Kellermann & Lim 1989) have given sustained attention to another kind of situation that evokes quite uniform performance from different individuals—initial interactions. Their work suggests that individuals not only have a standard, and standardly ordered, set of topics that are pursued in interaction, but also that the elaboration of these topics is governed by a standardized agenda.

While studies such as those by Kellermann et al. and by Linde and Labov testify to the existence of genres in which behavior is highly uniform, other researchers have argued that some communication situations demand one of a small set of structured responses. For example, the concept of the adjacency pair (for a review and discussion, see Levinson 1983) was invoked to explain how the occurrence of a particular kind of communicative act (a "first pair part") calls for the occurrence of a second act (the "second pair part") that is directly responsive to the demands of the first pair part. While the hearer may have opinions about which of the seconds he or she will use, the list of appropriate seconds is finite (for instance, a request can be met with either a grant or a turndown).

Finally, the communicative situations and tasks on which I have focused tend to elicit highly variable performance from different individuals. Indeed, these situations—those involving conflict management, regulation, comforting, persuasion, and other complex tasks—have been selected for study precisely because they generate message diversity.

In short, it appears that communicative tasks can be ordered in terms of their ability to elicit diverse performances from different individuals. This property of tasks has not been an explicit focus of concern for research on discourse organization. But, as I argue below, it is a quality that has serious, and largely unappreciated, implications for theories of message design. Because of this, the relationship between communication task and message variability needs to be a central concern of theories of communicative adaptation.

Communication Tasks and Message Variation

Perhaps because of the general presumption in favor of diversity in studies of message production, the tendency among communication researchers has been to define communication tasks broadly, thereby ensuring the widest possible range of variation in messages employed to address a task. A case in point is the method used in constructing Marwell and Schmitt's (1967a, 1967b) classic typology of compliance-gaining strategies. They surveyed the research literature to identify the kinds of message strategies researchers had observed across the range of compliance-gaining tasks and then systematized these diverse responses as a list of sixteen distinctive types of compliance-gaining strategies.

A conception of communication tasks as broad categories into which specific problems can be classified has also shaped research conducted under very different methodological assumptions. For example, constructivist research on message design processes is based on an explicit rejection of the kind of "strategy checklist" methodology employed by Marwell and Schmitt (for a review of this controversy, see Burleson, Wilson, Waltman, Goering, Ely, & Whaley 1988; also see commentary by Boster 1988; Burleson & Wilson 1988; Hunter 1988; and Seibold 1988). Instead, constructivist research generally proceeds through the analysis of diverse responses made to quite specific communication problems.

In some studies, subjects have been given scenarios that describe, quite concretely, interpersonal problems such as a friend who has experienced a distressing event or a work associate who is behaving unreliably; subjects have been asked to imagine themselves in that situation and write what they would say (for reviews of this work, see Burleson 1989; O'Keefe & Delia 1988). In other studies, subjects have been faced with realistic laboratory simulations of communication problems, such as a co-interactant who exhibits distressed feelings or disagrees with them, and the resulting interactions have been recorded for later analysis (see O'Keefe & Shephard 1987; Samter & Burleson 1984). But even though constructivist methods involve the identification of message strategies based on responses to singular, specific communication problems, nonetheless, each of the problems studied is treated as exemplary of some broader class of communication problems ("conforming," "regulation," "argument," and the like) and the message types identified with these methods are interpreted as the alternative strategies available for pursuing, not a specific problem, but the general type of task that the specific problem is taken to exemplify.

This conceptual and methodological approach—seeking to identify the types of messages employed to address a general type of task rather than a specific problem—seems natural and logical to most researchers. After all, what is wanted from research on message design is not simply information about how people behave in specific situations, but rather information about how people behave in general; we want to know in general how compliance-gaining messages differ in effectiveness, not just how their effectiveness differs in some particular situation. Hence, the standard approach, which focuses on broad types of tasks and situations and compares messages across different specific examples of a given type of communication problem, appears to be the only reasonable way to conduct research on message design.

But if the objective is to understand the relationship between communication tasks and message diversity, then precisely the opposite approach is needed: rather than defining communication tasks in a very general way, tasks should be defined as narrowly as possible. Consider, for example, the wide range of situations that might be classed as "compliance-gaining" situations: some involve relatively simple and straightforward kinds of tasks, such as asking a friend for a favor; some involve more complex and undefined problems, such as getting a subordinate to identify with an organization and its goals. There are fairly clear, culturally prescribed methods for asking friends for favors; but it is much less clear what sort of method is required to foster organizational identification. We would expect to see much more diverse methods suggested for addressing the latter kind of problem than for the former.

I am not suggesting that the category "compliance-gaining situation" is incoherent. A similar objection would apply to the subcategories that were just constructed. Take, for instance, the problem of asking a friend for a favor. With some kinds of favors, and some kinds of friends, the communication problem can be handled with a routine solution (a simple request) that anyone would employ; but by changing the nature of the favor, or changing the profile of the friend, we can construct a problem about which individuals will disagree—some people will advocate one method, others another, for managing the situation.

Similarly, we can imagine some kinds of organizational situations, say those in which what it means to be a "team player" is very clear and in which it is easy to see how to suggest appropriate behavior to a subordinate, where the problem of encouraging identification with the organization could be reduced to a simple solution that is virtually uniformly endorsed by different message producers. We can also imagine kinds of situations involving the socialization of subordinates where there will be vast disagreement about how one should properly proceed.

What this discussion suggests is that if one is interested in the relationship between communication tasks and message diversity, one should proceed in a way that recognizes that within the broad functional categories that have been traditionally employed in research on message design, there are some tasks that elicit uniform performance across individuals (low diversity tasks) and some tasks that elicit highly variable performance (high diversity tasks). Moreover, in the effort to isolate those factors that contribute to diverse performances, we should employ methods that permit us to see what the range of variation actually is for a particular task; this generally entails investigating responses to concrete and well-specified tasks. And finally, having observed that a particular range of variation is produced by a particular task, one should avoid the assumption that other tasks in the same functional domain will necessarily show the same (or even a similar) range of variation.

In summary: Recognizing some straightforward and basic facts about message diversity leads to a rather different view of how message variation should be conceptualized and studied. Rather than assuming that all tasks will elicit a similar range of functional variation, we should recognize that some tasks elicit high diversity and some tasks elicit low diversity. Since message variation is such a crucial backdrop to theories of message design and message effects, explaining the causes and conditions that lead to message diversity is a problem of some importance to interpersonal communication research.

EXPLAINING DIVERSITY IN MESSAGE DESIGN

Two very different kinds of explanations of message variation currently coexist in the research literature. The first type of explanation, which has been called the "Strategy Choice Model," treats message production as a process of act selection. The second type of explanation, which I call the "Message Design Model," treats message production as a process of managing or adapting the expression of relevant thoughts and intentions.

The Strategy Choice Model

As Seibold et al. (1985) note, the dominant model of message production and adaptation is the Strategy Choice Model. According to this model, message producers have a list of possible types of messages to employ in any type of communication situation; message production is a process of selecting the appropriate type of message and then instantiating the abstract message format as a specific message. As I have noted in an earlier paper (O'Keefe 1990), the key features of a Strategy Choice explanation of message design are (1) reifying message types as message "strategies"; (2) conceptualizing alternative message types as strategy repertoires; and (3) equating message production with strategy selection.

First, Strategy Choice Models are generally developed in concert with descriptive work that seeks to identify the types of messages employed in responding to a particular type of task; such descriptive work has been conducted both by researchers constructing message typologies (e.g., Marwell and Schmitt 1967a, 1967b; Wiseman and Schenk-Hamlin 1981) and those developing message analysis systems in which message types are defined and ordered in terms of some abstractive dimension like listener-adaption (e.g., "constructivist coding systems; see Clark and Delia 1976; Delia, Kline, and Burleson 1979). Strategy Choice Models posit that for each message type identified, there is a corresponding internal, psychological structure (a "strategy") that is used to produce the message. This theoretical move—from observed message types to underlying psychological processes—is seldom justified, but rather is finessed by calling message types "strategies" and thereby introducing the psychological explanation in the process of describing the behavioral structure to be explained.

Second, Strategy Choice Models equate observed variation with individual options. From an analysts's viewpoint, looking across individuals and across particular situations, the set of message types presents itself as a set of alternatives for message production. It is the common practice to refer to the set of alternative message types for a given type of task as a "strategy repertoire" and to assume that message producers have all or part of the "strategy repertoire" available as a set of options for message design.

Finally, given the assumption that each individual possesses a strategy repertoire for a given type of situation or task, the process of message production is conceptualized as the selection of a strategy from the repertoire. That is, individuals are seen as reviewing the list of available message options, selecting one of these options based on its fit with situation features, and then "filling" in appropriate message content to instantiate the general "strategy" as a concrete message.

The first thing to notice about Strategy Choice Models is that they presuppose, but do not explain, message variation. To see that this is so, consider what a Strategy Choice Model has to say about low diversity communication situations, such as the one Linde and Labov (1975) studied. In such situations, where messages are uniform, all one can say is that people use such-and-so type of message. To extend the illustration, imagine that in every situation, there is one type of message that is overwhelmingly employed. In that case, all a Strategy Choice Model can do is indicate the match between situations and messages. In fact, if this were the case, a Strategy Choice Model would be very misleading, since no one would ever have a choice—choice would be an illusion created by collapsing a set of situations into a larger task-type category and then constructing a list of all the strategies employed.

From this, one can see that a Strategy Choice Model presupposes a high diversity task. This kind of model cannot explain why a task would elicit either high or low diversity in responses, and it has nothing to say about how messages are designed as responses to low diversity tasks. And consequently, a Strategy Choice Model constructed for a broad task category that includes both high and low diversity tasks (e.g., compliance-gaining or comforting) will necessarily give an inaccurate and misleading explanation of how behavior is produced in a large number of situations.

Not only does the image of a strategy repertoire provide a misleading depiction of communicator competence, but the vision of message design as strategy selection is cognitively implausible. Those who have developed Strategy Choice Models have generally given a great deal of attention to the factors that influence preference for message types but virtually no attention to describing the actual processes of choice that putatively govern message production. The metaphor of choice appears to be little more than a device for systematizing observed preferences: there are observable relationships between, on the one hand, situational and individual difference variables, and, on the other hand, preference for particular types of messages. In describing this state of affairs, the Strategy Choice Model constructs a hypothetical communicator who constantly has at the ready all the available types of messages and chooses among them based on the system of preferences. But there is no evidence that demonstrates that the hypothetical Strategy Chooser corresponds to any actual person, much less all communicators.

In fact, there is no direct evidence that individuals choose types of messages or that they have a strategy repertoire from which to choose. It is important to keep in mind that the only individual who we know has a list of all possible message types is the communication analyst, who has purposely set out to describe the range of message variations produced for a given type of situation. The fact that different people use different messages in a given situation is not good evidence that any of them could have chosen to produce any message from the analyst's list; similarly, the fact that a given person uses different messages in different situations is not good evidence that the person could have chosen to use either message in either situation or that the person produced his or her message by selecting its type from a master list. In short, the analyst's ability to find and describe message variation is not relevant evidence about the cognitive processes used in designing messages.

As a way of summarizing the system of preferences, the idea of a Strategy Chooser seems fairly harmless. But suppose one takes it seriously, as a model of message design (as Marwell and Schmitt, 1967a, apparently did, and as others have). Strategy Choice Models have come under increasingly heavy criticism from researchers who take the problem of explaining language production seriously (see, for example, Greene 1987; Lambert and O'Keefe 1991; O'Keefe 1990). These arguments are reviewed, with application to a broad range of active selection models, by Lambert (1992). The cognitive implausibility of the Strategy Choice Model derives from its basic conceptual move, namely, to equate the message types an analyst observes (or alternately the "types" that emerge from clusters of messages defined by perceivers' dimensions of evaluation) with a "strategy repertoire" in people's minds and to equate message design with strategy selection and instantiation.

As I have argued previously (O'Keefe 1990), Strategy Choice Models lead to some absurd conclusions when taken seriously as models of message production. On the one hand, there is the problem that genuinely rational selection of a message cannot be done on the basis of its abstract type. What can be said in a given situation depends on what is true (or can be true) of that situation, and so messages must be designed and evaluated in relationship to the specifics of a given situation. Consider request situations: whether one should elaborate a request by listing one's own needs, counterarguing against possible objections, or mentioning advantages accruing to the other depends on what is true of the specific situation one faces. Does the requestee have objections and can they be met? Is it the case that this specific proposal will be advantageous to the requestee? The requester cannot select among these kinds of elaborating arguments without knowing what is true of the situation; and knowing what is true of the situation will give the requester his or her lines of argument.

So, to make any considered assessment of the viability, let alone the utility, of the available message types, one would have to choose among specific instantiations of the strategies rather than simply among the strategy types. Notice that this problem is exacerbated by the fact that given message types might be instantiated in any of a number of different ways in the situation, with different instantiations being differentially effective. There might be multiple, different advantages to the requestee in a given request situation. A rational choice would depend on selecting the most effective instantiation from among the available advantages to be mentioned. And all the possible messages would have to be evaluated against each other in order to select the best available strategy. Although I have no estimates of the processing time required to make these kinds of decisions, it seems most implausible that individuals should first instantiate and then compare all possible messages before speaking. Certainly it seems unlikely that these computations could be performed in the time allowed for floor exchange.

Since strategies cannot be rationally evaluated in the abstract, but only as concrete sets of ideas about the situation, a rational version of the Strategy Choice Model presupposes a very inefficient process with huge information processing demands. But the alternative is to suppose that strategies are selected irrationally, based on factors other than that the message is true or likely to be effective.

There are, in fact, versions of the Strategy Choice Model that treat strategy selection as governed by peripheral concerns rather than ends-means reasoning. For example, Hunter and Boster (Hunter and Boster 1978, 1979, 1981; Williams and Boster 1981; this work is cited and summarized in Seibold et al. 1985) have argued that the strategies in strategy lists can generally be ordered in terms of their positiveness or negativeness, and that selection is based primarily on this feature. But this sort of procedure leaves the message producer in the position of having to somehow instantiate whatever strategy is selected, even though it was selected on a basis other than truth or relevance or likely effectiveness. If this were the way message production worked, we would expect to see a great many more lame messages than we do. Imagine the predicament of the message producer: "Golly, I've got to correct my subordinate here, but I really like him. What's the least positive strategy I'd feel comfortable using here? I guess I'll bribe him. I'll say; Hey, Frank, if you'll start coming to work on time, I'll get you a big raise."

So although it is possible to imagine a Strategy Choice Model in which strategies are selected purely on the basis of abstract qualities (like how "positive" they are), such a view makes it virtually impossible to explain how people manage to say things that are true, relevant, and effective. With such models, message variation and adaptation are seen as the effects of peripheral factors (e.g., how much the message producer likes the target or how nice the message producer is) on the message design. Consequently, these kinds of Strategy Choice Models, cannot, in principle, offer any account of real adaptation, i.e., the fit between messages and the jobs they are meant to do.

In sum: Strategy Choice Models rest on a number of unexamined assumptions, including (1) that individuals have mental representations that correspond to analysts' lists of message types, and (2) that message design begins with the selection of a message type which is later instantiated. Such models presuppose, but do not explain, message diversity; at best, they provide a framework for the analysis of preferences among message types as a function of situational or individual differences.

However, most Strategy Choice Models conceptualize such preferences as residing in processes of individual decision-making that are employed in strategy selection. Models of message production that assume that messages begin as abstract message types are implausible: either they require indefinitely large amounts of processing or they assume that what people say is a function of factors that are peripheral to the communication event.

Finally, in realizing that the Strategy Choice Model is little more than a device for summarizing facts about preferences for types of messages, it becomes quite clear that the Strategy Choice Model has nothing to say about message adaptation. What is it about a given message that makes it suitable or unsuitable for its task? Knowing that a message is preferred or dispreferred for a given task is not the same as having an account of its adaptive qualities. The Strategy Choice Model fails to provide a genuine explanation for either message variation or message adaptation, and tells an implausible story about language production.

Message Design Models

Message Design Models, by contrast with Strategy Choice Models, focus on adaptation: they assume that what people say is, first and foremost, what they need to say in order to accomplish their aims. In general, Message Design Models presuppose that messages begin, not as abstract formats or types, but as expressions of the message producer's situated thoughts and intentions; since message design is seen as the management of available content, and not the selection of abstract message types, they are not subject to problems related to strategy instantiation. What is actually said, and how it is said, is a function of processes that modify and elaborate the message so that it will better serve the message producer's goals.

The object of a Message Design Model is to explain form-function relationships, why a given type of message takes a particular form in order to perform a particular function or set of functions. The best known and most influential message Design Model is Brown and Levinson's (1978) treatment of universals in politeness. I have discussed their views in detail in an earlier paper (O'Keefe 1990), and the following discussion is a summary of that work.

Brown and Levinson argued that the various forms of politeness within a language could be understood as rational resolutions of goal conflicts that naturally arise when a speaker undertakes a face-threatening action: to achieve his/her goal, the speaker needs to be clear, but being clear will mean being more face-threatening; and conversely, to save face, the speaker must sacrifice getting the point across.

In Brown and Levinson's account, message variants arise from the coordinated deployment of two linguistic structures: indirectness and face-relevant elaboration. Each of these message structures can be analyzed and described independently of its role in shaping types of messages.

Most theorists agree that indirectness essentially consists of communicating by implication. A speaker says one thing, which under the circumstances, would warrant the inference that the speaker means to communicate a second intention or idea as well. Indirectness is used to address a variety of communication problems, among them the problem of communicating face-threatening information or intentions.

The fact that "face" is part of one's "front" makes indirection a useful way to convey face-threatening intentions. In Goffman's (1967) formulation, which serves as the foundation for Brown and Levinson's analysis, face is defined as "the positive social value a person claims for himself" (5). Face is an aspect of the person as publicly defined and represented. By keeping face-threatening intentions unspoken, "off-record," indirect messages can convey potentially face-threatening messages without affecting the hearer's face; by speaking the face-threatening message "on-record," the hearer's face will necessarily be diminished.

But communication by implication depends on the hearer's making the correct inference about the speaker's intentions and so it is less certain to make the point of the message clear to the hearer. Hence, both direct and indirect communication have payoffs and tradeoffs: being direct makes it more likely that one will get one's point across, but creates increased possibilities for face-threat; being indirect reduces face-threats, but may fail to get the point across or secure the hearer's acknowledgment of the point.

Message producers have a second linguistic device to use in managing conflicts between their intentions and the hearer's face-relevant elaborations, which Brown and Levinson call "forms of redress." Since face is a symbolic entity that is created through communication, it can be manipulated symbolically. A person can give "face" by offering verbal descriptions, accounts, or reassurances to another. Although it is more efficient to simply perform a face-threatening act baldly, with no redress, adding in redress mitigates the face threat by giving face in return. Consequently, as a speaker gives higher priority to saving face, he or she should be more likely to employ forms of redress; the lower the priority given to saving face, the less likely a speaker should be to use redress.

If we assume that speakers have both indirectness and redress at their disposal to use in designing messages, we can see that there are four possible types of strategies an individual might use when faced with the possibility of performing an act that would threaten another's face (a face-threatening act or FTA). First, the person might choose not to perform the act (Don't do the FTA). Second, the person might choose to perform the act, but indirectly (Do the FTA off record). Third, the person might choose to perform the act on record, but append some form of redress (Do the FTA with positive or negative redress). Finally, the person might perform the act on record, with no attempt to support the other's face (Do the FTA baldly). Given the analysis of payoffs and tradeoffs associated with each possible message feature, it is possible to order these strategies in terms of politeness, that is, in terms of the degree to which the message protects face rather than clearly communicating the FTA, with Don't do the FTA being most polite and Do the FTA baldly being least polite.

In addition, Brown and Levinson argue that the level of politeness employed can be predicted from the weightiness of the FTA, which in turn is a function of the intrinsic qualifiers of the act and the relationship between speaker and hearer. The greater the weight of the FTA, the greater the preference for politeness.

Now it might appear that Brown and Levinson's analysis of politeness is nothing more than a complex version of a Strategy Choice Model. After all, their model could be described as a list of basic politeness "strategies" and an equation that expresses the preference system that operates to associate strategies with situations (see Brown and Levinson 1978, 76). If this were an adequate summary of their theory, it indeed would be a Strategy Choice Model.

But in Brown and Levinson's work, the list of message types and the preference system that governs their distributions in use are just general facts which must be accounted for through detailed analysis of message features and the payoffs and tradeoffs associated with those message features. The general politeness strategies are not a set of empirically derived types of messages; they are a set of abstract possibilities, the logical kinds of messages that might be produced by exploiting the features of indirectness and redress. Because the politeness "strategies" are constructed theoretically, rather than through simple observation of message diversity, Brown and Levinson's approach provides an explanation of how the variant message types arise, as opposed to taking diversity for granted.

In addition, each message feature is independently analyzed both for its form and its functions. It is this aspect of their analysis that enables them to offer principled accounts of form-function relationships.

This is not to suggest that Brown and Levinson's model of politeness is not empirically grounded; in fact, they offer quite detailed and extensive evidence about the varying forms politeness can take, across several languages. But their project is to construct a general model of the fit between specific message forms and message functions. The identification of diverse message forms, which is the conclusion of message analysis for a Strategy Choice Model, is simply the beginning of an analysis like Brown and Levinson's.

In short, Brown and Levinson's analysis of the use of indirectness and forms of redress in designing polite messages provides an exemplary account of the adaptive properties of interpersonal messages, of the fit between messages and the jobs they are meant to do. Forms become more polite as lower priority is given to clear communication and higher priority is given to saving face; the priority given each goals is a function of situational variables; hence, messages vary because situations vary and cause different priority to be given to clarity and face protection.

Most important, a model like Brown and Levinson's offers a principled explanation of the existence and use of variations in politeness forms. In previous work on face-protection and identity management (e.g., Gross and Stone 1964; Scott and Lyman 1968; Weinstein 1969), researchers have constructed lists of face-managing strategies but have failed to adequately explain why message variations occur and why there should be diversity within a given situation in the types of messages produced by different individuals (for an elaborated discussion of this point, see O'Keefe 1990). Brown and Levinson's model offers a unified account of why messages differ, why they take the specific forms they do, and why they are differentially successful in being clear and polite.

THE LOGIC OF MESSAGE DESIGN

Brown and Levinson's (1978) work generated a great deal of excitement among researchers studying message design; it provided a new model for theorizing about the adaptive properties of messages and a principled account of message diversity. Their work prompted efforts among communication researchers to construct similar analyses of a range of communication phenomena. For example, Baxter (1984) proposed that the range of compliance-gaining message strategies identified by diverse research programs essentially reflects a common differentiation of message types in terms of the priority given to the face wants of the addressee.

Evidence of Diversity in Reasoning About Communication

In a paper published shortly after the publication of Brown and Levinson's (1978) work, I argued that constructivist research on the relationship between cognitive complexity and "person-centered" communication could be more profitably understood in terms of a framework modelled on the analysis of politeness (O'Keefe and Delia 1982). As noted previously, the constructivist model of message production is one version of the Strategy Choice Model (for very clear examples of the use of Strategy Choice concepts and reasoning, see Delia and O'Keefe 1979; O'Keefe, Murphy, Meyers, and Babrow 1988).

O'Keefe and Delia (1982) attempted to reformulate the agenda for research on message design. This paper criticized earlier constructivist research on the grounds that the early studies identified relations between individual difference variables and message preferences without providing any genuine explanation of either message production or message adaptation.

O'Keefe and Delia (1982) also offered an explicit analysis of the role of the communication task in promoting message diversity: message diversity is a function of task complexity. Complex tasks are those (such as communicating face-threatening messages) in which the speaker has multiple, conflicting objectives and in which the speaker encounters obstacles to goal achievement. Simple tasks are those in which speaker goals are in harmony and in which goal achievement is relatively unimpeded.

Finally, O'Keefe and Delia (1982) offered an analysis of message adaptation: when faced with contradictory requirements, speakers can use any of three distinct methods for resolving conflicts among goals or between goals and obstacles: selection, separation, or integration. Selection resolves conflicts through simple prioritizing, by choosing one goal to pursue and thereby transforming the task into a simple one. Separation relies on prioritizing as well, but goes beyond simple selection by elaborating the message to address lower priority aims. With separation, the high priority goal dominates the message, but low priority goals are addressed in message features such as indirection, redress, and the like. Integration resolves the conflict by finding a solution that addresses multiple aims simultaneously; this often involves rhetorical manipulation of the context to evade conflict among goals.

Greg Shepherd and I designed a study to test the hypothesis that individuals who exhibit high levels of cognitive complexity would show a preference for messages that address multiple goals and resolve goal conflicts through integration, whereas those low in cognitive complexity would show a preference for messages embodying a strategy of selection (O'Keefe and Shepherd 1987, 1989). We asked people who were known to disagree strongly about a topic to discuss the topic and try to persuade each other. We videotaped the resulting interactions. After the interaction, interactants rated each other's performance and provided their impressions of each other.

The videotaped interactions were segmented into message units; messages were classified in three ways. First, we classified the messages in terms of the kind of basic posture an individual adopted toward the conflict—whether the message expressed agreement or disagreement with the position advocated by the message recipient. Second, we classified the messages in terms of how the basic posture was expressed whether the message was explicit in taking a position or conveyed agreement or disagreement only by implication.

Third, we classified each message in terms of the method used to manage subsidiary objectives. Following Brown and Levinson (1978), we initially constructed an abstract analysis of the payoffs and tradeoffs associated with each posture. An individuals's decisions about whether to agree to disagree and how to express agreement/disagreement define a set of goals that are being pursued and traded off: Someone who explicitly agrees is trading off being clear about his or her own position and avoids threatening the face wants of the other person. Someone who explicitly disagrees is able to clearly express his or her own views but commits an overtly face-threatening action. Someone who conveys agreement or disagreement implicitly resolves the trade-off between clear communication and face by trading off the possibility of continuing the conversation by refusing to say anything to which they will be committed. Following this analysis, we were able to classify messages in a third way, according to their method of goal reconciliation (selection, separation, or integration).

Selection reflects the practice of simply trading off subsidiary goals. Individuals who employ selection make no effort to address the goals that are traded off. Separation strategies address subsidiary goals in a separate and discrete part of the message, as an "add-on" that is not integrated with the primary action being performed. These involve redressive elaborations added to the basic message, such as compliments, hedges, apologies, accounts, etc., designed to satisfy the goals traded off by the basic posture and manner of expression. Messages that employ integration strategies "defuse" the basic posture and manner of expression by explicitly manipulating the meaning of the enacted posture; they do this through embedding and act that would otherwise be problematic in a context that alters its significance for the subsidiary goals. Such messages avoid he tradeoffs that would ordinarily be associated with agreeing or disagreeing, being implicit or being explicit.

In interpreting the results of this study, I realized that they could not be accounted for in terms of a model, like Brown and Levinson's, that assumes everyone uses the same techniques in designing messages. Both separation and integration strategies were used relatively infrequently, and their use was related to cognitive complexity. People who were less cognitively complex used these types of messages (particularly integration) much less frequently than those who were more cognitively complex.

When they employed the "separation" method of dealing with subsidiary goals, people acted in ways that fit Brown and Levinson's model fairly neatly. They chose to pursue the goal of persuasion by advancing assertions and trying to get the other person to agree; the objective assigned to them (persuade the other) led them to produce communicative acts with indentifiable points. There were a wide variety of messages that employed separation: some used indirect action, some used redressive forms in their messages, and so on. But these message variations are all easily understood as instantiations of Brown and Levinson's four basic politeness strategies. Moreover, people in this study were asked to rate their partners's behavior for politeness and persuasiveness, and our results supported the view that use of such conventional politeness forms in fact results in a trade-off of clear and effective communication against politeness (O'Keefe and Shepherd 1987, 1989).

But what we called "integration" appears to involve a qualitatively different way of reasoning about message design. For example, some of the individuals in our study explicitly altered the situation by defining it as cooperative rather than competitive (e.g., by describing the goal of the encounter as trying to find a consensus that would satisfy both parties or by locating common ground). Such individuals would pursue the goal of securing agreement, but defined and organized agreement as a common understanding achieved jointly rather than as a backdown of the other party.

This kind of strategy does not fit well within any of Brown and Levinson's four categories. Arguments presented as attempts to reach consensus do avoid performing any face-threatening action, since the agendas of both speaker and hearer are affirmed. But it does not make sense to call this an instance of avoidance, of "Don't do the FTA," since there was no FTA to be performed. And in addition, the act is performed; it just is not face-threatening when performed in this way. It is not a case of indirectness: in indirectness the FTA is performed, but off record, and with this approach, the performed act is quite direct and no face-threatening act is implied. it is not a case of using redress; explicitly naming the common objective to be sought has no logical connection to giving the hearer face. And it is not a case of doing a bald FTA; no on-record FTA is performed. So whatever this approach represents, it reflects a message design strategy different in kind from the ones Brown and Levinson have described.

It is a strategy that cannot be described within any model that assumes that communication situations consist of a set of fixed parameters that dictate goals and in turn dictate actions, since it depends on altering the situation to fit the action to be performed. Brown and Levinson's analysis is based on the assumption that people alter their communicative actions to fit the communicative situation. By altering the situation, rather than the desired action, people who use integration manage to escape the trade-off between clear communication and face support, and so are able to be both polite to their fellows and effective in pursuing their own argumentative aims.

Since it is possible to approach a situation we studied in a way that makes face threat irrelevant, why would anyone choose to pursue an intrinsically face-threatening line of action? The only answer Brown and Levinson can give is that avoiding the FTA trades off efficiency in communication and thus makes it more difficult for the speaker to achieve his/her personal agenda. But several recent studies (Bingham 1988a, 1988b; O'Keefe and McCornack 1987; O'Keefe and Shepherd 1987, 1989) have found that even though messages employing integration strategies were judged as the most effective messages for managing face issues, they were not rated as ineffective in advancing the speaker's own aims. One study (O'Keefe and McCornack 1987) found they were actually more effective in achieving both the dominant communication goals and face protection.

So integration strategies seem to avoid the trade-off between clear communication and face support, while separation strategies embrace the trade-off. Selection strategies, by contrast, often appeared completely ineffectual and irrational. For example, some interactants in our study blatantly lied about their position on the issue, refusing to disagree with their partners (we know they lied because they reported their beliefs on a pretest questionnaire); other subjects wouldn't discuss the issue or anything else, refusing to give uptake to their partners; others made incoherent contributions that introduced irrelevant personal topics; and so on.

If we try to interpret these behaviors as instantiating any of Brown and Levinson's four strategies, the most straightforward classification is that these are all instances of avoidance, of "Don't do the FTA." But such a suggestion preserves Brown and Levinson's category scheme at the expense of their assumption of rationality: all of these "avoidance" behaviors are radically uncooperative by conventional standards. Lying, being irrelevant, refusing to get the point, and so on, involve gross flouting of every standard of cooperative conduct in conversation (see Grice 1975). They do not involve withholding the FTA, in any normal sense; there is no point to be made and hence no intrinsically face-threatening action that follows from getting the point across. These acts involve withholding communication itself.

In light of the number of effective and utterly conventional ways there are to disagree politely, it hardly seems rational for individuals to perform such radically uncooperative acts, with their attendant costs, simply in the interest of not disagreeing with another person. It is easy to imagine circumstances in which the threat of self-exposure would lead any person to at least consider lying or behaving in some other uncooperative fashion; but in the situation we examined everyone already knew the person's views. People reported their views on the pretest; their self-reports were explicitly discussed part of the experimental induction. Lying served no apparent purpose and left the partner in an uncomfortable position. For these reasons, this too seems to be a form of behavior that stands outside the kind of analysis Brown and Levinson have offered. At the very least, it seems to embody a very different sense of rationality than the one that Brown and Levinson assume.

So, although Brown and Levinson have offered a convincing analysis of conventional forms of politeness, their model could not be extended to cover the full range of messages we observed in our study of face-to-face arguments. We were left with the question of how to explain the diverse performances we observed.

The answer to this question lies in recognizing that there are two sources of diversity in responses to a communicative task. Brown and Levinson's model assumes that all communicators reason in the same way: a person has a set of goals, orders them as to priority, derives an act that will accomplish the primary goals, and expresses the act in a way that reflects the weightiness of the FTA. Clearly, some of the variation in individual performance can be attributed to differences in the priority given to different goals by different individuals; but not all variations can be explained this way. Some of the variation is associated with individuals differences in reasoning about the relations between message forms and message functions.

The uncooperative communicators we observed seemed to focus on the expressive qualities of their messages rather than functional considerations: their reasoning seemed to be dominated by concerns about revealing their thoughts and feelings to the partner. Hence, their actions were designed defensively rather than painfully and reflected a self-oriented design (Don't reveal yourself) rather than an other-oriented design (Don't do the FTA). They appeared to view the communication situation as an occasion for self-exposure rather than an opportunity to influence the addressee.

The people we observed using integration strategies also seemed to reason in ways that diverge from Brown and Levinson's model. Communicators who design messages using integration strategies appear to assess the situation; they seem to begin by envisioning a state in which all the relevant goals are maximally satisfied; and then they determine how the situation would have to be changed in order to bring about this state. So, for example, consider a person who wants to do her best to persuade the partner, using all her best arguments, but who does not want to be disagreeable or disrespectful to the partner. She envisions a situation in which her persuasive behaviors are not offensive—say, a situation in which the goals is to pool arguments or find all their common arguments or create the best joint analysis of the issue. By explicitly describing the situation in this way, a context is created in which the desired line of action is uncoupled from what would ordinarily be its face-threatening implications.

Based on these reflections, I hypothesized that there are, in fact, three distinct methods that individuals employ in designing messages. The first method involves simply thinking about the situation in relation to the self, evaluating thoughts in terms of whether they are disagreeable, repressing or misrepresenting disagreeable thoughts if uttering them might have negative consequences, but otherwise saying what comes to mind. If this is the method an individual has available to design messages, then one rational response to a conflict situation is to refuse to discuss the topic or to lie about what one's views are. Another rational response is to simply say what one thinks about the topic or about the arguments made by the other part, without showing any concern for face.

The second method of message design can be assumed to involve the kind of ends-means reasoning Brown and Levinson posit. The speaker (a) assesses the situation, and in particular assesses the rights and obligations of parties to each other; (b) selects an action that trades on these rights and obligations to induce the hearer to do or believe what is wanted; (c) determines the effect of performing the action on subsidiary objectives; and (d) says what is necessary to get the point across in an appropriately polite way. By assuming that some people use this kind of message design process we can account for messages that employ standard techniques for performing FTA's, such as indirectness and redress.

The third method of message design involves a different kind of ends-means reasoning. The speaker (a) projects a state of affairs in which both parties play their roles, without conflict or offense; (b) determines the differences between that state of affairs and the present situation; and (c) attempts to change the hearer's representation of the situation to conform to the desired state of affairs. By assuming that some people use this sort of message design process, we can explain how those people could produce messages that recontextualize what would have been FTA's, thereby rendering the message inoffensive.

Explaining Diversity in Reasoning about Communication

The question is, why would people employ such variant reasoning in designing messages? These different modes of designing messages are differentially effective, with reasoning focusing on self-expression being least effective and reasoning about situation manipulations being most effective. If people are oriented to the payoffs and trade-offs of their messages, it would seem that everyone should use the most effective approach to message design.

My theory of message design logic (O'Keefe 1988) is designed to explain why people's messages can be very similar in some situations and, in other situations, display such markedly different ways of approaching communication tasks. On the basis of studies of individual differences in message production across a number of different genres, I have argued that individuals may employ any of three different functional principles ("message design logics) in producing and understanding messages. The three message design logics identified in my original formulation are called expressive, conventional, and rhetorical.

An expressive message design logic manages the substance of messages. It reflects the view that communication is a process of expressing and receiving encoded thoughts and feelings. Characteristically, those using an expressive logic fail to distinguish between thought and expression; in producing messages, they "dump" their current mental state, and they assume that others produce messages the same way. Expressive communicators do not generally alter expression systematically in the service of achieving effects, nor do they ordinarily find anything other than "literal and direct" meaning in incoming messages. Their messages have a distinctively "reactive" quality, in the sense that they react to contingencies rather than anticipating them.

A conventional message design logic manages the force or point of messages. It is based on an image of communication as a game played cooperatively, according to social conventions and procedures. Within conventional logic, thought and expression are related in a less direct way, since expression is subordinated to the achievement of other instrumental goals. Language is still treated as a means of expressing propositions, but the expressed propositions are specified by the social effect one wants to achieve (utterance content is specified in the sense that uttering a given set of propositions under certain conditions counts as performing an action that is associated in socio-cultural practice with the effect the message producer wants to achieve; for example, uttering a certain kind of proposition under the right conditions counts as performing a request, and performing a request is a way to get certain wants satisfied simply by exploiting conventional obligations among persons). Conventional communicators treat communicative contexts (the roles, rights, and relations situations contain) as having fixed parameters (that is, they take social structure—roles and norms—to be both manifest to all and relatively inflexible) and design messages by performing what they take to be the contextually appropriate actions.

A rhetorical message design logic manages the context of messages. It reflects a view of communication as the creation and negotiation of social selves and situations. The rhetorical view subsumes knowledge of conventional ways to achieve goals within the view that social structure is flexible and created through communication. For the rhetorical communicator, social reality is created by what and how something is said or written, and so messages are designed to portray a scene that is consistent with one's wants; the discourse of others is closely interpreted to determine the nature of the drama and the perspective they are enacting. Individuals using a rhetorical logic anticipate interactional problems and evade them by offering explicit redescriptions of the situation.

The three design logics are developmentally related and ordered. O'Keefe and Delia (1988) summarize research on the development of oral and written communication skills that documents a progression, across tasks and media, from expressive to rhetorical functioning. This progression reflects the natural ordering of the logics: an individual first develops general techniques for managing the relation between thought and talk ((expressive design logic); then learns to subordinate expression to the conventions governing social situations (conventional design logic); and finally, learns to invoke situations through enactment of their features and conventions (rhetorical design logic). There is evidence that the acquisition of design logic is a lengthy process, extending into adulthood (Logan 1991).

Uniformity and Diversity in Message Design

Consistent with the general goal of explaining why people sometimes produce uniform messages and sometimes very different messages, the theory of message design logic predicts that in some situations individuals will differ and in others they will all behave similarly. Some kinds of tasks elicit low diversity: those in which there are few if any limits on relevance and in which saying what is on one's mind is the appropriate and effective thing to do. Other tasks elicit diverse responses from individuals relying on different design logics.

Because the theory of design logic predicts that in some situations messages will be uniform and in other situations messages will vary, some readers have expressed the view that the theory of design logic is incomplete without a "theory of situations" that spells out which situations will elicit high diversity and which low diversity. No ordinary "situation variable" (e.g., intimacy of the speaker-hearer relation) is likely to be a value in predicting where diversity attributable to design logic differences will appear. Even "situation complexity," a condition that promotes message diversity, will not always be sufficient to elicit design logic differences, since not every high diversity situation will be one in which design logic differences are clearly displayed.

In fact, the relevant "theory of situations" is integral with the theory of design logic itself. The theory of design logic is a theory of the circumstances that make differences in design logic visible. Those who use an expressive design logic to not distinguish between what they happen to think and what others think is relevant or what will help to get the job done. To separate those who use expressive logics from those who use conventional or rhetorical logics, then, one must find a situation in which people do different things depending on whether they make this distinction. Those who use a rhetorical design logic appreciate that goals can be achieved by manipulating situations, even though it is not always profitable to do so; to separate those using rhetorical logics from those using other logics, one must find a situation in which it is profitable to alter the identities or beliefs of the participants.

To illustrate this point, consider messages (1) through (6). These messages were produced in response to the Group Leader problem, which has been used extensively in our studies of interpersonal competence. This problem asks people to say how they would handle a situation in which they, as the leader of a class project group, must deal with a procrastinating group member who has requested an extension just before a major project deadline.

The Group Leader problem has several features that are important from the standpoint of detecting differences in design logic. First, the procrastinator, Ron, is represented as having repeatedly failed to conform to the group's decisions and procedures; this leads people to have a negative impression of Ron and a number of salient beliefs about his past conduct that are not particularly relevant for dealing with the present situation. Second, the group is portrayed as having a particular organization and set of commitments that might or might not be subject to renegotiation but which are relevant to dealing with Ron's failure to perform; the ways that the group's arrangements might be altered to secure a good outcome are fairly easy to see and plainly advantageous. The presence of salient but irrelevant and negatively balanced beliefs about Ron's past behavior and the desirability of reorganizing the situation make this scenario especially useful for detecting differences in design logic.

Messages (1) through (6) are quite diverse in content and effects. Messages (1) and (2) are sparse, ineffectual, and highly effectively toned. They express highly affective reactions to Ron's behavior without speaking to the issue of how the group is to complete its work. What functional principle could connect these messages to the communicator's larger objective to complete the project and get a good grade? Only an expressive design logic allows the communicator to follow his or her impulses or say whatever he or she thinks regardless of how it affects larger goals, because an expressive message design logic focuses on the relation between one's own stream of consciousness and the message rather than the effects of the message. Someone using an expressive design logic may evaluate and repress "bad" thoughts, but the thoughts available for expression are the reactions of the message producer to the situation, and not ideas about how to get the task accomplished.

1. You stupid ass fucker. Why did you wait so long to tell us you were getting behind on your part. You fucked up all our grades. I'm getting you out of this group. Everybody feels the same way. I hope you have fun when you take the class next semester.

2. Ron, I can't believe you haven't finished your research. You have been inconsiderate to the group all along. Several members even suggested that you be taken out of the group but we decided to give you a chance. Now what are we supposed to do? It was your responsibility and you backed out. I'm afraid that I'm going to tell the TA that you haven't done your share. I will be so mad at you if we get a bad grade on this—I need an A in this course.

Messages (3) and (4) message contrast strongly with the expressive messages, in that they explicitly instruct Ron to get the work done. However, it is notable that little is done other than instructing him to finish his work. The details of how to get Ron out of his predicament are left unaddressed. The message depends for its success on the force of the order to get the work done; no effort is made to go beyond mentioning rights and obligations to discuss, say, how Ron's time could be organized or why he should be motivated to finish. The connection between these messages and the goal of getting the work done is a conventional design logic, in which the speaker assumes that message design is a process of insuring that he or she has the right to make a demand (or that someone else does) and then making and defending that demand.

3. Ron, you idiot, this speech is due next week and you are not getting anything done. Now number one you owe it to other people in the group who have spent a great deal of time and energy working on this to at least do your part. Number two, you have been slacking off together on this project, I hope you realize you will be getting an individual grade—and at this point I seriously doubt that it will be a high one. There is no excuse for this laziness, and I really don't appreciate it, so get going now, and have that material prepared by tomorrow.

4. I would ask Ron if he had serious family problems or was he just blowing us off. If he had serious problems, I would ask him to call the T.A. and tell him/her the situation with our group. If he was blowing us off, I would talk to my T.A. and explain the problem. If Ron had serious problems I would encourage him to talk to someone. I would ask him to please consider what he is doing to our group. If he was blowing us off, I would insist he get his butt to the library and research.

Messages (5) and (6) treat the conditions described in the scenario not as givens, but as resources that can be called on in transforming the situation to facilitate goals attainment. The linguistic mechanisms through which these transformations are effected are motivational appeals, rhetorical labelling, explicit redescriptions of the context, and the like. In the course of talking about one thing (what Ron should do), these communicators elaborate the message in such a way as to reconstitute some important set of features of the situation (own identity, Ron's identity, Ron's motives, the group's procedures, and so on). The message rationalizes goal attainment; it is as though the message producer began with the goal to be achieved (Ron does his work well so the group can be successful) and then described a situation in which those goals can be achieved easily; the redescription, if accepted by Ron, is one that will lead him to complete his work. Example (5) is particularly striking in explicitly managing multiple features of the context for Ron's behavior as a way of orienting him to finish the work. It is in this sense that these messages reflect a rhetorical design logic.

5. Ron, I'm sorry you won't have everything ready by tonight. Can you give me some good reasons I can tell the group? I know you've been having problems all along and that's obvious to the rest of the group too. You need to be able to see how your personal problems have interfered in the group's completion of the project. I'll be the first to sympathize with you but now we'll have to come up with some concrete solutions. You can't expect someone else to take over your research workload.

6. Well, Ron, it's due next week and we have to get it all to the typist. OK, if it's not done it's not. Tell you what. Why don't you jot down your main ideas so that we can include them in the introduction and conclusion. Also, tell me when you think your section should come in the whole project. Then get it to my apt. by 10:00 the next day because I have to get it to the typist by 2:00. Is this okay? I'll just explain to the group that you'll have it done but not by meeting time. We all want a good grade, so if you need the time to make your part better, go ahead. But if I can't get it to the typist in time, you'll have to type it. Alright, take it easy.

So messages (1) through (6) can be seen as varying in terms of the functional principle that connects the message (specifically, central features of the message) to the speaker's goals. Whenever a person produces a message, the message can be seen as reflecting at least one design logic. In using that message, the person may be said to have relied on that design logic.

It is important to emphasize that different design logics can lead to uniformity in messages as well as diversity. Suppose we have a low diversity situation, one in which everyone produces very similar messages. Each of those messages reflects the operation of some design logic. Even though it is not possible to see what design logic was employed in constructing the message, the message is typical of the operation of that design logic in this situation. It is typical of different design logics to generate just this one type of message in this kind of situation.

Suppose we have a situation in which those using rhetorical, conventional, and expressive design logics all produce different kinds of messages. Again each message reflects the operation of design logic, and again the messages are typical of the operation of the design logic they exemplify. It happens to be typical of different design logics to produce differing kinds of messages in this other kind of situation.

The fact that in one situation the messages are all the same and in the other they are all different does not make the messages either more or less typical of their design logics; both outcomes—uniformity and variability—are expected, depending on circumstances.

But what does change from situation to situation is how useful the message is as an index of its design logic. If we want to know which design logic serves as the rationale for a particular message, just by looking at the message, then we have to do so in a situation in which we know that people relying on different design logics typically produce different kinds of messages.

Variation, Adaption, and Message Effectiveness

The theory of message design logic is not just an analysis of diversity; it is an analysis of why diversity in message design results in differential message effects. Notice that a move up the hierarchy of message design systems opens up additional possibilities for the use of language. Attaining a conventional level of functioning makes expression an option, a goals one might choose rather than the guiding principle behind the message production system; attaining a rhetorical level of functioning makes affirmation of preexisting roles and routines a choice, rather than a necessary foundation from which all action derives. The difference between an expressive and a conventional message design logic is, in large part, the difference between a system that simply reacts to circumstances and a system that responds to exigencies with some appropriate remedy; the difference between a conventional and rhetorical system is the difference between a system that is limited in its response by historically evolved structures and a system that draws on a wider range of resources by changing structures. Hence, differences in message design logic should lead to difference in the ability to accomplish whatever tasks are confronted in the situation. Messages generated by an expressive design logic should be judged as least effective and messages generated by a rhetorical design logic should be judged as most effective in meeting situational demands. In the case of regulative situations, these demands include attaining own wants and objectives, getting the message target to perform, and satisfying norms of civility and politeness that are relevant to all social situations (Brown and Levinson 1978; Goffman 1959)

Hence, as level of message design logic increases, messages should be perceived as more effective in managing the immediate practical task faced in the situation, in eliciting the desired performance from the message target, in satisfying the various parties involved in the situation, and in showing respect and consideration for the message target. These expectations received initial support in an experiment conducted by O'Keefe and McCornack (1987). They found that as level of message design logic increased, so did perceived effectiveness in regulation, perceived effectiveness in giving support to the message recipient, and the attractiveness of the message producer.

Explaining Message Production

As I have emphasized (O'Keefe 1989), my published work on design logics addresses the question of how differences in design logic can lead to message variation and adaption. Some readers (e.g., Logan 1991) have taken this account to be a literal model of mental representations underlying message production. Because of this, it is important to emphasize what a design logic is and how the analysis of design logic can be incorporated into explanations of message production.

A design logic is the rationale that connects a function to a form (and this in any design medium; e.g., architecture). In the case of message design, it is an account of why uttering these words under these circumstances has this particular meaning or effect. In this sense, Searle's (1975) theory of speech acts is an explicit and formal message design logic.

The relationship between design logic and message is like the relationship between an equation and the curve it describes. It would not be proper to say that the equation is one of the "characteristics" of the curve. Similarly, it would not be proper to say that the equation "causes" the curve, in the way that "cognitive complexity" supposedly "causes" "person-centerdness." And while it might be proper to say that the equation "generates" the curve, one should not assume that a design logic "generates" messages in the sense of machining or extruding them. A curve might be made by some natural process (e.g., the process by which a nautilus builds its shell, which is shaped as a particular curve); even though the curve is truly described by a particular equation, the equation may play no causal role in the creation of an actual physical object that is shaped along that particular curve. Similarly, what we make explicit in describing a design logic probably has no identifiable correlate under a human skull, but may nonetheless by a true description of the form-function relationships in a set of messages produced by a person.

If descriptions of design logic are not offered as literal descriptions of mental processes employed in message production, then (a) what is the model of message production implicit in the model, and (b) what is the role of functional explanation in a model of message production?

There is a specific view of message production processes implicit in the characterization of message design logics, a view of message production as the transformation of situation representations into expressions (for a detailed discussions of this issue, see Lambert 1992; Lambert and O'Keefe 1991; O'Keefe and Lambert 1989). This view of message production can be seen in work such as that of Linde and Labov (1975), Grosz (198), Hermann (1983), and Sibun (1991). In this work, messages are seen as constructed through accessing and selecting specific message content to be expressed; speakers focus on and describe elements of their active representations of situations and situation-relevant knowledge.

Bruce Lambert and I (Lambert 1992; Lambert and O'Keefe 1991; O'Keefe and Lambert 1989) have argued that in general, messages originate in speakers' representations of situations; that is, messages begin not as abstract message types, but as thoughts that are available for expression. What we call a design logic is a way of thinking about communication situations, selecting thoughts for expression, and modifying expression to meet goals. A design logic is a description of the way thought, transformed as messages, related to desired message outcomes.

Hence, we should model differences in message production processes as differences in patterns of thoughts about communication situations and differences in the mapping of thoughts to messages. This project is the focus of ongoing work discussed by O'Keefe and Lambert (1989), Lambert and O'Keefe (1991), and Lambert (1992).

In an earlier section, I argued that the Strategy Choice Model treats a preliminary stage of message analysis, identification of varying message types, as the endpoint of analysis. The identification of message types is the beginning for a Message Design Model; the analyst's task is to account for variation in message content and effects in terms of a detailed model of message features, their functions, and their rational deployment in message production. In a similar manner, functional analysis is a preliminary stage to the construction of models of message production. By providing a description of the variations in performance to be accounted for, a Message Design Model serves as the basis for, but is not equivalent to, development of cognitive models of message production.

Summary

Although Brown and Levinson's (1978) analysis of universals in politeness provides a useful model for theories of message variation and adaption, Message Design Models must take into account the fact that there are multiple sources of functional variation in messages. While some variation is attributable to variations in speaker goals, other variations reflect differences in the way individuals conceive of the possible functions of communication in solving everyday problems; individuals may employ any of three different conceptions of the relationship between communication forms and functions (message design logics). The theory of message design logic provides an account of message variation and adaptation, and can serve as the foundation for models of the process of message production.

THE INTERPLAY OF THEORY, DATA, AND METHOD IN THE DEVELOPMENT OF A RESEARCH PROGRAM

This chapter has reconstructed the development of my research program as a response to one specific issue: finding the best account of variation in message design. Since that is the issue my work is currently focused on, this reconstruction is the best way to explain where the work is now. But it creates a very misleading picture of the way the ideas actually developed. In particular, the formulation of the problem of message variation, as it is laid out in the opening section of this chapter, is quite recent—the last ten years of my work should be described as the effort to bring this problem into focus and formulate it properly, rather than as a search for a theory that responds to the problem as it is formulated here. In this sense, the work is more accurately characterized as the discovery of a problem than a search for a solution.

The problem I thought I was addressing was understanding social inference processes and their role in communication behavior. This is the defining problem of constructivism, which originated as a model of impression formation (Crockett 1965). The core of constructivist theory is the assertion that cognitive complexity—skill in impression formation—is a key factor influencing preferences for message types. Constructivist research has provided impressive documentation for this assertion, a long list of studies that have found significant relationships between cognitive complexity (considered as construct differentiation, abstractness, perspectivism, or integration) and preferences for certain types of messages (for reviews see Burleson 1989; O'Keefe and Delia 1988).

This research presupposed a Strategy Choice Model; this is quite clear and explicit in constructivist theory (see, e.g., Delia and O'Keefe 1979; Delia, O'Keefe, and O'Keefe 1982; O'Keefe and Delia 1982; O'Keefe, Murphy, Myers, and Babrow 1989). The Strategy Choice Model embodied in constructivism was unproblematic as a way of summarizing the observed system of preferences, but when we began to take its account of message production seriously (O'Keefe and Delia 1982; O'Keefe, Murphy, Myers, and Babrow 1989), the logical defects of the model became increasingly apparent. The forces that led me to begin examining the constructivist account of message production are difficult to pinpoint, since they are never mentioned in any of the published work; but the increasing influence of cognitive science on the intellectual scene and the need to move beyond simply documenting preferences would seem to be sufficient conditions to have motivated such an effort.

The early research also reflected a narrow reliance on a particular observational method: asking subjects to give their responses to role-played, hypothetical scenarios, usually in writing. But it soon became clear that we needed to demonstrate that the effects observed using written (and other monologic performances) would generalize to interactional behavior. This impulse led to several projects that analyzed messages produced in face-to-face interaction (Applegate 1980; O'Keefe and Shepherd 1987; Samter and Burleson 1984). This methodological shift highlighted the problem of describing functional variation in messages, since types of messages identified using monologic tasks do not correspond to easily identifiable structures in conversation.

Quite naturally and unreflectively, then, developments in the research program shifted attention toward the problem of describing messages, and in particular of describing message variation. This shift in attention is evident in a number of papers published in the mid- to late-1980s, including Dan O'Keefe's (1987) widely circulated paper on the problem of message description and my own work on the logic of message design.

The message design logic model was developed as an account for observed individual differences in communication behavior; in its initial presentation, the problem of explaining message diversity and uniformity was not yet crisply formulated (O'Keefe 1985). But it did not take long to discover that the problem of variation and adaptation was addressed very well by this model, and that by making the problem of diversity central one could develop a more careful and detailed treatment of message adaptation. By the time the theoretical presentation of message design logic was published in 1988, the problem of understanding message uniformity and message diversity was an integral part of the argument and analysis (O'Keefe 1988; O'Keefe and Delia 1988; O'Keefe and McCornack 1987).

The theory of message design logic does address standard constructivist problems concerning the relationship of social inference to message production and the development of communication skill (for a discussion, see O'Keefe and Delia 1988). It also promises to provide a useful foundation for message analysis and models of message production. But in the end its primary contribution may be neither the methodological developments it has spawned nor the conception of communication it embodies; it may well be that the chief value of this way of looking at communication is that it has led to a sharper analysis of a key problem, the problem of message variation and adaption.

REFERENCES

Alvoy, K. T. (1973). The development of listener adapted communication in grade school children. *Genetic Psychology Monographs* 87, 33–104

Applegate, J. L. (1980). Person- and position-centered teacher communication in a day-care center. In N. K. Denzin (Ed.) *Studies in symbolic interaction,* Vol. 3 (pp. 59–96). Greenwich, Conn.: JAI Press.

Baxter, L. A. (1984). An investigation of compliance-gaining as politeness. *Human Communication Research 10,* 427–456.

Bingham, S. (1988a). *Interpersonal responses to sexual harassment.* Unpublished doctoral dissertation, Purdue University.

Bingham, S. (1988b). *Message design logic, communication competence, and the management of multiple situational demands.* Paper presented at the annual meeting of the Speech Communication Association, New Orleans, La.

Britton, J., Burgess, T., Martin, N., McLeod, A., and Rosen, H. (1975). *The development of writing abilities (11–18).* London: Macmillan.

Brown, P., & Levinson, S. (1978). Universals in language usage: Politeness phenomena. In E. R. Goody (Ed.), *Questions and politeness* (pp. 56–323). Cambridge: Cambridge University Press.

Burleson, B. R. (1989). The constructivist approach to person-centered communication: Analysis of a research exemplar. In B. Dervin, L. Grossberg, B. J. O'Keefe, and E. Wartella (Eds.), *Rethinking communication, Vol. 2: Paradigm exemplars* (pp. 29–46). Newbury Park, Cal: Sage.

Burleson, B. R., & Wilson, S. R. (1988). On the continued undesirability of item desirability: A reply to Boster, Hunter, and Seibold. *Human Communication Research* 15, 178–191.

Burleson, B. R., Wilson, S. R., Waltman, M. S., Goering, E. M., Ely, T. K. and Whaley, B. B. (1988). Item desirability effects in compliance-gaining research: Seven studies documenting artifacts in the strategy selection procedure. *Human Communication Research 14,* 429–486.

Boster, F. J. (2988). Comments on the utility of compliance-gaining message selection tasks. *Human Communication Research 15,* 169–177.

Clark, R. A., & Delia, J. G. (1976). The development of functional persuasive skills in childhood and early adolescence. *Child Development 47,* 1008–1014.

Crockett, W. H. (1965). Cognitive complexity and impression formation. In B. A. Maher (Ed.), *Progress in experimental personality research,* Vol. 2. New York: Academic.

Delia, J. G., Kline, S. L., & Burleson, B. R. (1979). The development of persuasive communication strategies in kindergartners through twelfth-graders. *Communication Monographs 46,* 241–256.

Delia, J. G., & O'Keefe, B. J. (1979). Constructivism: The development of communication in children. In E. Wartella (Ed.), *Children communicating* (pp. 157–186). Beverly Hill: Sage.

Flavell, J. H., Botkin, P. T., Fry, C. L., Wright, J. W., and Jarvis, P. E. (1968). *The development of role-taking and communication skills in children.* New York: Wiley.

Goffman, E. (1959). *The presentation of self in everyday life.* Garden City: Doubleday Anchor.

Goffman, E. (1969). *Strategic interaction.* Philadelphia: University of Pennsylvania Press.

Greene, F. (1987). *The language of action: Symbolic representation in the output system.* Paper presented at the annual meeting of the Speech Communication Association, Boston.

Grice, H. P. (1975). Logic and conversation. In P. Cole & J. L. Morgan (Eds.), *Syntax and semantics, vol. 3: Speech acts* (pp. 41–58). New York: Academic.

Gross, E., & Stone, G. P. (1964). Embarrassment and the analysis of role requirements. *American Journal of Sociology 70,* 1–15.

Grosz, B. J. (1981). Focusing and description in natural language dialogues. In A. Joshi, B. Webber, and I. Sag (Eds.), *Elements of discourse understanding* (pp. 84–105). Cambridge: Cambridge University Press.

Hermann, T. (1983). *Speech and situation: A psychological conception of situated speaking.* Berlin: Springer-Verlag.

Higgins, E. T. (1981). The "communication game": Implications for social cognition and persuasion. In E. T. Higgins, C. P. Herman, & M. P. Zanna (Eds.), *Social cognition: The Ontario symposium, Vol. 1.* Hillsdale, N.J.: Laurence Erlbaum.

Hunter, J. E. (1988). Failure of the social desirability response set hypothesis. *Human Communication Research 15,* 162–168.

Hunter, J. E., & Boster, F. J. (1978). *An empathy model of compliance-gaining message production.* Paper presented at the annual meeting of the Speech Communication Association, Minneapolis.

Hunter, J. E., and Boster F. J. (1981), *Compliance-gaining message experiments: Some evidence for an empathy model.* Unpublished manuscript, Michigan State University.

Jacobs, S. (1985). Language. In M. L. Knapp & G. R. Miller (Eds.), *Handbook of interpersonal communication.* Beverly Hills: Sage.

Kellermann, K., Boretzmann, S., Lim, T., & Kitao, K. (1989). The conversation MOP: Scenes in the stream of discourse. *Discourse Processes 12,* 27–61.

Kellermann, K., & Lim, T. S. (1989). Conversational acquaintance: The flexibility of routinized behaviors. In B. Dervin, L. Grossberg, B. J. O'Keefe, and E. Wartella (Eds.), *Rethinking Communication, Vol. 2: Paradigm exemplars* (pp. 172–187). Newbury Park, Cal.: Sage.

Lambert, B. L. (1992). *A connectionist model of message design.* Unpublished doctoral dissertation, University of Illinois, Urbana-Champaign.

Lambert, B. L., & O'Keefe, B. J. (1991). *Modelling message production.* Paper presented at the annual meeting of the International Communication Association, Chicago.

Levinson, S. C. (1982). *Pragmatics.* Cambridge: Cambridge University Press.

Linde, C., & Labov, W. (1975). Spatial networks as a site for the study of language and thought. *Language 51,* 924–939.

Logan, C. (1991). *Message design logics and moral reasoning: Developmental processes of communication function and social cognition.* Paper presented at the annual meeting of the Speech Communication Association, Atlanta.

Marwell, G., & Schmitt, D. R. (1967a). Dimensions of compliance-gaining behavior: A synthesis and model. *Sociological Quarterly 8,* 317–328.

Marwell, G., & Schmitt, D. R. (1967b). Dimensions of compliance-gaining behavior: An empirical analysis. *Sociometry 30,* 350–364.

O'Keefe, B. J. (1985). *The functional integration of communication concepts: Evidence for individual differences in reasoning about communication.* Paper presented at the annual meeting of the Speech Communication Association, Denver.

O'Keefe, B. J. (1988). The logic of message design: Individual differences in reasoning about communication. *Communication Monographs 55,* 80–103.

O'Keefe, B. J. (1990). The logic of regulative communication: Understanding the rationality of message designs. In J. Dillard (Ed.), *Seeking compliance: The production of interpersonal influence messages* (pp. 87–106). Scottsdale, Ariz.: Gorsuch-Scarisbrick.

O'Keefe, B. J. (1991). Message design logic and the management of multiple goals. In K. Tracy (Ed.), *Understanding face-to-face interaction: Issues linking goals and discourse* (pp. 101–117). Hillsdale, N.J.: Laurence Erlbaum.

O'Keefe, B. J., & Delia, J. G. (1982). Impression formation and message production. In M. Roloff and C. Berger (Eds.), *Social cognition and communication* (pp. 33–72). Beverly Hills: Sage.

O'Keefe, B. J., & Delia, J. G. (1988). Communicative tasks and communicative practices: The development of audience-centered message production. In B. Rafoth and D. Rubin (Eds.), *The social construction of written communication* (pp. 70–98). Norwood, N.J.: Ablex.

O'Keefe, B. J., & Lambert, B. L. (1989, November). *Effects of message design logic on the communication of intention.* Paper presented at the annual meeting of the Speech Communication Association, San Francisco.

O'Keefe, B. J., & McCornack, S. A. (1987). Message design logic and message goal structure: Effects on perceptions of message quality in regulative communication situations. *Human Communication Research 14,* pp. 68–92.

O'Keefe, B. J., Murphy, M. A., Myers, R. A., & Babrow, A. S. (1988). The development of persuasive communication skills: The influence of developments in interpersonal constructs on the ability to generate communication-relevant beliefs and on level of persuasive strategy. *Communication Studies 40,* 29–40.

O'Keefe, B. J., & Shepherd, G. J. (1987). The pursuit of multiple objectives in face-to-face persuasive interactions: Effects of construct differentiation on message organization. *Communication Monographs 54,* 396–419.

O'Keefe, B. J., & Shepherd, G. J. (1989). The communication of identity during face-to-face persuasive interactions: Effects of receiver's construct differentiation and target's message strategies. *Communication Research 16,* 375–404.

O'Keefe, D. J. (1987). *Describing messages.* Paper presented at the annual meeting of the Speech Communication Association, Boston.

Samter, W., & Burleson, B. R. (1984). Cognitive and motivational influences on spontaneous comforting behavior. *Human Communication Research 11,* 231–260.

Seibold, D. R. (1988). A response to "Item desirability in compliance-gaining research." *Human Communication Research 15,* 152–161.

Seibold, D. R., Cantril J. G., & Meyers, R. A. (1985). Communication and interpersonal influence. In M. L. Knapp and G. R. Miller (Eds.), *Handbook of interpersonal communication.* Beverly Hills: Sage

Searle, J. (1969) *Speech acts.* Cambridge: Cambridge University Press.

Scott, M. B., & Lyman, S. M. (1968). Accounts. *American Sociological Review 48,* 46–62.

Sibun, P. (1990). The local organization of text. *In Proceedings of the Fifth International Workshop on Natural Language Generation* (pp. 120–127). Los Altos, Cal: Morgan Kaufman.

Weinstein, E. A. (1969). The development of interpersonal competence. In D. A. Goslin (Ed.), *Handbook of socialization theory and research* (pp. 753–775). Chicago: Rand-McNally.

Williams, D., & Boster, F. (1981). *The effects of beneficial situational characteristics, negativism, and dogmatism on compliance-gaining message selection.* Paper presented at the annual meeting of the International Communication Association, Minneapolis.

Wiseman, R. L., & Schneck-Hamlin, W. (1981). A multidimensional scaling validation of an inductively-derived set of compliance-gaining strategies. *Communication Monographs 48,* 251–270.

5

A Theory of Speech Codes

GERRY PHILIPSEN

Every person is connected to other people, whether the connection is obvious or subtle, tacit or announced, strong or weak, active or passive, pleasing or repugnant. These connections always exist in a particular time and place, circumstances that provide not only the sites of human connectedness but the resources as well. Thus, human connections, a universal phenomenon, are realized in particular ways which are contingent upon the milieu in which, and the resources with which, they are constructed. This chapter is about such situated resources, the public, discursive resources in and through which the connections between and among people are thematized, constituted or reconstituted, and managed. Speech codes is the name I apply to such resources. Drawing from selected example of speech codes research, this chapter essays the nature of such codes and their workings in social life. To introduce such research, I begin with a brief mention of three exemplary instances of its practice.

Tamar Katriel reported an Israeli way of speaking which she labeled *dugri* speech. Translated from the Hebrew as straight or direct talk, *dugri* speech refers to an utterance or exchange in which one interlocutor confronts another so as to display images of honesty, assertiveness, naturalness, solidarity, and matter-of-factness. Katriel demonstrated that in saying something like, "I'll tell you *dugri,* I don't like what you're doing," an Israeli speaker implies that the hearer is strong enough to put aside concerns for self in order to accomplish the greater good of correcting a situation that the speaker treats as socially undesirable. The larger social and political context of such an appeal is the interlocutors' shared understanding of Israel as society which must be internally strong so as to preserve its very being. Thus, in speaking *dugri,* the speaker enacts a particular identity, that of the "Sabra," and expresses a powerful message of shared identity with the other person (Katriel 1983, 1986).

Donal Carbaugh reported a way of speaking which he observed on a television talk show in the United States, the DONAHUE show. In episodes of that show, he found evidence that the interlocutors actively resisted efforts to assert what he calls a transindividual standard. When speakers on the show expressed a social standard (a rule of "society") for guiding conduct, others spoke out against such a standard, arguing instead for the "rights" of others to follow their own personal lights in matters of conduct. Carbaugh quotes the host of the program as saying, on one occasion, "No one is going to deny you your position, but the question is why do you impose it on others? (Carbaugh 1987, 42). In terms of the give and take or argument, the proponents of individual "rights" prevailed over those who advocated a transindividual standard. Although the DONAHUE speakers' insistence on the priority of personal over communal standards of self-presentation is itself a communal standard, it is a different one from that of the Israeli who speaks *dugri* (Carbaugh 1984, 1987, 1988).

Kristine L. Fitch reported the ways Colombians address each other, focusing on how people addressed women, including those with no kinship relation to the speaker, with some form of the word *madre* (mother). She reported, for example, that a male service person, around forty years of age, said to a female stranger, in her fifties, "No, *madre,* sorry but you can't park here. You have to move your car somewhere else." With *madre* forms of address, Fitch found, Colombians not only designate the addressee of an utterance (one of the functions of address terms) but also do a kind of interpersonal work in and through the use of such a term. Fitch shows that the service person, in using *madre* rather than, say, *señora,* was heard by his interlocutor as "asking a favor" rather than "giving an order." It is through such habits of linguistic expression, Fitch shows, that the Colombians not only refer to people and smooth the social process, but also reveal their outlook on types of persons and the proper conduct obtaining among interlocutors (Fitch 1991, 267). By examining some Colombians' modes of address, Fitch discovered a particular sense of social reality which her interlocutors invoke and establish in their talking with each other.

These reports each focus on three interrelated aspects of communication and interpersonal connection, aspects that help to introduce the nature of speech codes.

First, in each instance reference is made to an observed use of a term or notion about communicative conduct. These terms and notions include a symbol about a style of speaking (*dugri*), a rule (that one should not impose her or his "position" on another), and an interpretive principle (that the use of a madre term can be taken as "asking for a favor" rather than as "giving an order"). Such symbols and notions which interlocutors deploy to talk about talk are the elements of the systems I call speech codes.

Second, the words and notions involved in each instance derive from distinctive linguistic and cultural circumstances. *Dugri* is a Hebrew slang term derived from Arabic that has a distinctive meaning in its Israeli (as opposed to its arabic) use. The rule that one should not impose one's "position" on another was found expressed in discourse spoken in English in the United States. The notion about the situated meaning of *madre* was expressed, in Spanish, by a Colombian speaker of Spanish. Although these elements are not necessarily restricted or unique to the places in which they were found, each is an artifact that was constructed in and through a process of social interaction, in a nameable time and place. A speech code is a system of such locally situated, artifactual elements.

Third, in each instance the invocation of a particular term or notion was socially consequential. Such terms and notions, the elements of speech codes, are developed when interlocutors are concerned with thematizing, managing, or negotiating the ends and means of social action. In the reported instances, the use of a culturally distinctive term or notion about talk constituted an expression of social meaning which, in turn, established a particular connection between or among the interlocutors who produced and interpreted it. Those expressions were, in the *dugri* utterance, an assertion of social solidarity and an insistence on the political accountability of one's interpersonal conduct, in the DONAHUE utterance an assertion about the kinds of rhetorical self a proper person should and should not enact, and in the *madre* appellation the expression of deference through the casting of another into a particular persona.

These three instances help to introduce the concept of speech codes and the rationale of speech codes research. The reports suggest that the study of speech codes is motivated, at least in part, by the desire to understand particular, socially constructed discursive worlds, such as those portrayed in the examples, as the historical, spatial, and cultural sites in which human connections are accomplished. Beyond the motive of understanding such discursive worlds for their own sake, there are many practical motives for studying speech codes, including, at least, those of participation, appropriation, critique and defense. That is, the understanding of a particular, socially constructed discursive world can be applied toward such overlapping, potentially conflicting practical ends as participating intelligibly and appropriately in such a world, of appropriating judiciously its resources for one's use, of generating a sound and penetrating critique of it, and of defending it against its critics. Thus, although the study of speech codes, like their use, always serves a practical agenda, the agenda varies with the purposes of the particular application.

The rationale for speech codes research can be developed further by focusing on some of the key questions it has been pressed to answer. From its inception, speech codes research held out the promise for demonstrating that the kinds of local knowledge people deploy to talk about—to characterize, interpret, or rationalize—their communicative conduct is indeed local, particular knowledge. This suggested *the question of the existence of distinctive speech codes,* and has prompted the search for evidence of distinctiveness, across cultures, in the resources people deploy to invent, characterize, interpret, and rationalize their communicative conduct. If evidence could be found for the existence of such culturally particular resources, then there followed *the question of the substance of speech codes,* whether they provide a vocabulary, as it were, in and through which their users express and constitute distinctively coded social meanings and social worlds. The questions of the distinctiveness and the substance of speech codes suggested, in turn, *the question of how speech codes could be observed and formulated,* a question of method, broadly speaking, of concern to scholarly investigators as well as to those with immediately practical concerns. Finally, given that speech codes appeared to contain resources that interlocutors deploy in the service of practical ends, *the question of the force of speech codes in social life* was raised. The speech codes theory presented in this chapter is an effort to answer those four questions.

The chapter proceeds in three parts. First, the *concept* of speech codes is introduced and explicated. Second, I survey some of the *fieldwork* I have done that has contributed to my understanding of the nature and functions of speech codes. Finally, I propose *five propositions* about speech codes which are supported by my own and others' fieldwork research, and which form the core of speech codes theory.

1

The concept of speech code was fashioned from Berstein's concept of coding principle and Hymes's programmatic approach to the ethnography of communication.

The British sociologist Basil Bernstein (1972) demonstrated that, within the same society, there can exist different social groups or social classes whose communicative practices differ in important ways. Such differences, he argued, go beyond surface features in language use to differences in the coding principles that govern communicative conduct. Furthermore, he argued, ways of speaking are shaped by and, in turn, reinforce speakers' understanding of and affective orientation toward themselves, other people, and social life.

For Berstein, a coding principle is a rule governing what to say and how to say it in a particular context. An elaborated coding principle, for example, directs the speaker to use novel, complex, and diverse linguistic means to communicate individual intent, to emphasize the communication of unique personal meanings, and to adapt to the unique personal circumstance of listeners. A restricted coding principle directs its speakers to rely relatively less on verbal expression of intent to signal meaning, to rely heavily on (presumed) shared context in the signalling of meanings, and to emphasize the expression and continuing ratification of shared identity—such as shared gender or social status—among interlocutors.

Bernstein's theory links the differential use and valuation of these coding principles to socioeconomic differences at the level of social organization and to correlative differences in family structure and family interaction patterns (Bernstein 1972). His data suggest that the use of these ways is highly sensitive to the socioeconomic background and the situational context of speakers and hearers. In particular, he applied his approach to the study of middle versus lower working-class groups in contemporary England, showing that speakers in these groups made systematically different use of, and differently valued, ways of speaking, even though they spoke the same language. He did not claim that there are only two coding principles or that any social group or class uses only one. He did claim that specifiable socioeconomic conditions influence the degree to which the members of a social group or community use and value such principles. The empirical work of Bernstein and associates (collected in Bernstein 1971 and 1973) contains evidence that speakers from the English middle class were predisposed to use and value an elaborated coding principle, and those from the English lower class were predisposed to use and favor a restricted coding principle, although neither was confined to only one in all circumstances (Robinson 1965).

Bernstein has been criticized on several counts. He was accused of privileging the elaborated over the restricted coding principle, thus revealing a middle class bias (Labov); of objectifying and reifying class membership, thus ignoring nuances of social and personal qualities (Rickford); and of overstating the deterministic effect of socioeconomic conditions on conduct (Cook), thus neglecting the artfulness and diversity that "working class" speakers display in the deployment of their linguistic repertoires (Rosen 1972).

Although I believe Bernstein's critics gloss over the subtlety in his moves, particularly as these are deployed over time (see, for example, Bernstein 1973), it is not my purpose here to defend his program against the specific charges mentioned above. But at the very least it should be said that Bernstein's extensive research program as well as important extensions of it (Douglas 1970; Halliday 1973) show that his work raises fundamental questions about the communication process: (1) Are there different coding principles operative in communication? (2) If so, what are they? (3) How do coding principles influence, and how are they influenced by, the conditions of social life?

Contemporaneous with Bernstein's program, another approach to cultural differences in communicative practices was given a programmatic formulation. In 1962, Dell Hymes, an anthropologist and linguist, introduced "the ethnography of speaking" (1962), an approach to the study of communicative conduct which posits that there is, among the peoples of the world, great variety in culturally distinctive communicative practices and ways of conceptualizing communication. In a series of papers (Hymes 1962, 1964, 1972), Hymes proposed that students of communication direct their attention to the study, *in situ,* of a wide range of societies, in order to discover and describe, in particular cases, how communication is distinctively practiced and conceptualized. Shortly after he made his proposal, several important studies were published that suggested that his assumptions about cultural variety in communicative practices were well founded (see, for example, Abrahams and Bauman 1970; Albert 1964; Basso 1970; Bauman 1970; Philips 1970, and the collections of Gumperz and Hymes 1972 and Bauman and Sherzer 1974). By 1996, Donal Carbaugh and I (Philipsen and Carbaugh 1986) were able to find some 250 studies that had answered Hymes's call for fieldwork, and the number has grown substantially since that time.

The work of Bernstein and Hymes, taken together, suggested to me the possibility that communicative conduct is an activity that is radically cultural—something practiced and formulated distinctively across speech communities and cultures. While both Bernstein and Hymes demonstrated the existence of distinctive communicative practices, Hymes's ethnographic approach differed from Bernstein's approach in two important ways. First, where Bernstein formulated a limited number of communicative possibilities (two coding principles, two socioeconomic strata), Hymes proposed a framework to guide an exploratory search into the variety of communicative practices of a given social milieu. Second, where Bernstein observed the presence of specified objective properties in the speech he examined, Hymes prioritized the meanings, to those who used them, of communicative practices.

In the ethnography of speaking, the emphasis on exploration suggests a belief that when a given world of discourse is examined, it will be found to house discursive particulars (ways of speaking and resources for producing and interpreting communicative conduct) that are locally distinctive. For example, an associate of Bernstein's (writing in a volume edited by Bernstein) suggested that the study of certain worlds of discourse in English life could reveal the use of the term "brow" (as in "highbrow" and "lowbrow"), presumably a term that its users use to characterize or appraise certain communicative acts (Halliday 1971). Where Bernstein's framework had ignored such phenomena, Hymes's was designed explicitly to find and examine them. Where Bernstein made no provision for what speech judged as "highbrow" might mean to someone, Hymes provided explicitly for that. Hymes's approach took the observer "close to the ground" (Hymes's phrase), as it were, to observe and report the means of speech and their meanings to those who use them in a given circle of discourse.

Halliday's mention of the word "highbrow" was little more than an incidental part of his larger commentary, but I have focused on it here because it helps to reveal something about the study of speech codes, as that study was made possible by the ethnography of speaking. A study of the ways of speaking of a particular speech community can proceed by an investigator's formulating in advance that certain phenomena will be attended to, and the nature of these phenomena can be formulated quite explicitly according to some pre-formulated scheme. The empirical work of Bernstein and his associates exemplifies such an approach. They formulated such concepts as the context-dependence of speech and observed and recorded the degree to which such speech was present or absent in the communicative behavior of people drawn from different social classes. But the ethnography of speaking allows an investigator to hear and then attend to indigenous expressions, such as "highbrow," *dugri,* "sharing," and *madre*. Rather than treating such expressions as ephemera or insignificant local details, the ethnography of speaking provides that such phenomena themselves be made the object of theoretical and practical interest. It is precisely such phenomena which can form the starting point of inquiries which reveal practical resources that are crucial to the lives of individuals and societies. Such phenomena are not only the starting point of inquiries—their discovery, description, and interpretation are as well the ends of investigation, that is, they are phenomena of interest in their own right.

The exploratory search for local, socially constructed resources, patterns, and meanings is an activity that some people would call the study of a culture, and I turn now to the specialized sense in which I use that term. I take culture to refer to a socially constructed system of symbols, meanings, premises, and rules. A symbol is defined as a "vehicle for a conception," and symbols are "tangible formulations of notions, abstractions from experience fixed in perceptible forms, concrete embodiments of ideas, attitudes, judgments, longings, or beliefs. The "conceptions" are the "meanings, notions, definitions, and so forth, which symbols express" (Geertz 1973, 91). Premises express beliefs of existence (what is) and of value (what is good and bad). A rule is a prescription for how to act under specified circumstances.

The definition of culture used here does not equate it with a group, nation, or people. Rather, it focuses on culture as a code–as a system of such code elements as symbols, meanings, premises, and rules. Although, in the course of investigating codes, I initially found evidence for them in the spoken life of nameable groups of people, when I use "culture" it is used in reference not to a group but to a code as a system. Just as the English language is found in many places, and just as many people speak more than one language, so it is with cultures: Culture refers to a particular system and not to the geographic or political unit in which it is found.

Every common culture of which interlocutors might partake, and which they might use in speaking together, includes, among its parts, a part devoted to the symbols and meanings, premises, and rules pertaining to communicative conduct. For this specialized subset of a cultural code, I use the term speech code. *A speech code, then, is defined here as a system of socially constructed symbols and meanings, premises, and rules, pertaining to communicative conduct.*

2

The empirical part of this story begins with the experience of having commonsensical notions about communication tested in the crucible of social life. In 1969, a few years after graduating from college, a degree in communication in hand, I was employed as a youth worker in a neighborhood on the near south side of Chicago. This was a job in which I had occasion to practice such noble arts of communication as persuasion, negotiation, and instruction, as well as the baser but lively arts of detecting deception, deflecting insults, and assessing threats to bodily harm, the body in question frequently being my own. The youths with whom I worked were, in the language I used then, "tough kids," and it was my job to soften them a bit or at least to channel their energies into constructive activities and to provide them with character-building experiences.

In college, I had learned that working effectively with other people was enhanced by the use of certain communicative practices, such as sitting down to talk things through, listening carefully to what people said, and involving other people in decisions that affected them. Although I have stated them rather simply here, these were what could be called theoretically grounded learnings. That is, the use of these strategies was sanctioned by certain assumptions, propositions, and empirical evidence which were widely credited and which were roughly consistent with the positions not only of such writers as Carl Rogers and Irving Lee, but also of the more obviously empirical and theoretical Kurt Lewin.

Although these strategies for encompassing a situation were theoretically and commonsensically legitimated, they were not always effective in the Chicago neighborhood, as they had been elsewhere. In the neighborhood, which I labeled "Teamsterville" (after the modal occupation of its residents: truck driver), these strategies were ineffective not because I or my interlocutors were artless or malicious, but because they and I assigned very different meanings to my actions. Thus, on many occasions, the results of using these strategies were misunderstanding, suspicion, and alienation. After several years of working and studying in Teamsterville, I developed an understanding of a locally deployed speech code such that I realized that much of the misunderstanding and suspicion to which I had contributed centered around cultural differences in the meanings and value of speaking as a mode of social interaction. Where I valued, and used, speaking as a means to assert influence and secure cooperation, my neighborhood interlocutors heard my acts of speech—in the particular contexts in which they were performed—as a sign of weakness and incompetence in dealing with the adolescent boys and girls who were under my supervision. To the Teamstervillers, a man who merely talked with these young people, instead of using his power to discipline and punish them, was not a proper man.

After spending several months in Teamsterville, I began to notice there a practice, a habitual way of speaking, reinforced by the expressions of Teamstervillers. It was difficult to detect and not much easier to describe, but it was salient enough that it was hard to ignore, both practically and theoretically. That practice consists of infusing a concern with "place" into every conversation. Where persons stand in relation to each other according to a social code of power and position—a person's place in the social hierarchy—was mentioned directly or indirectly in virtually every conversation in which I participated. For example, if one's interlocutor did not know one's "nationality" it would be asked at the beginning of the conversation, and it seemed that every reference to a person included a reference to that person's ethnicity. The same is true for residence: references to where the person lived, or was from, permeated everyday speech.

Teamsterville concerns for social and physical placement were, in their pervasiveness and importance, alien to my ways of thinking and speaking. It took some time for me to notice that there was something there to notice—a pattern of emphasis and salience of the cultural category place, expressed in many symbols and expressions of social and physical space. To the extent that I was learning what potentially significant aspects of the world the Teamstervillers thought and spoke about, and that I was learning the local vocabulary and expressions for symbolizing those experiences, to that extent I was learning about a culturally distinctive system of symbols and meanings, that is, what I would now call a speech code.

The experiences in Teamsterville led to the formulation of two aspects of Teamsterville culture that bear directly on communicative conduct. The first of these pertains to neighborhood norms—rules that were widely endorsed—for the use and non-use of speaking in male role enactment. Teamsterville culture proscribes the use of speaking as the means for encompassing a situation when the participants' social identity relationship is asymmetrical. Such relationships are, for the adult man in Teamsterville, those with a wife, child, boss, outsider to the neighborhood, or a man of different ethnicity. Certainly, Teamsterville men do speak to their wives, girlfriends, children, and employers, but these are not contexts of relationship that call for high quantity of speaking nor are these the natural situations in which to engage others in a state of talk. Thus, speech is proscribed for a man in critical symbolic ways—as protector and master of a house and as breadwinner. If an assertion of power is deemed necessary, custom sanctions other means of expression than speech. If one's addressee is of lower status—a child, a woman, a member of another Teamsterville ethnic group—the power assertion may rely on nonverbal threat or physical combat. When one's addressee is of higher status—a boss, an outsider from a more prosperous neighborhood, a government official—male power assertion may properly employ personal connections with an intermediary who states the man's case for him.

When the social identity relationship of the participants in a situation is symmetrical, the situation can appropriately realize a great amount of talking by a Teamsterville man. Specifically, the participants in a speaking situation should be matched on such identity attributes as age, sex, ethnicity, occupational status, and location of residence. The participants should be longtime friends. Speaking is a dominant focus of all-male social interaction in corner groups and corner bars. For boys the street corner, and for men the corner bar, is the principal setting for sociability. Speaking is a dominant activity in these settings. Typically, small groups of boys "hang" on their own corner, and groups of men have their own corner bar, a public drinking establishment claimed by them as their "turf," a territory to which outsiders are not invited or welcomed. Teamsterville men seek out other men of like identity, in well-established locations. These are the situations in which it is most appropriate for a man to produce a great quantity of talk.

A second aspect of Teamsterville culture that bears on communicative conduct pertains to a symbolic and ideational thematization of speaking in terms of place or setting. In terms of self-presentation and gender, I had participated in neighborhood life according to a model for action which I brought to the neighborhood, and learned eventually that actions that conformed to my (imported) model could be deeply problematic in Teamsterville. So too, I brought to the experience an understanding of settings which proved to be quite different from the understanding provided by Teamsterville culture. One manifestation of this is a system of indigenous terms for places, including "neighborhood," "street," "corner," and "porch," which designate the settings in which speech is properly conducted. Looking—or listening—for speech in the places where I was accustomed to finding it, and not finding it there, I concluded initially, as had one observer, who said to me, that "there is no communication in Teamsterville." That observer and initially I, too, did not know that Teamsterville culture specified a system of scenes in which speaking can appropriately, and in fact did, occur.

A sense of neighborhood has a deep and compelling significance to the dweller of Teamsterville. The socio-spatial boundaries that residents perceive as "the neighborhood" make up the largest region within which it is considered most appropriate and natural to engage in talk. The residents think of these boundaries as coextensive with a particular style of speaking, which is characteristic of the community and to which its residents are expected to conform. Definitions of neighborhood as scene, then, relate to indigenous judgments about when to talk and ways of speaking, and both kinds of judgment are linked to cultural views of place.

In addition to locating occasions of speaking within the boundaries of the "neighborhood," Teamstervillers also locate on a scale of social worth the style of speaking they associate with the neighborhood. Awareness of their own speaking style as one distinct from others is reflected in their readily reported assessment, consistent across informants, that their speech is inferior to the Standard English of middle-class people—people who live on "the north side" (of Chicago)—but superior to the speech of, respectively, "hillbillies," "Mexicans," and "Negroes." They respect and resent the speech of people who have a better control of Standard English than they do, are insecure about their own speech outside neighborhood contexts, and find reassurance in what they perceive to be the defects of others presumably lower than they on the socio-economic scale.

For several years after completing the Teamsterville fieldwork, I worked at understanding a second speech code, one that is, so to speak, closer to home. This is drawn, to a great extent, from the culture I brought with me to Teamsterville. It consists of a system of symbols and meanings, premises, and rules which some have labeled "Nacirema" culture ("Nacirema" is "American" spelled backwards: cf. Miner 1956). The books and essays of many writers (Schneider 1976, Hsu 1963, and Varenne 1977 stand out prominently) had helped me to grasp that a system of symbols and meanings, premises, and rules, with which I interpreted the world is, indeed, a socially constructed system—and not simply a given.

But the Teamsterville experience, the experience of living in a social world whose members regularly deployed a speech code different from the one to which I had been socialized, helped to reveal to me that my own ways of being in the world are deeply cultured. And so, I set about the task of discovering and describing what I have come to call Nacirema communicative conduct as a cultural system. This involved a new period of fieldwork research into a second speech code.

The Nacirema fieldwork began in southern California, when my student Mary Jo Rudd and I observed, and listened intently to tape recordings of, Nacirema conversations at family "dinner time." This is a speech event about which participants insist relentlessly that all family members be allowed a turn at talk, indeed be encouraged to talk—because each person has "something to contribute." We found that the people we observed believed strongly that one's place in the family, defined by a role such as "father," should not be a basis for interrupting or curtailing the speech of others, because each person's contribution is believed to be uniquely valuable. For these Nacirema, speech is a way to express one's psychological uniqueness, to acknowledge the uniqueness of others, and to bridge the gap between one's own and another's uniqueness. It is a means by which family members, for example, can manifest their equality and demonstrate that they pay little heed to differences in status—practices and beliefs that would puzzle and offend a proper Teamsterviller.

In Seattle, my student Tamar Katriel and I listened to many people tell their life stories—stories in which great moral weight was placed upon interpersonal "relationships" in which each person was not only free, but also felt a sense of pressure, to express and celebrate their uniqueness and to explore and understand the other's distinctive individuality. The sense of boundary sharply dividing occasions and personae, so prominent among the Teamstervillers, was either not expressed or, where it threatened to be present, was aggressively opposed. Observing Nacirema communicative conduct provided a rich corpus of metacommunicative commentary—a corpus of, to put it simply, talk about talk. We heard a variety of symbols and expression, like "highbrow," being invoked. As we scanned this material, we found, among other things, two clusters of terms pertaining to everyday ways of speaking. One of these clusters includes:

"communication"

"real communication"

"really talking"

"supportive communication"

"open communication"

This is what we labeled the "communication" cluster. The other cluster includes

"mere talk"

"small talk"

"normal chit-chat"

We labeled it the "mere talk" cluster.

We noticed, and our respondents confirmed our hunch, that in this Nacirema speech the terms in each cluster could be substituted for each other in some expressions and the sense of the expression would be maintained, but that in some expressions the terms could not be substituted across clusters. For example, in the statement, supplied by one of our respondents (the person labeled "K" in Katriel and Philipsen 1981), "Communication allows me to grow . . . it scares me to be stagnant," other Nacirema respondents said that the sense of the expression is maintained if "real communication" or "open communication" is substituted for "communication": that is, the Nacirema informants heard "Real communication allows me to grow" as a meaningful, sensible statement, but they felt that "Small talk allows me to grow" was not a sensible statement.

The discovery, in Nacirema speech, of the two clusters labeled by "communication and "mere talk" prompted us to search for the meaning, to the people who produced the materials we had collected, of the term "communication." "Communication," it seemed to us, was a prominent and important term in Nacirema speech about interpersonal life, and thus we set ourselves the task of delineating its meanings to those who used it in the highly poignant ways some of our informants did. We discovered that "communication" indeed was a symbol that figured prominently in Nacirema discourse about interpersonal life and that it carried a rich array of meanings. These meanings were revealed by examining the words with which "communication" co-occurred, such as "self," "relationship," and "work," as in a statement such as "things can be worked out, as a family you can learn to communicate" (Katriel and Philipsen 1981), or in the statement about "open marriage as a relationship where there is a value in good communication . . ." (Philipsen, Corpus). Note in the last statement the co-occurrence of the terms "communication" and "relationship"; it was such co-occurrences, among other things, that we located, analyzed, and interpreted.

In the course of examining such expressions, we followed a strategy of interpretation (see Katriel and Philipsen 1981, Philipsen 1992, chapters 3, 4, and 5) designed to uncover the meaning of the term "communication." That strategy consisted of several tactics. These included examining the utterances in which the term occurred and noting the terms with which it co-occurred, searching for semantic dimensions of the meaning of the term, analyzing the metaphors (such as "work") which the term was linked to in the speech we examined, and tracing the use of the term in prominent cultural episodes and public stories. This strategy enabled us to interpret what is meant by "communication" in the Nacirema speech we examined, and in so doing we discovered not only a definition but part of a complex cultural system of symbols and meanings, premises, rules, and discursive forms.

Based on the materials and the analytic and interpretive procedures outlined above, we (Katriel and I) formulated a definition of "communication" as "close, open, supportive speech." The phrase is our gloss, our interpretive definition, of what the term "communication" means in the discourse we collected and examined. This was our interpretation of what the symbol "communication" meant to the people who used it in the instances we recorded. Our formulation of the symbol "communication" and the meaning "close, open, supportive speech" was a finding grounded in observation and interpretation.

We also found that, for the people whose discourse we studied, "communication" could co-occur meaningfully with such Nacirema symbols as "self," "relationship," and "work," and that these terms derived their meaning, in part, by virtue of their co-occurrence with others of these terms. Thus, the symbol "relationship" meant something different in the utterance " 'communication' is essential to our 'relationship' " than it did in an utterance about a "statistical relationship." We had found, that is, that these terms constituted part of a cultural system, in that we had found several elements (symbols and meanings) whose meanings were interdependent.

Having initially formulated part of a speech code, one in which "communication" was a key term, we were able to find this term, and other symbols such as "relationship," occurring together in a wide array of Nacirema speech, including the telling of several life stories by informants, a popular television talk show which was broadcast nationally, and contemporaneous Academy Award-winning movies about contemporary American life. The importance of these discoveries was not so much that we found the culture we had formulated being used widely in American life but that we found the terms, premises, and rules we had discovered being used by speakers and hearers as one integrated code of meanings. Our concern, that is, was not so much with documenting that the culture we had formulated is widely used, but that the way of using "communication" and other terms we had formulated was indeed a systematic way of speaking and, thus, a portion of a culture.

Although it might appear that the Nacirema, with their penchant for individualism, do not have a common culture, we learned that among these individualistic, seemingly relativistic, people, there is deployed a discernible, common speech code, one that underpins much communicative conduct. For the Nacirema, such folk terms as "self," "relationship," "work," "openness," "growth," and "communication" provide a systematic vocabulary of perception and motive. To understand some Nacirema speech, as its speakers and hearers understand it, to understand the motives they use in organizing and interpreting their social experiences, to know what it means to be a Nacirema—these all require that one have knowledge of the culture-specific meanings of these Nacirema symbols (Carbaugh 1988 extends and develops the account of Nacirema "communication").

It is hard to immerse oneself in an alien cultural world, as Teamsterville was to me, and be unchanged by it. For me the contact with Teamsterville life brought into sharp relief several aspects of Nacirema culture that, at one time, I had taken for granted. That such terms as "communication," "self," and "relationship," and the ideas to which they refer, are cultural constructions and not universally given experiences, was easier to grasp after struggling to learn a culture such as Teamsterville's. To hear a Nacirema's statement that "each of us is an individual," as a deeply cultured, even quaint, statement is made easier after having spent three years listening to Teamstervillers talk about persons as "Italians," "Poles," "Lithuanians," and so forth—as persons whose being is defined more by their social than by their psychological characteristics. To hear, as a deeply cultured statement, the Nacirema's insistence that each child should express himself because of the child's potentially "unique contribution" to a family conversation is facilitated by listening for three years to Teamstervillers insisting that a child should be seen and not heard.

In sketching some of the Teamsterville and Nacirema findings that I have reported, I have tried to show, in each case, how the fieldwork contributed not just to the collection of anecdotes but to the discovery and formulation of a distinctive code. The formulation of a speech code, I propose, is a theoretic move in that it is general, empirical, and explanatory.

First, to formulate a code is to move from the particular to the general. One can observe, record, and interpret a great deal of human behavior, but then to make the bold statement that one has formulated (even a part of) a code is to leave the relatively safe ground of description for the heights, as it were, of generalization. Such an interpretation says there is a code (a socially constructed system of symbols and meanings, premises, and rules) revealed in the record of human behavior which has been assembled, that that code consists of these particular elements and that these elements are related in this particular way. It is just such an interpretation that I have made in proposing my formulations of Teamsterville and Nacirema speech codes.

Second, the formulation of a code is an empirical task. In the Teamsterville and Nacirema fieldwork materials I found expressions of notions about communicative conduct, expressions that took the form of symbols, utterances, and patterned uses of symbols and utterances. In each case the analyses and interpretations of field materials, and combining them into a system of connected and related elements, constituted the formulation of a code as a system of symbols and meanings, premises, and rules, pertaining to communicative conduct. The systems were built up from empirical materials—observations and records of communicative conduct. In turn, each of these formulations can be subjected to empirical conduct. In turn, each of these formulations can be subjected to empirical disconfirmation—that is, new fieldwork data or the reinterpretation of extant data could lead to a revision of the formulation that was proposed.

In relation to this second point about ethnographic theories, mention should be made of the work of Donal Carbaugh in advancing the theory of Nacirema "communication" (particularly Carbaugh 1988). Carbaugh developed substantially the theory of "communication" which Katriel and I set out. First, his studies shored up empirically the earlier work by producing and interpreting new materials that corroborated the earlier proposal about "communication." Second, he added to the theory by providing (1) detailed studies of other symbols in the code, including "being honest," "sharing," "choice," and (2) a much more intensive examination of a Nacirema meaning of self (Carbaugh 1988). This is a theoretic advance because the formulation of the code was developed by showing that symbols and meanings other than those originally mentioned are important elements of the code and by showing the ways in which the initial symbols and meanings and the ones that Carbaugh examined independently relate to each other.

Third, a theory should provide a basis for explaining something. An account of a code provides a principle or principles by which a great number of particular observations are made intelligible. The formulation of a Teamsterville speech code posits that the theme of place ramifies throughout the culture's thematization of communicative conduct. The formulation of a Nacirema speech code posits that the theme of "communication" ramifies throughout the culture's thematization of communicative conduct. In each case, particulars are made intelligible that would otherwise seem inchoate, and particulars that would otherwise seem unconnected are integrated into a system. Thus, the formulation of a speech code is a device with which the observer interprets or explains an empirical record which has been assembled.

3

In this section of the chapter I formulate five propositions about speech codes. These propositions are suggested by, and consistent with, the empirical literature of the ethnography of communication. They are answers to the questions raised in the introduction of this chapter, the questions of the existence, substance, discovery, and force of speech codes. Although I illustrate and support these propositions here primarily through reference to the Teamsterville and Nacirema studies, because they are the ones most familiar to me, I emphasize that the propositions are grounded in a much larger fund of studies (which is available for further theory generation and for testing and refining such proposals as those I advance below). Braithwaite (1990), Carbaugh (1989), and Goldsmith (1991) are examples of theoretical work drawing from the fund of studies included in Philipsen and Carbaugh (1986). The first four of these propositions were presented earlier (Philipsen 1992), with some modifications here, and the fifth has been added to the earlier formulation.

1. The Distinctiveness of Speech Codes

In Teamsterville and Nacirema speech codes, it has been shown, speaking, as a mode of social interaction, has been thematized distinctively. In these two systems, speaking is assigned different purposes, valued differently, linked to distinctive cultural themes, and conceptualized by a different metacommunicative vocabulary.

This point can be expressed no less sharply because Teamsterville and Nacirema speech codes are each expressed in the same language, English. Each of these codes draws from the same language a distinctive set of terms and notions. And each makes of the same terms something distinctive. "Communication," a quintessentially Nacirema symbol, is certainly part of a Teamsterville lexicon, but "close, supportive, flexible speech," A Nacirema meaning for "communication," is a meaning not active in Teamsterville talk about talk. "Neighborhood," an important symbol in Teamsterville culture, is certainly also part of the Nacirema symbolic repertoire, but the sense of "neighborhood" as a culturally defined place for speaking is not a prominent part of Nacirema sensibility. Likewise, there are contrasting Teamsterville and Nacirema premises and rules about speaking, such that one can think of two distinctive speech codes built up from the same linguistic codes. The "same" linguistic code provides the basic symbols from which such contrasting orientations can be constructed as the Teamsterville notion that "children should be seen and not heard" and the Nacirema notion that "you can't keep a child quiet at the dinner table."

The point here is not that people who live in "Teamsterville" draw from only one code and that "Nacirema" code users draw from only one code. Rather, in the Teamsterville and Nacirema sites I found the respective codes being used prominently. In each case, the particular speech communities or social settings provided a place in which a code could be heard because it was deployed by interlocutors who found their speech mutually intelligible. Presumably, Teamstervillers and others speak in the terms of more than one code. What I found was that by listening to various people speaking together, in sites selected because they were likely to yield difference, I could find different codes deployed and that these codes had a kind of internal consistency or logic to them.

The finding that speaking is thematized in culturally distinctive ways is consistent with the large number of ethnographies of speaking that are now available for comparative analysis (Philipsen and Carbaugh 1986). In study after study, drawn from languages and cultures throughout the world, have come data that support the proposal, here formulated as Proposition One, that *wherever there is a distinctive culture, there is to be found a distinctive speech code.* These studies show cross-cultural distinctiveness in terms, semantic dimensions used to define those terms, metaphors, premises, and rules, pertaining to "speaking."

The Nacirema term "communication," with its dimensions of close-distant, supportive-neutral, and flexible-closed, is a useful point of contrast. Other speech codes, for which semantic dimensions for "speaking" terms have been reported, include that of the Afro-American peasants of St. Vincent in the West Indies, a code that makes prominent the semantic contrasts sensible-senseless and polite-impolite as dimensions for characterizing acts of speech (Abrahams and Bauman 1971); that of seventeenth-century New Englanders, in which a controlled-uncontrolled contrast is prominent (St. George 1984); that of the Haya, in which substantial-insubstantial is prominent (Seitel 1974); and that of *dugri* speech in Israel. The available literature suggests that for each cultural system of speaking there is a distinctive system of such semantic dimensions, which in part constitute the domain of "speaking."

Another way the cultural particularity of speech codes is manifested is in metaphors for "speaking." Again, the juxtaposition of "communication" to other codes is instructive. Katriel and I found the "work" metaphor—as in, " 'communication' is the 'work' which is necessary for a 'relationship' "—to be a cultural resource for conceptualizing and interpreting Nacirema speech. Speech codes in other cultures have a metaphorical theme, which ramifies throughout the domain of "speaking." The Haya, for example, conceptualize the domain of speaking in terms of an "alimentary process" metaphor (Seitel 1974). The Chamula (Gossen 1974) and seventeenth-century New Englanders (St. George 1984) conceptualize speaking in terms of a "heat" metaphor, which has different meanings in each case.

As it is with symbols and meanings, so it is with premises and rules. Consider Walter Ong's proposal that speaking links individuals in social relationships. He writes: "Because in its physical constitution as sound, the spoken word proceeds from the human interior and manifests human beings to one another as conscious interiors, as persons, the spoken word forms human beings into close-knit groups" (Ong 1982, 74). Ong's statement reveals a premise about speaking that emphasizes the interior of the individual as the starting point and source of experience of communication. This is, of course, a deeply cultured model, one whose evocation might be quite stirring to the Nacirema ear. But regardless of whether Ong's model is objectively true, the ethnographic literature suggests that other cultures implicate other premises.

For example, Michelle Z. Rosaldo's (1982) ethnography of speaking among the Ilongot in the northern Philippines, an "oral culture," portrays a people whose understanding of speaking deemphasizes the individual speaker as the intentional initiator of spoken meaning. The Ilongot's understanding presents a model of speaking as something quite different from what Ong proposes—individuals are, in the Ilongot code, already wedded to each other in unbreakable bonds of sociality, and speaking is merely a manifestation of that connection. Rather than proceeding from the interior of the person outward, speaking—and the meanings it embodies—originates outside the person.

Verschuren (1989) has conducted an eighty-one-language survey of what he calls "language action verbs," such as "to speak" or "to say." Seventy-seven of the eighty-one languages include a word for the English "to talk." But beyond that, there are many differences across languages as to what notions of linguistic action can be expressed in the language. Verschuren's finding that "to speak" is a linguistic universal suggests that in all cultures "speaking" is thematized in some way. But in the Teamsterville and Nacirema cases, and in many others in the ethnography of speaking literature, it can be seen that this linguistic universal is but a starting point for thematizing speaking, a point from which each language and culture takes its own distinctive course.

2. The Substance of Speech Codes

What do speech codes thematize? What is their substance? Of course, they are about speaking, but what, one might ask, is the substance or matter of speaking, as this is illumined by the study of speech codes? In the first full formulation of the ethnography of speaking, Hymes (1962) suggested that "speaking," with its connotations of interpersonal contact and engagement, might be a metaphor for social life, that by inquiring into a people's 'speaking' one might learn something about their social life. This applied not only to their habits or practices of speaking, that is to conduct, but also to native concepts and notions about speaking.

Hyme's suggestion that speaking is useful as a heuristic metaphor for the study of social life was supported by several studies of particular speech communities. Bauman (1970), for example, found that the historical records of the seventeenth-century Quakers provided data that suggest that Quaker speech practices, percepts, and precepts articulated with Quaker social and cultural patterns. Working in this way, Bauman (1970), Basso (1970), Seitel (1972), Stross (1974), Fox (1974), Sherzer (1983), and others were able to show that that attention to "speaking" opens up a view— or hearing—of the distinctive particularities of a people's social life.

In 1976, when I initiated the Nacirema studies and began to think about the contrasts in the Teamsterville and Nacirema codes, I formulated a scheme that laid the groundwork for subsequent studies. This is a scheme that suggests that speaking is a resource with which people accomplish human purposes, but a resource that is distinctively conceptualized in different codes. This line of thinking and the development of the working scheme were influenced by Richard McKeon's theory of communication, truth, and society (Mckeon 1971), which proposes a universalist thesis about the functions of speaking, and by Hymes (1962), Bernstein (1964), and Douglas (1970), which suggest cross-cultural differences in how these universal functions are realized. These sources, and my Teamsterville and Nacirema data, led me to suggest (Philipsen 1976b) that cultural definitions of the resourcefulness of speaking could be compared and contrasted in terms of three interrelated functions of discourse—discourse as a medium of self expression, embodiment of common values, and discovery of truth, categories inspired by Mckeon's categories "communication," "society," and "truth." In each culture,

I proposed, speech is defined as being resourceful for a particular kind of self-expression, for the embodiment of particular social values, and as differentially instrumental in the process of knowing, a claim suggested by the ethnographic studies of speaking then available as well as Hymes's programmatic essays (Hymes 1962, 1964, 1967, 1972).

Philipsen (1976b) provided an initial statement of how the Teamsterville and Sunnyville (Nacirema) findings mapped onto this comparative scheme. My strategy was to use these formulations of how speaking is a medium of personal expression, social linkage, and epistemic activity, and then to use the fieldwork in which I had been involved to propose differences, across communities, in terms of these three dimension of comparison and contrast. The preliminary formulation was illustrated in contrasts along two of the three dimensions. The Teamsterville code seemed to emphasize the appropriateness of speaking as a resource for (1) revealing to others those aspects of one's self that are similar to those of others in one's age-gender-nationality-block group within a community, and for (2) affirming one's continuing recognition and endorsement of the local sense of "place," boundary, and hierarchy. By contrast, the Sunnyville/Nacirema data suggested another configuration of cultural definitions of the resourcefulness of speaking—a system that emphasizes the use of speech for (1) expressions of personal uniqueness and (2) a community sense of rightness attaching to an equality ethnic in interpersonal relations (Philipsen 1976b). Such works as Berger, Kellner, and Berger (1970), Rosaldo (1982), and Silverstein (1979) suggested a revised formulation of the dimensions, one that I used in several reports (Philipsen 1986, 1987, 1989, and 1992), and that has been used and adapted by others (see, for example, Carbaugh 1994; Fitch 1994).

The revised formulation is that the thematization of speaking in Teamsterville and Nacirema cultures reveals a distinctive code of self, society, and strategic action. These codes, historically transmitted, socially constructed systems of symbols and meanings, premises, and rules about communicative conduct, are at once codes about the nature or persons, about the ways persons can and should be linked together in social relations, and about the role of symbolic action in forging, sustaining, and altering such interpersonal linkages.

This can be expressed as Proposition Two, *a speech code implicates a culturally distinctive psychology, sociology, and rhetoric*. A speech code does not provide simply an account of coding, encoding, and decoding, as neutral processes sealed off from other aspects of culture. Rather, it implicates a view of what a person is and of how persons are constituted, of the particular kinds of social relations that persons can and should enter into, and of the appropriate and efficacious symbolic resources available to interlocutors for constituting themselves as persons in social relationships. This was shown elsewhere in a lengthier treatment of these codes (Philipsen 1992, chapter 6).

Proposition One points to differences across codes, Proposition Two to the substance of such codes. These two principles can be joined to comprise the following elaboration of Proposition Two: *speech codes are distinctive thematizations of the ends and means of social action.* Each implicates a distinctive conception of what goods humans should aim to secure, how to secure those goods, and how to judge efforts to attain them. A speech code, as a culturally distinctive "social rhetoric" is part of a common culture that can provide individuals with a kind of practical knowledge about what to feel and what to do (Scruton 1979). It provides a system of meanings and beliefs that provides answers to questions about ends to seek, as well as answers to questions of the proper and efficacious means for achieving those ends. In particular, a speech code provides a system of answers about what linkages between self and others can properly be sought, and what symbolic resources can properly and efficaciously be employed in seeking those linkages (Philipsen 1987, 1989, 1992).

The matter, or substance, of speech codes is, by this account, social life. This general point is woven through the literature of the ethnography of communication, echoing and supporting Hymes's (1962) suggestion that speaking or communication can be thought of as a metaphor for social life, and that as communication (including speaking) is thematized and enacted distinctively across cultures, and across speech communities, so cultural thematizations of communication and speaking should reveal a culturally distinctive code of social meanings and conduct in particular cases.

3. The Meanings of Speaking

Proposition One refers to the distinctiveness, and Proposition Two to the substance, of speech codes. Proposition Three is concerned with the part that speech codes play in the process of communication.

It has long been assumed that whenever interlocutors speak with each other, they potentially create shared meaning. They do this, for example, by referring to experience in such a way that the interlocutors can find common meanings in the use of language. It has long been assumed as well that users of language, and of other media of communication, not only express and interpret communicative acts in terms of what is said—or talked about—but also in terms of what is being done (Austin 1962). Attention has been drawn to such "actions" performed in speaking as "persuading," "entertaining," "uniting," "chatting," "conversing," and so forth. A parallel move is made by practitioners of the coordinated management of meaning, who posit as one of the interpretive resources interlocutors bring to bear in constructing a sense of social acts, the idea of speech act (Pearce and Cronen 1980, see also Philipsen in press for a comment on this approach).

Still another parallel move is the axiom of Watzlavick, Beavin, and Jackson (1967) that communications have both a content and a relationship aspect.

Proposition Three is that *the significance of speaking is contingent upon the speech codes used by interlocutors to constitute the meanings of communicative acts.* When I spoke to unruly Teamsterville boys in order to discipline them I was judged by them to be unmanly because, in such circumstances, I spoke. From my perspective, my acts of speech were gentle but firm administrations of discipline and the benign exercise of adult power. My interlocutors constituted from my behavior a different act. In each case, what the behavior counted as was contingent upon the speech codes which the interlocutors used to constitute the meanings of the acts.

"Constitute" is used here with deliberate cognizance of its use in the speech act theory of the philosopher John Searle (1976). That theory holds that there is a definite range of what can be done, what acts can be performed, in speaking. And it holds that what a given speech behavior counts as is determined by the universal conditions necessary and sufficient for a behavior to count as, for example, a promise, a command, and so forth. Searle is concerned with a set of philosophical possibilities and the logical requirements for an observer to say that one of these possibilities was realized in a given utterance. For example, Searle posits that it is possible, in an act of speech, for the speaker to make a promise, and that a promise is made if and only if certain conditions are fulfilled. In uttering, for example, "I will take you to the cleaners tomorrow," certain conditions must be met for the locution to count as a promise (for example, the speaker must think the hearer wants to go to the cleaners, or else the utterance might count as a threat rather than a promise). If a speaker said, "I will take you to the cleaners tomorrow," and all the logical requirements were met for classifying the utterance as a promise, Searle would call it a promise even if the speaker and the hearer called it an expression of sorrow. Searle would say, I believe, that although the utterance was mistaken as an expression of sorrow, a promise was indeed made, because the conditions for making a promise were met.

To propose that speech codes are used by interlocutors to constitute speech acts as meaningful says something different from, but not necessarily in conflict with, what Searle says about speech acts. My move has been to interpret what interlocutors, singly or jointly, experience their speech acts and interactions to be. To Searle's set of logical possibilities this adds, in particular instances, a further component of the speech act or of spoken interaction, and that is what the interlocutors experience the meanings of their speech acts to be. These meanings are such outcomes as "communicating," speaking "like a man," speaking in a way that is "supportive," and speaking like "one of us." Each of the meanings expressed in quotation marks refers to what Teamstervillers or Nacirema interlocutors might take their communicative acts to be. Although Searle's system might be perfectly adequate to determine the conditions under which an observer can say that an utterance counts as a directive or a promise, it is through knowledge of particular speech codes that the observer can hear and interpret such experienced meanings as those I have instanced here.

Cultural types of speech acts and cultural meanings do not necessarily meet any philosophical or logical criteria, only the criterion of shared significance among interlocutors. The cultural formulation of these acts and meanings might have its own logic but that is not necessarily the logic of the philosopher of language. The Nacirema term "communication" illustrates these differences between the philosophic and the cultural account of speech acts. "Communication" is a Nacirema term that, in some contexts, refers to "close, supportive, flexible" speech. To say that "we are really communicating" requires that interlocutors engage in spoken interaction that is highly disclosive, in which the interlocutors are supportive of each other as unique persons, and in which both parties are committed to the possibility of negotiating their perceptions of self and other. This is not a philosophical or a philological account of what conditions must be present to say we are "really communicating"—it is an observer's formulation of what some interlocutors take "really communicating" to be.

The question, What happens when people talk?, is thus reconfigured here as, What do interlocutors interpret—or experience—themselves to be doing in speaking? And the answer is: it depends upon the speech code they use to constitute—to construct, to define, to interpret—their communicative acts. To the extent that this claim is true, and the claim is consistent with the data consulted for this chapter, then the meaning of speaking is always, at least in part, a function of culture.

This was, for me, a hard-won learning. Perhaps it is obvious to others that when people speak they also perform certain actions—certainly Austin and Searle had made the point, and it seems plainly enough put in Watzlavick, Beavin, and Jackson (1967). But thinking through the abundance of field experiences in the Teamsterville and Nacirema studies helped me to understand that this is true and that it is important in the lives of people. Quite simply put, when people speak they understand themselves to be doing something, and when other people experience others speaking they take those others to be performing some kind of action. A speech code is the resource that people deploy to do that taking, or interpreting.

The distinctive contribution of ethnographic studies to this idea is the telling, in many studies of many codes, that there are many codes of speaking which interlocutors bring to bear in hearing speech acts as one thing or another. And each distinctive code provides a distinctive system of resources for doing the hearing.

The ethnographic studies that can be used to substantiate this point merely point to the use of distinctive resources and the organization of those resources into socially constructed codes. The accumulated studies do not suggest that cultural codes are more powerful as resources for constituting the meanings of speech acts than are idiosyncratic personal codes. But they do suggest that cultural speech codes are one important source of such meaning construction.

4. The Site of Speech Codes

In formulating Teamsterville and Nacirema speech codes, I have been concerned with auditing utterances and interpreting their significance to those who make or hear them. In many instances, I have interpreted instances or collections of instances of speaking that, upon first hearing, sounded culture-free, or at least culture-neutral. For example, in the early part of the Teamsterville fieldwork, when I heard people talk about "the neighborhood," "around here," or "connections" (to a political figure), I was not aware that they were speaking terms that, although they are common English words, are also code terms in Teamsterville culture. Likewise, when I first listened to Nacirema parents say that "communication" is vital to the parent-child "relationship," I did not hear such expressions as deeply cultured. The data-rich experience of auditing and interpreting Teamsterville and Nacirema communicative conduct has suggested Proposition Four, that *the terms, rules, and premises of a speech code are inexplicably woven into speaking itself.* This suggests that a speech code is something that is and can be learned by all who might have an interest in it. In elaborating this proposition, I suggest four ways that speech code elements are woven into speaking.

Patterns in speaking. In formulating the Teamsterville speech code, I used the organizing frame of participants, setting, ends, and topic, taken from Hymes's (1962) scheme, to examine who talks to whom, in what settings, toward what ends, and about what topics, in order to learn fundamental aspects of a Teamsterville speech code. Such central categories in Hymes's scheme as speech events, components of speech events, and functions of speech events, provided a way to organize many separate instances of spoken behavior into a pattern that could be, and was, tested against further events and validation by local consultants. The use of Hymes's framework enabled me to hear, in the stream of Teamsterville behavior, a culturally distinctive pattern where initially I had heard no culture pattern being implicated.

It was by applying these categories that I was able to hear the Teamstervillers not simply as speaking but as speaking in culturally organized ways. For example, it was only by applying the framework that I was able to appreciate that one never merely speaks in Teamsterville but that one always speaks as a bearer of a culturally defined social identity—that is, that if one is male one always speaks as a man, as that category is thematized in Teamsterville culture. The local pattern for speech behavior, as well as the local commentary upon behaviors that do not fit the pattern, comprises ways that Teamsterville communicative conduct invokes and implicates a code. So too, in the earliest Nacirema studies, Mari Jo Rudd found one speech event, family "dinner time," in which our informants and subjects experienced a way of speaking that is highly patterned and the object of a good deal of moral and temporal energy. One way that a code is woven into speaking is that interlocutors pattern their speaking in culturally distinctive ways.

Metacommunicative vocabularies. A second, immediately obvious way that culture is woven into speaking is in the use of a culturally distinctive metacommunicative vocabulary (and other talk about talk). When, for example, I asked a Teamsterviller about who his preferred interlocutors are and he replied by saying they are people from "around here," he used a culturally distinctive term, one whose meaning was different from that which I supplied prior to studying Teamsterville culture. When a Nacirema talks about the importance of "communication in a relationship," cultural terms with very particular definitions are being used—and displayed.

Attention to metacommunicative terms is a tactic proposed by Hymes, who wrote that "One good ethnographic technique for getting at speech events . . . is through words that name them" (Hymes 1962, 110). Several years later, there was a substantial fund of studies that had taken up Hymes's (1962) suggestion. In a review of some of these studies, Carbaugh wrote that "As speech is identified and labeled through cultural categories, its efficacy as an action—what it is doing, what it should and should not do, what it can and can not do—is displayed" (1989, 124).

There is now a substantial literature that draws attention to the thesis that terms for talk and other metalinguistic references thematize the means of communication and the meanings that these means have to those who use and experience them. Much of this work is conducted under the auspices of the ethnography of speaking (see, especially, Stross 1974, Abrahams 1974, Sherzer 1974) and more recently under the heading of metapragmatics (Collins 1987; Verschuren 1987; Lucy 1992). Katriel's study of dugri is an exemplar of such research in that it begins with a folk term for a kind of speaking, traces the meanings of the term dugri, and delineates the social understandings implicit in the term's situated use. Fitch has demonstrated a particularly useful approach to such research, emphasizing one type of speech act, directives (Fitch 1994).

The rhetorical invocation of metacommunicative vocabularies. Applying a methodological principle articulated by Kenneth Burke, that one should not merely compare "verbalizations . . . [but should] also correlate the situations behind them" (Burke 1965[1954], 183), suggests a third way that interlocutors weave culture into speaking. In the reports of Teamsterville and Nacirema fieldwork (Philipsen 1992, chapters 2 through 5), I have attended to how speech code elements are expressed in the naming, interpreting, explaining, evaluating, and justifying of communicative acts. If, following Burke (1950) again, one thinks about utterances as addressed to some hearer for a persuasive purpose, one can hear—or at least interpret—interlocutors as using speech code elements to serve rhetorical ends.

The use of metacommunicative vocabularies in culturally distinctive forms. Cultures (and the speech codes that comprise one part of them) are not unordered arrays of elements, displayed without pattern or form. Some elements of any culture are more important than others in terms of their significance to the interlocutors who use them; some cultural themes ramify more widely throughout the lives of those who use them; and some elements of culture are expressed more prominently than are others. The particular studies that make up the empirical literature of the ethnography of communication suggest that a fourth way to hear the articulation of speech code elements is to listen for the use of them in three communicative forms whose structure enables one to notice the cultural significance of the symbols and meanings, premises, and rules displayed in them. Those forms are totemizing rituals, myths, and social dramas.

The following part of the descriptive framework is based on Philipsen (1987) and slight modifications of it in Philipsen (1992). Initially, it was proposed as part of a theory of cultural communication, which includes a specification of key communicative forms in and through which interlocutors enact, articulate, and negotiate and test their personal identification with a code or a speech community (Philipsen 1987) have been used as a descriptive framework in several published studies (including Katriel 1986; Carbaugh 1988; Fitch 1991; Sequeira 1993). Its successful use is, in part, evidence of its general utility.

All routinized episodic sequences—known, repeatable ways of structuring an interaction event—entail the use of cultural ways of speaking and interacting. All episodic sequences do this because they are routinized—stereotypical, predictable—and because their routinization marks some aspect of share practice. Greeting rituals are example. A *totemizing ritual* (Turner 1988, 161–163), a particular type of ritual, is a structured sequence of actions the correct performance of which pays explicit homage to a sacred object of a group or culture. Thus, a totemizing ritual is routinized but it also is a particularly poignant (meaning-full) ritual. They are infused with the expression of emotional content such as anger, frustration, and joy. And the referent of the situation—the sacred object of the group—is made explicit. Katriel and I have shown how the Nacirema display a kind of "communication" ritual, in which a structured sequence of communicative acts honors and explicitly affirms the importance of things taken to be sacred among the Nacirema, notably selves, relationships, and communication (see Philipsen 1992, chapters 4 and 5).

All stories, which string together cultural symbols in meaningful sequences of activity, potentially implicate cultural content. *Cultural myths,* a special kind of story, make key elements of a cultural code particularly salient. A myth is a story of some type of person who confronts a type of problem and responds effectively through the use of some type of action or resource. A cultural myth is a story that, in the telling, provides its hearers with resources for interpreting their own experiences and for telling their own stories in ways intelligible to them and their interlocutors. In the course of developing the Nacirema speech code we not only listened to people tell us their personal stories, but I also examined some prominent public stories told in mythic form, stories in which, like the everyday stories, Nacirema speech code elements were prominently displayed (Philipsen 1992, chapter 5).

A third communicative form in which significant cultural symbols are made salient is the *social drama*. In the social drama, someone invokes a moral rule in challenging (criticizing) the conduct of another. In the next step of the sequence, a reply, consisting of a repair, a denial, or the like, is made to the challenge. The reply is either honored or dishonored, with the consequence that the offender either reintegrates with the group of evidence of moral schism is revealed. In this process of invoking rules and replying to rule-invocations, code elements are pressed into service. They are pressed into service in a form that, like rituals and cultural myths, provides not only for the invocation of the code element but also for the discursive co-ratification of its legitimacy by the interlocutors. In this way, interlocutors deploy significant code elements, and their discursive force is revealed in and through how their use either does or does not have force for the interlocutors (Philipsen 1992, chapter 3).

Interlocutors organize and interpret spoken activity in ways that can be detected by the application of such frames as participants and setting. They express and articulate meanings about speech in their use of a culturally distinctive metacommunicative vocabulary. They seek to accomplish things by invoking elements of a speech code. They participate in rituals, myths, and social dramas, forms of discourse infused with the elements of a culture. In all these ways, and this is an illustrative but by no means an exhaustive account, speaking is revealed to be richly woven through with the resources of a culture (see Fitch 1994 for an extension of the argument).

The proposition that speech codes are woven into speaking is both a methodological and a substantive point. It is methodological in that it suggests a general framework for the discovery and description of speech code elements. As such, the particular way in which the proposition has been developed here is subject to empirical testing—that is, one could ascertain, in and through the examination of cases, whether this formulation of a descriptive framework is adequate to extant and new cases, whether it is sufficiently parsimonious, and what prejudices it privileges, either knowingly or unknowingly. That it has been used successfully by others is one kind of rough validation of its utility. But it is presented here, as it has been presented elsewhere, as a working proposal, which is to be modified in the light of criticism, both conceptual and empirical.

The proposition that speech codes are woven into speaking suggests that the latter can be permeated with elements of the former. Research in the ethnography of speaking suggests that speaking is more permeated with speech code elements than one might ordinarily suspect. This discovery, when made by an individual trying to listen perceptively to the speech she or he hears or when made by a theoretically-oriented observer, opens up and important investigative possibility—the code, as it were, is deployed in social interaction, and thus made accessible to the auditor who listens to speaking with these categories in mind. As a theoretical and practical matter, then, and not just a methodological one, the proposal that speech codes are woven into speaking is of considerable consequence—the proposal locates the site of one important class of human action, that is, metacommunicative action. And what is the consequentiality of that? For that I turn to a fifth and final proposition.

5. The Discursive Force of Speech Codes

Propositions One, Two, and Three point, respectively, to the distinctiveness, the substance, and the function, of speech codes. Proposition Four is concerned with their site or location. Proposition Five answers the question, What force do culture in general and speech codes in particular have in social life? The question is whether knowledge of speech codes, in particular discursive situation, enables a practitioner or an observer of spoken life to predict and control some aspect of communicative conduct. Faced with the kind of human situations encountered in Teamsterville and the Nacirema studies, it is difficult to feel that culture is not a powerful force in spoken life. Teamsterville and Nacirema speech were noticeable as remarkably cultured precisely because each is expressed in a distinctive code. Furthermore, when speaking in the terms of these codes, speakers and hearers evoke and invoke standards of social expression which are brought to bear in characterizing and evaluating oneself and others. To hear the responses that Teamstervillers make to those of one's actions that do not meet the standard of the Teamsterville code, and to hear a response to one's actions that is grounded in the Nacirema code is to feel, firsthand, the force of Teamsterville or Nacirema culture.

One thesis about the culture-conduct relationship attributes to culture a deterministic force in conduct. In this view, culture is one of the springs of action that impels humans to act in particular ways and that provides the meanings humans use to construct the sense of the actions that they and others perform. There is, of course, a great deal of anecdotal and systematic evidence to support the idea that people experience a kind of social pressure to make their behavior conform to social norms (Coleman 1989; Enker 1987;

Richman 1988; Schwartz 1973). But there is a substantial literature that criticizes this approach as theoretically flawed and empirically unsupportable. Hall developed this critique more fully and situated it within the ongoing debate in the social sciences over norms and conduct (Hall 1988/89, see also Philipsen 1989).

My fieldwork observations suggest that the individuals I observed on occasion violate and resist various cultural imperatives, while nonetheless not challenging their general legitimacy. That is, the people I observed did not behave as cultural automatons, even as they did behave as culture bearers. In Teamsterville, for example, residents who themselves deployed the code in their talk, nonetheless did, on occasion, talk reflectively about it—hey described, interpreted, and evaluated their own and others' violations of the code. In his theory of dueling structures, Huspek underscores this point more generally in referring to social actors as "purposive" and "reflective" (Huspek 1993).

Given that there is widespread evidence for the force of culture in human communicative conduct, but nonetheless a substantial body of evidence and argument to suggest that humans not only follow but also flout their cultures, the code-conduct relationship must be treated as an issue. The theoretical resolution I have proposed for this issue is what I call the discursive force position. This position, expressed here as Proposition Five, is that *the artful use of a shared speech code is a sufficient condition for predicting, explaining, and controlling the form of discourse about the intelligibility, prudence, and morality of communicative conduct.* This is a complex proposition which can best be amplified by discussing several of its key aspects.

One, the studies cited in this chapter provide substantial evidence that *discourse about the intelligibility, prudence, and morality of communicative conduct is a prominent and consequential feature of human lives.* People talk about talk—they label, interpret, explain, evaluate, and justify their own and others' communicative acts. And in the course of doing that, they claim for themselves and others particular social identities, and they express social meanings which constitute, for themselves and others, social experience. It is the pragmatics, or effects, of such claiming, expressing, and constituting, in particular cases, which Proposition Five seeks to explain.

Two, the proposition points to an aspect of discourse to which the proposition applies: *the form of discourse about the intelligibility, prudence, and morality of communicative conduct.* A crucial distinction is made between predicting and controlling (1) the production or interpretation of a particular kind of communicative act and (2) the form of discourse about communicative acts. (1) refers to predicting and controlling whether someone will, faced with a decision, produce an act that is congruent with a particular code's meanings and expectations. (2) refers to a subset of (1), those acts that are part of a metacommunicative discourse—that is, are part of a sequence of talk about talk. Proposition Five does not generate predictions that in all circumstances interlocutors will perform actions that are congruent with a code, but does generate predictions about how interlocutors will talk about such performances.

Data from the Nacirema studies illustrate and substantiate this aspect of the proposition. For example, the Nacirema code thematizes and legitimates a parent's listening carefully to a child's expressions of opinions and feelings, say at the dinner table; but parents who themselves pay lip service to the Nacirema code on occasion do not realize its ideals. Such anomalies are not threatening to the speech codes theory, because not all code-conduct congruencies are predicted by the theory. Rather, the theory predicts that, under the circumstances described, if a parent did not respond "openly" and "supportively" to the child, this might be the occasion for discourse about the parent's communicative conduct. If another parent observed the conduct and then commented on it, involving Nacirema code elements in the comment, and then the first parent responded to the comment, there would be discursive chain of comments, the form of which is predicted by speech codes theory. The theory predicts that if the commentary is artfully formulated and the code is shared between (or among) the interlocutors, then interpretations or evaluations grounded in it will be treated as intelligible and legitimate. A case in point is the following report:

> At the family dinner table, a parent said to the children at the table that they must be silent for the remainder of the meal. Later, the other parent characterized the first parent's actions as "uncommunicative"; furthermore, the second parent admonished the first that such conduct would result in "your children not liking you."

In this episode, the second parent initiated discourse grounded in a speech code, with particular comments on the prudence of the first parent's action ("If you are uncommunicative, your children will not like you"). Speech codes theory predicts the range of likely responses to be: a repair, an argument about the pertinence on this occasion of the code principles appealed to, or an effort to negotiate the situational legitimacy of the code's force; all of these responses implicate the responder's orientation to appeals grounded in the code as intelligible and at least of sufficient legitimacy to require some kind of reasoned response to the appeal. Philipsen (1989) and Hall (1988/89) develop this aspect of the theory more fully.

In this matter, I follow a strongly developed literature on vocabularies of motives. This literature, which is grounded in Burke (1935/1954) and Mills (1940), proposes that we should think about "motives not as inner dispositions that cause action, but rather as rhetorical constructs that define action with respect to particular social contexts" (Hopper 1993, 801). For Burke and

Mills, "motives" encompasses not only rules of action but symbols, meanings, and premises as well. Furthermore, Burke and Mills argue that the seeming orderliness of social life is constructed in and through the use, by interlocutors, of verbalizations that are grounded in symbols and reasons that are given credence by those who share the vocabularies of motives from which the symbols and reasons are drawn. Hopper (1993) provides important empirical evidence in support of this position.

Three, we can focus on *how the process of discursive force works* as it does. Why are appeals grounded in speech codes efficacious in the way I have proposed they are? The answer to this question lies in three features of speech codes—their systematicity, their social grounding, and their expression in formal elements. Each of these will be considered.

Code systematicity, refers to the fact that code elements derive their meaning from their place in a network of reinforcing and interanimating code elements. When the criticizing parent, reported in the episode above, commented on the "uncommunicative" quality of the first parent's actions, the word "uncommunicative" invoked a network of symbols, premises, and rules, thus endowing the remark with a kind of force that an unconnected word would not have had. This is similar to what Leslie J. Miller calls "macrosocial supports" (Miller 1990).

Socially legitimated refers to the fact that the code was learned in and through social interaction in significant socializing contexts (Bernstein 1972). The association of code elements, which are involved in discourse, with the memory of life experiences in these socializing contexts, endows them with a sense of legitimacy and normalcy. Socially legitimated is more a temporal concept, in that the person who hears a code invoked can think back to previous invocations of the code. This suggests a sense of precedence and the presumption that precedence might entail. This is similar to what Miller calls "microsocial supports" (Miller 1990; see also Simon, Eder, and Evans 1992).

Code elements as forms refers to the fact that the forms in which cultures are expressed are devices that are used to influence or control others. In my discussion of Proposition Three I identified several communicative forms or patterns which are widely believed to be among the carriers of culture: contextual patterns, symbols, arguments, routines (including rituals), stories, (including myths), and social dramas. These can be treated as vehicle or carriers of culture and examined as sites where codes are deployed. This is the heuristic use of these forms to notice or learn code elements. But there is a long-established practice of treating these forms as rhetorical—or control—devices as well as heuristic devices. In a paper titled "How to Control Things with Words," Cnarniawska-Joerges and Joerges (1988) focus on labels, metaphors, and platitudes as linguistic artifacts that social actors use as control instruments. They show that these linguistic devices, like material artifacts, are built with design features that make them implements of linguistic control.

Symbols, metaphors, arguments, platitudes, stories, et al., are not only sites in which culture is displayed, they are also sites in which culture is deployed.

Cnarniawska-Joerges and Joerges (1988) argue that such communicative forms as labels, symbols, metaphors, and platitudes are not only forms but devices, each of which embodies a linguistic control mechanism. For example, metaphors, by transferring aspects of one object to another, fit meanings into imagination-stimulating messages. To hear the phrase, invoked by a marriage counselor, "the relationship is the patient" (based on Lear 1988, 64) invites the hearer to imagine things about the "relationships" or marriages that are, presumably, stimulated by the metaphorical linkage between "relationship" and "patient." Platitudes, by implicating a link between the general past and the specific present, conventionalize or normalize the conduct the speaker characterizes or assesses. The platitude, "You can't keep a child quiet at the dinner table," uttered by a Nacirema parent, can be invoked to explain as well as to appraise a child's conduct or a parent's response to it. I am arguing, following Cnarniawska-Joerges and Joerges (1988), that a third feature of a code, its expression in formal elements, is conducive to the rhetorical effectiveness of its use, that is, when an interlocutor invokes a code element in interpreting or evaluating communicative conduct, the interlocutor's deployment of the code draws its efficacy from its expression in a particular rhetorical form or device.

In this section of the chapter I have suggested some of the conclusions that might be drawn from a review of a large body of speech codes research. As with the fieldwork studies referred to in the previous section, these conclusions are grounded in a body of empirical particulars. As with particular ethnographic formulations of speech codes, these propositions at once formulate a tested and testable generalization and serve a particular explanatory function. They draw attention to a phenomenon, speech codes, and point to their existence, diversity, and importance in social life. Taken together, these propositions help to explain why it is that, in concrete situations, people pay the attention they do to their own and others' talk; they help to explain how it is that interlocutors (including investigators) can come to know the particularities of communicative conduct and of its meanings to those who produce it in particular discursive worlds; and they help to explain the particular function and force that speech codes have in social life.

Proposition 1 draws attention to the phenomenon of speech codes and to their distinctiveness. Someone experiencing a given discursive world for the first time could, as is the case with myself in relation to Teamsterville, fail to notice that the talk that, in part, makes up that world, is deeply and distinctively cultured. This was also true for both Tamar Katriel and, in a different way, for me, in our early experiences of some Nacirema speech. Proposition 1 raises the empirical possibility that, in any given circumstance, a distinctive speech code is a substantial component of a particular discursive world, and thus Proposition 1 serves to draw attention to an important phenomenon which can be overlooked (or not heard) by participants and observers.

Proposition 2 helps to explain why it is that speech codes and the phenomena that people thematize with the resources of a particular code are consequential to those who use and partake of them. Specifically, Proposition 2 suggests that these phenomena are important to people because they are intricately implicated with notions and experiences of self, other, and strategic action. Like speech codes themselves, such notions and experiences can be missed—that, is, not noticed—and what is noticed, when communicative conduct is perceived through the "lens" of a speech code, is the constructions people make of talk. These constructions are important to people because they are intricately involved with such questions as, What does conversing intelligibly and appropriately among this people require and entail? What kind of man or woman or person will I be if I converse intelligibly and appropriately in these distinctive terms? What kinds of social experiences will be enacted in and through such conversations? In using and adapting to the use of a particular speech code, such questions as these are raised and, at least implicitly, answered. Proposition 2 thus explains the consequentiality of the use of particular speech codes.

Propositions 1 and 2 are more fully elaborated when they are joined with Proposition 3, the proposition about the use of speech codes to constitute the meanings of communicative acts. Specifically, the distinctiveness of speech codes (P1) and the social ideological aspect of speech codes (P2) together help to explain that the adoption of a particular speech code can bring into play distinctive expressions and experiences of social reality. The distinctiveness of speech codes (P1) and the use of speech codes to constitute the meanings of speech acts (P3) together help to explain how interlocutors who deploy different codes can systematically misunderstand each other. And the social ideological aspects of speech codes (P2) and the use of speech codes to constitute the meanings of speech acts (P3) together help to explain the importance interlocutors attach to their own and others' acts of speech.

Proposition 4 locates the display of speech codes elements in talk and, having sited it there, further specifies some of the particular places in which interlocutors (and researchers) can look or listen for such elements. Proposition 4 has a double edge. It *characterizes* speech code elements as public, observable resources, and it *points to particular sites* in which the deployment of these resources can effectively be observed. Thus, it simultaneously focuses on the deployment and the discoverability of speech code elements.

Proposition 5 presents a complex argument about the nature, limits, and conditions under which the deployment of speech codes has force, or traction, for the interlocutors who use them and experience their use. It specifies a limited but powerful domain in which the deployment of speech codes has force in shaping communicative conduct. Furthermore, it specifies three variables that influence the force that speech code deployment has in particular encounters: code systematicity, social legitimation of a code, and the form of code elements. Proposition 5 thus not only explains the circumstances under which the deployment of speech codes has rhetorical traction, it also provides an explanation of why they have the force they do.

When Propositions 4 and 5 are joined, they point to the use of speech codes theory in providing for prediction and control of communicative conduct. They reference an observable phenomenon, elements of speech codes, and they specify where these phenomena can reliably be found. Furthermore, they specify a particular rhetorical function that the deployment of these code elements serves and they specify the conditions under which their deployment has certain predictable effects. When Propositions 1, 2, and 3 are joined to Propositions 4 and 5, a powerful combination of explanatory and heuristic themes is provided, themes that provide the resources for noticing and explaining a consequential dimension of communicative conduct.

CONCLUSION

Talk is important to people, but in distinctive ways across distinctive circumstances of time, place, and culture. The distinctive ways talk is important to people are manifested in the symbols, meanings, premises, and rules about communicative conduct which they deploy to talk about talk and which, when examined, can be understood to constitute what I have called speech codes. The deployment of speech codes—their use by interlocutors in communicative conduct is consequential for those who use them, in that in and through their deployment social meanings are expressed and constituted. Such codes can be discovered and described through the examination of their public display in communicative conduct. These are some of the conclusions to be drawn from research on speech codes.

The five propositions presented here constitute the working core of a speech codes theory. In this chapter I have set forth some particulars in the development of that theory, by tracing some of the history of the theory's core concept, speech codes, have surveyed some of the fieldwork that has contributed to the theory's development, and have articulated five propositions that form the core of a theory. Although the story of the development of the theory has been presented sequentially in three parts, an accurate telling of the story would interweave conceptual development, fieldwork, and the process of generalization rather than separating them.

The empirical status of the propositions is twofold. First, they were each generated in and through an interweaving of conceptualization, data collection and analysis, and speculation based on the data. It is important to emphasize that the data from which they were constructed include not only my own original research into several speech codes but also, indeed primarily, the work of others, as cited. Thus, each of the propositions is, having been formulated, subject to empirical testing. That is, new data or reinterpretation of extant data can be used to disconfirm, refine, or develop these propositions.

Finally, the theory itself, as formulated here, is designed to thematize a phenomenon, speech codes, explore its attributes, and assess its workings in the process of communication. As such, its value is twofold. First, it suggests a particular way of perceiving and thinking about communicative conduct in particular social milieux, and its value can be assessed in terms of whether the use of this approach will continue, as it has in the past, to stimulate discoveries about particular ways of speaking. Second, it proposes generalizations about the phenomenon it essays, and its value can be assessed in terms of whether those generalizations stand the test of further work.

REFERENCES

Abrahams, R., and Bauman, R. (1971). Sense and nonsense in St. Vincent: Speech behavior and decorum in a Caribbean community. *American Anthropologist 73,* 762–72.

Albert, E. M. (1972). Culture patterning of speech behavior in Burundi. In Gumperz, J. J., and Hymes, D. (Eds.), *Directions in Sociolinguistics: The Ethnography of Communication* (pp. 72–105).

Austin, J. L. (1962). *How to Do Things with Words.* Oxford: Oxford University Press.

Basso, K. (1970). "To give up on words": Silence in western Apache culture. *Southwestern Journal of Anthropology 26,* 213–30.

Bauman, R. (1970). Aspects of seventeenth century quaker rhetoric. *Quarterly Journal of Speech* 56, 67–74.

Bauman, R., and Sherzer, J. (Eds.) (1974). *Explorations in the Ethnography of Speaking.* Cambridge: Cambridge University Press.

Berger, P., Berger, B., and Kellner, H. (1973). *The Homeless Mind: Modernization and Consciousness.* New York: Vintage Books.

Bernstein, b. (1971). *Class, Codes, and Control. Volume 1. Theoretical Studies towards a Sociology of Language.* London: Routledge and Kegan Paul.

Bernstein, B. (1973). *Class, Codes, and Control. Volume 2. Applied Studies towards a Sociology of Language.* London: Routledge and Kegan Paul.

Bilmas, J. (1976). Rules and rhetoric: Negotiating the social order in a Thai village. *Southwestern Journal of Anthropology 32,* 44–57.

Braithwaite, C. A. (1982). *Cultural uses and interpretations of silence.* M. A. thesis, University of Washington, Seattle.

Burke, K. (1935, 1954, 1965). *Permanence and Change: An Anatomy of Purpose.* Indianapolis: Bobbs-Merrill.

———. (1968). *Counter-statement.* Berkeley: University of California Press.

———. (1950, 1969). *A Rhetoric of Motives.* Berkeley: University of California Press.

Carbaugh, D. (1987). Communication rules in Donahue discourse. *Research on Language and Social Interaction 21,* 31–62.

———. (1988). *Talking American: Cultural Discourses on DONAHUE*. Norwood, N.J.: Ablex.

———. (1989). Fifty terms for talk: A cross-cultural study. *International and Intercultural Communication Annual 13*, 93–120.

Coleman, J. (1989). Response to the sociology of education award. *Academic Questions 2*, 76–78.

Cook, J. (1973). Language and socialization: A critical review. In Bernstein, B. (Ed.) *Class, Codes, and Control. Volume 2. Applied Studies towards a Sociology of Language* (pp. 293–342).

Douglas, M. (1970). *Natural Symbols: Explorations in Cosmology*. London: Cresset Press.

Enker, M. (1987). Attitudinal and normative variables as predictors of cheating behavior. *Journal of Cross-Cultural Psychology 18*, 315–330.

Fitch, K. (1989). *Communicative enactment of interpersonal ideology: Personal address in urban Colombian society*. Unpublished doctoral dissertation. University of Washington, Seattle.

Fitch, K. (1990/91). A ritual for attempting leave-taking in Colombia. *Research on Language and Social Interaction 24*, 209–224.

Fitch, K. (1991). The interplay of linguistic universals and cultural knowledge in personal address: Colombian madre terms. *Communication Monographs 58*(3), 254–272.

Fitch, K. (1994). The issue of selection of objects of analysis in ethnographies of speaking. *Research on Language and Social Interaction 27*, 51–93.

Fox, J. (1974). "Our ancestors spoke in pairs": Rotinese views of language, dialect, and code. In Bauman, R., and Sherzer, J. (Eds.), *Explorations in the Ethnography of Speaking* (pp. 65–85).

Geertz, C. (1973). *The Interpretation of Cultures: Selected Essays*. New York: Basic Books.

Goldsmith, D. (1989/90). Gossip from the native's point of view: A comparative analysis. *Research on Language and Social Interaction 23*, 163–194.

Gumperz, J. J. (1982). *Discourse Strategies*. Cambridge: Cambridge University Press.

Gumperz, J. J., and Hymes, D. (1972). *Directions in Sociolinguistics: The Ethnography of Communication*. New York: Holt, Rinehart & Winston.

Hall, B. (1988/89). Norms, action, and alignment: A discursive perspective. *Research on Language and Social Interaction 22*, 23–44.

Hall, B. (1991). An elaboration of the structural possibilities for engaging in alignment episodes. *Communication Monographs 58*, 79–100.

Halliday, M. (1973). Preface. In Berstein, B. (Ed.) *Class, Codes, and Control, Volume 2. Applied Studies towards a Sociology of Language* (pp. ix–xvi).

Hopper, J. (1993). The rhetoric of motives in divorce. *Journal of Marriage and the Family 55*, 801–813.

Hsu, F. (1963). *Clan, Caste, and Club*. New York: Van Nostrand.

Huspek, M. (1993). Dueling structures: The theory of resistance in discourse. *Communication Theory 3*, 1–26.

Hymes, D. (1962). The ethnography of speaking. In Gladwin, T., and Sturtevant, W. C. (Eds.) *Anthropology and Human Behavior* (pp. 13–53). Washington, D.C.: Anthropological Society of Washington.

———. (1964). Introduction. Toward ethnographies of communication. In Gumperz, J. M., and Hymes, D. (Eds.) The ethnography of communication, *American Anthropologist 66* (part 2), 1–34.

———. (1967). Models of the interaction of language and social setting. *Journal of Social Issues 23,* 8–28.

———. (1972). Models of the interaction of language and social life. In Gumperz, J. J., and Hymes, D. (Eds.) *Directions in Sociolinguistics: The Ethnography of Communication* (pp. 35–71).

Katriel, T. (1983). *Toward a Conceptualization of Ways of Speaking The Case of Israeli 'Dugri' Speech.* Dissertation, University of Washington.

Katriel, T. (1986). *Talking Straight: 'Dugri' Speech in Israeli Sabra Culture.* Cambridge: Cambridge University Press.

Katriel, T., and Philipsen, G. (1981). "What we need is communication": "Communication" as a cultural category in some American speech. *Communication Monographs 48,* 302–317.

Labov, W. (1969). The logic of nonstandard English. *Georgetown University Monograph Series on Languages and Linguistics 23,* 1–31.

Lear, M. (1988). The new marital therapy. *The New York Times Magazine* (March 6), 63–64.

Miller, L. (1990). Violent families and the rhetoric of harmony. *British Journal of Sociology 41,* 263–288.

Mills, C. (1940). Situated actions and vocabularies of motive. *American Sociological Review 5,* 904–913.

Moerman, M. (1988). *Talking Culture: Ethnography and Conversation Analysis.* Philadephia: University of Pennsylvania Press.

Philips, S.U. (1970). Acquisition of rules for appropriate speech usage. *Georgetown University Monograph Series on Languages and Linguistics 23,* 77–94.

Philipsen, G. (1975). Speaking "like a man" in Teamsterville: Culture patterns of role enactment in an urban neighborhood. *Quarterly Journal of Speech 61,* 13–22.

———. (1976a). Places for speaking in Teamsterville. *Quarterly Journal of Speech 62,* 15–25.

———. (1976b). Speaking as a cultural resource. Paper presented at the Annual Convention of the Speech Communication Association, Chicago.

———. (1987). The prospect for cultural communication. In Kincaid, D. (Ed.) *Communication Theory from Eastern and Western Perspectives* (pp. 245–54). New York: Academic Press.

———. (1989). Speech and the Communal Function in Four Cultures. *International and Intercultural Communication Annual 13,* 79–92.

———. (1992). *Speaking Culturally: Explorations in Social Communication.* Albany: State University of New York Press.

Philipsen, G., and Carbaugh, D. (1986). A bibliography of fieldwork in the ethnography of communication. *Language in Society 15,* 387–98.

Richman, J. (1988). Deviance from sex-linked expressivity norms and psychological distress. *Social Forces 67,* 208–215.

Rickford, J. (1986). The need for new approaches to social class analysis in sociolinguistics. *Language & Communication 6,* 215–221.

Robinson, W. (1965). The elaborated code in working class language. *Language and Speech 8,* 243–252.

Rosaldo, M. (1982). The things we do with words: Ilongot speech acts and Speech Act Theory in philosophy. *Language in Society 11,* 203–217.

Rosch, E. (1987). Linguistic relativity. *Et cetera 44,* 254–279.

Rosen, H. (1972). *Language and Class: A Critical Look at the Theories of Basil Bernstein.* Bristol: Falling Wall Press.

St. George, R. (1984). "Heated" speech and literacy in seventeenth-century New England. In Hall, D. D., and Allen, D. G. (Eds.) *Seventeenth-Century New England* (pp. 275–322).

Schneider, D. (1976). Notes toward a theory of culture. In Basso, K., and Selby, H. (Eds.) *Meaning in Anthropology* (pp. 197–220). Albuquerque: University of New Mexico Press.

Schwartz, S. (1973). Normative explanations of helping behavior: A critique, proposal, and empirical test. *Journal of Experimental Social Psychology 9,* 349–364.

Scruton, Roger. (1979). The significance of common culture. *Philosophy 54,* 51–70.

Searle, J. (1976). A classification of illocutionary acts. *Language in Society 5,* 1–23.

Seitel, P. (1974). Haya metaphors for speech. *Language in Society 3,* 51–67.

Silverstein, M. (1979). Language structure and linguistic ideology. In Clyne, P. R. Hanks, W. F., and Hofbauer, C. L. (Eds.) *The Elements: A Parasession on Linguistic Units and Levels* (pp. 193–247). Chicago: Linguistic Society.

Simon, R., Eder, D., Evans, C. (1992). The development of feeling norms underlying romantic love among adolescent females. *Social Psychology Quarterly 55,* 29–46.

Swidler, A. (1986). Culture in action: Symbols and strategies. *American Sociological Review 51,* 273–286.

Turner, J. (1988). *A Theory of Social Interaction.* Stanford: Stanford University Press.

Turner, J. (1980). Social dramas and stories about them. *Critical Inquiry 7,* 141–168.

Varenne, H. (1977). *Americans Together: Structured Diversity in a Midwestern Town.* New York: Teachers College Press.

Verschuren, J. (1989). Language on language: Toward metapragmatic universals. *IPrA Papers in Pragmatics* 5, 5–144.

Watzlawick, P., Beavin, J., Jackson, D. (1967). *Pragmatics of Human Communication: A Study of Interactional Patterns, Pathologies, and Paradoxes.* New York: W. W. Norton.

6

Developing Communication Theories

JOHN STEWART

The original premise drawing together this collection of papers was that communication theory emerges when careful empirical observation is creatively and insightfully blended with equally careful conceptual analysis. Professors Albrecht and Philipsen first reasoned that it would be useful for a community of graduate students and faculty to discuss with several active researchers how the researchers worked concepts and empirical observations into theory. Then they reasoned that a larger audience might be interested in these matters—hence this book.

Albrecht and Philipsen were clearly right. The colloquium series, which also included discussions with professors Janet Beavin Bavelas, Edna Rogers, and John Wilson, was stimulating and productive. Listener-discussants had the rare privilege of hearing the people responsible for some of the most often-cited research in the field report on their struggles to devise fruitful ways to observe communication phenomena, to understand how concepts guided observations and were in turn guided by them, and to develop, test, and revise theoretical formulations to make sense of the empirical observations and concepts. The result was a series on "developing communication theories" that aptly illustrated both senses of this strategically ambiguous title: (a) that there are various, incremental, often nonlinear, and even serendipitous ways to build communication theory, and (b) that several important communication theories are unfinished and still in process.

The colloquium presentations were, of course, revised extensively for this volume. They now display these scholars' understandings of the process they go through in their work even more explicitly than did the original oral versions. Thus, these chapters offer the reader the opportunity to examine the general model of theorizing that is operating here and the sometimes subtle but important variations among these theorists' approaches. In some cases, other essays by these authors—works that helped make them important contributors to the colloquium—are useful in fleshing out the various theorist-researchers' views.

I propose in this chapter to exploit the opportunity for metatheoretical analysis that these essays provide by responding to two questions about these chapters and related publications by these same authors:

> What are the views of theory and theorizing that emerge in these essays? and What are some of the most fruitful and the most potentially problematic theoretical moves made by each of these researchers?

I hope in this way to indicate how the papers interrelate, to highlight some important contributions, and to contribute to the ongoing conversation about communication theorizing that engages these and other researchers.

WHAT IS THEORY OR THEORIZING?

As I noted, all the chapter authors appear to accept the general formula:

$$\text{Empirical Observations} \longleftrightarrow \text{Concepts} \rightarrow \text{Theory}$$

But there are distinctions among their approaches. Albrecht sketches a roughly chronological or evolutionary view of theory-building which consists of first posing a series of research questions, then making and testing predictions which are fulfilled, unfulfilled and/or modulated, and finally using these experiences to construct a "story" based on the process. O'Keefe indicates that her theorizing is less systematic; she notes that her post-hoc reconstruction makes it appear that her research program was much more chronologically linear than she believes it actually was. Cappella claims, on the other hand, that "little of value can be said in general about how to construct subtle, testable, and useful theories," but that the products of theorizing should be understood and tested, not as "stories" but as "causal arguments." Philipsen's emphasis on the "local, particular knowledge" that governs communicative conduct might imply that he agrees with Cappella's resistance to general theorizing, but his five propositions are presented as the core of a *general* speech codes theory.

Related writings by some of these same authors underscore the differences among their views of communication theory and theorizing. For example, in two widely-cited essays Berger (1991, 1992) speculates about why there are so *few* communication theories, relying primarily on the view of theory described in his and Chaffee's *Handbook of Communication Science* (Berger and Chaffee 1987, chapters 1 and 3). In another exchange, O'Keefe (1993) defines the problem differently: in an essay entitled "Against Theory," she argues that "there is little justification for the continuing search for a unifying theoretical consensus" among communication scholars (81), and that these scholars and teachers should respectfully encourage multiple theoretical voices. Robert T. Craig (1993), founding editor of the journal *Communication Theory,* concludes from evidence like that, "what communication theory should look like, what it is for, the boundaries and internal divisions of the field, how communication research should be conducted, and how such research properly relates to the development of theory—all must be regarded as open questions at the present time" (1993, 26). Craig also contends that one reason why these questions are so open is that most discussions of these issues by communication scholars pay relatively little attention to complementary and parallel metatheoretical developments in the broader human sciences.

I believe Craig is right on both points. I will describe later what strike me as some of the important and subtle theoretical contributions made by this volume's authors, but I also believe that the theoretical work done by these and other communication scholars could be even more productive were the field's most active researchers to attend more closely to the broader intellectual context that frames their theorizing efforts. One part of this context germane to the chapters making up this volume is the historical controversy among European and American theorists and metatheorists over whether *explanation* or *understanding* is the appropriate goal of social science. Another concerns the difference between treating theory as *process* vs. *product,* and a third clarifies the ramifications of treating theory as *story* or as *argument.* I believe it can be shown in the chapters of this volume, first, that theoretical work reflects the degree with which the theorist sees himself or herself as engaged in explanation or understanding, theorizing or developing a theoretical product, and constructing a story or making an argument; and second, that the work of both inexperienced and experienced theorists can be fruitfully assessed and productively fine-tuned using these criteria.

Explanation and Understanding

As a variety of influential authors demonstrate (e.g., Winch 1958; von Wright 1974; Dallmayr and McCarthy 1977; Apel 1984; Gadamer 1989; Bohman 1991), the terms "explanation" and "understanding" have been widely used to summarize fundamental distinctions in theoretical perspectives and research approaches, especially among those who call themselves social scientists. Those who foreground "explanation" have relied on such philosophers of science as August Comte, John Stuart Mill, Carl Hempel, Theodore Abel, and Richard Rudner. These writers have argued for the methodological unity of the natural and social sciences, claiming, as one commentator puts its, "that progress in the social sciences requires adoption of the methods and standards of the natural sciences [so that social scientists can] construct causal *explanations* of human behavior, *explanations* based on general laws and theories that can be verified by empirical observation and are not influenced by the personal values of the scientist" (Warnke 1984, vii, italics added).

Proponents of understanding rather than explanation have been persuaded by the arguments of such philosophers of inquiry as Wilhelm Dilthey, Hans-Georg Gadamer, Peter Winch, and Charles Taylor, who emphasize the similarities between the social sciences and the humanities, not between the social and natural sciences. These and other metatheorists maintain that, because social scientists study humans, context-dependent meaning is an inherent feature of each phenomenon researched, which is to say that each "variable" or object of study is connected somehow to individual and relational self-definitions and cultural traditions. On this view, the social sciences necessarily involve an interpretive dimension (Taylor 1971); they cannot rely on observation and explanation alone. As Dilthey put it in the late nineteenth-century "Nature we explain; [human] life we understand" (Quoted in Dallmayr and McCarthy 1977, 4).

Recently, some "post-empiricist" philosophers of inquiry have questioned the efficacy of the traditional explanation-understanding distinction itself, on the grounds, first, that it obscures or ignores the impact on theories and disciplines of the larger social and historical contexts in which they are applied, change, and develop; and second, that it oversimplifies the histories and actual practices of various scientific programs (Bohman, 3). Kuhn's (1962) *The Structure of Scientific Revolutions* has been labeled the "first major post-empiricist work (Bohman, 3) because of its development of the first of these arguments, while ethnomethodological and ethnographic studies of particular research efforts have fleshed out the second argument (e.g., Knor-Cetina and Mulkay 1983).

Issues addressed in these literatures surface at several points in the preceding chapters. For example, Berger and Chaffee (1987) define communication science as an enterprise that "seeks to *understand* the production, processing, and effects of symbol and signal systems by developing testable theories, containing lawful generalizations, that *explain* phenomena associated with production, processing, and effects" (17, italics added). The indication in this definition that explanation produced understanding is reinforced in this book when Berger complains that the practice of labeling social interaction patterns "communication rituals" constitutes a "non-explanation." Berger's point is that research outcomes only *explain* phenomena when they tell *why some pattern occurs,* which is to say both that explanation is the proper goal of social scientific theorizing, and that proper explanations posit verifiable *causes.* Albrecht appears to share this viewpoint when she complains that Kanter's (1982; 1983) research "did not adequately explain for theory-building purposes *why* highly multiplex ties are the most probable pathways for talk about innovation" (italics added). On the other hand, Philipsen argues in his chapter that the study of speech codes is motivated "by the desire to *understand* particular, socially constructed discursive worlds . . . as the historical, spatial, and cultural sites in which human connections are accomplished" (italics added). Here he pointedly does not say that the goal is to *explain* these worlds, and his characterization of these sites as "*particular,* socially constructed discursive *worlds*" (italics added) resonates with the concerns of the anthropologist, philosophical anthropologist, or ethnographer who would, like Dilthey, Gadamer, Winch, and Taylor, link the social sciences with the humanities. Later, however, Philipsen asserts that *"the artful use of a shared speech code is a sufficient condition for predicting, explaining, and controlling the form of discourse about the intelligibility, prudence, and morality of communicative conduct."* This proposition embodies the primary goals of, and rings with the tones of, the "explanation-focused" social scientist. Read alongside the first claim, it might well lead a person familiar with the historical distinction between understanding and explanation to puzzle about the central thrust of Philipsen's research agenda, or perhaps to assume that his orientation is post-empiricist in Bohman's (1991) sense.

There is not space here for a full exploration of all the issues raised in these chapters by the various uses of "explanation" and "understanding." But a closer look at the central construct of *causality* ought to demonstrate the potential value of integrating these literatures into communication theorizing. As Cappella notes in his chapter in this volume, many theorists have argued that "one of the most important ways that humans achieve . . . the 'click of comprehension' is by grasping the causal relationships that exist among a set of events, items, ideas, works, and so on." Most of this book's contributors would probably concur. But historically the causality construct has been problematic, in that theorists have disagreed fundamentally about what constitutes an adequate account of causal links in the human world. For example, in the late nineteenth-century Max Weber attempted to work out an empirical science of concrete human actions that would produce "valid" and "objective" knowledge but from a perspective that acknowledged the inherently value-laden (*werbezügliche,* value-relative) character of scientific investigation. One of Weber's most important moves was to give to *motive* the key role in the human world that cause had in the natural world. As he wrote, "Thus we understand in terms of *motive* the meaning an actor attaches to the proposition twice two equals four, when he states it or writes it down, in that we understand *what makes him do this* [italics added] at precisely this moment and in these circumstances" (Dallmayr and McCarthy 1977, 42). Thus, Weber concluded, "A correct causal interpretation of a concrete course of action is arrived at when the overt action and the motives have both been correctly apprehended and at the same time their relation has become meaningfully comprehensible (1977, 45).

Early in this century, Talcott Parsons's positivist interpretation of Weber deemphasized motive in an effort to restore causality to something approaching its natural scientific structure and function. Parsons argued that causal explanation required not an analysis of motives but a relating of particular facts "through analysis by means of a generalized theoretical scheme which is in the nature of the case abstract." Moreover, he argued, "the conception of generalized theory as has been developed in the great tradition of the natural science [sic] is an essential component of all empirical science" (1971, 61).

Carl Hempel (1965) had a similar interest in reducing the distance between the human and natural sciences, but he returned to Weber's belief in the power of reasons to function as causes. For example, Hempel claimed that the French Revolution could be "explained" in terms of the general law: "A revolution will tend to occur if there is a growing discontent, on the part of a large part of the population, with certain prevailing conditions" (1965, 236). As many critics of this line of thinking pointed out, however, reasons or motives cannot be treated as causes analogous to, for example, the mass on one end of a lever that causes the lever to move, because they cannot be identified and measured in any "objective" way. Thus, a central problem with treating reasons as causes is that "the agent's full preferences can only be established in her choice behavior and not by any independent means" (Bohman 1991, 22), which means that any theoretical claim about the relationship between reason or motive and outcome is merely analytically true. In Hempel's example, the only objective evidence of the existence of the motive "discontent" among French citizens is the existence of revolutionary behavior. So the law "explains" nothing outside itself; it is simply analytically true.

Difficulties like these have led interpretivist and post-empiricist social scientist to underscore the danger of importing into the human studies such natural scientific constructs as causality—even when efforts are made to modify them significantly—and claiming that theories of such human events as organizational, interpersonal, or cultural communication can produce what have historically been called *explanations*. Bohman (1991) concludes from his review of both metatheoretical studies and empirical reports making up four prominent research programs (rational choice, ethnomethodology, interpretive social science, and Habermas's theory of communicative action) that contemporary social science is inherently "indeterminate," which is to say that it cannot successfully construe tis theories as *causal*. In fact, Bohman argues that social actions—which include all communicative events—must be viewed as "doubly indeterminate: they are performed by reflective and knowledgeable actors in interaction with other reflective and knowledgeable social actors." This means that when social scientific theories fail, it is most often not because their laws or models are weak, but because they are too rigid in that their premises "fix" agents' purposes or goals "making them into 'judgmental dopes' or 'rational fools,' to borrow apt characterizations of the failures of Parsonian sociology and rational choice theories" (1991, 7). Bohman insists, however, that the inherent indeterminacy of the social sciences does not exclude rigorous theorizing; the goal of his book is "to show how explanatory rigor is possible without necessity or determinacy" (1991, 7), that is, how rigorous social science can and must be done without recourse to such a "fixed" construct as causality.

How might Cappella's treatment of causality change if he were to take into account some of the discussions I have just sketched? First, Cappella argues that "causal accounts are explanatory," which is to say that knowledge about the linkage between antecedent and consequent is a necessary part of complete comprehension. He supports this argument in part with two examples, one involving a light switch and its connected wiring and the other involving the carburetor in a standard combustion engine. He concludes, "causal explanation is central to theory building because causal explanation is central to ordinary human understanding." But one might ask whether Cappella's analysis is valid for *human* events as contrasted with natural ones—electrical transmission and combustion. Do humans actually come to comprehend an election, a family conflict, or a committee meeting by grasping the *causes* of what happens? Antecedents and consequents in an election, for example, are as likely to be understood as functionally, politically, logically, psychologically, or even chronologically related as they are to be comprehended as causally linked. In the context of some of the related literatures, it appears that Cappella is working here from a rather limited view of "ordinary human understanding." Against the position Cappella takes, Charles Taylor argues that comprehension of social events centrally involves not causality but the participants' "constitutive self understandings," and that "what one could call a moral context" is more important than the "causal context" of a series of events (1985, 94–95).

This literature is also relevant to Cappella's discussion of myths about the empirical confirmation of theories. The point of his second myth is that no causal relationship can be established unequivocally. Bohman (1991) would agree with the mythic status of this belief. He would agree with Cappella that, at least in the human studies, "no general, informative conception of causality is possible." But unlike Cappella, Bohman would not continue to insist that "Good theories are good causal arguments," or that the best theories favor "low as opposed to high inference linkages in the causal story" and "deeper causal accounts." The reason is that Bohman is led by his analysis to disconnect causality and explanation, while Cappella works to keep them connected. And the difference is not just a matter of preference, but of coherence. Cappella acknowledges the problematic status of the concept of causality, but he appears to believe that these problems can be finessed by treating theories as arguments rather than demonstrations. His position is that, even though human events may be causally indeterminate, theory can (or more accurately, must) still be causal, so long as theory is viewed as an argument, open to challenges by rival theory.

The problem with this move is that one cannot solve a *conceptual* problem like this one with a simple *methodological* shift. To say that "no unassailable logical explication of the concept of causality is possible," is to say that causality is in this sense an incoherent construct. This incoherence is not salvaged by simply reducing the criterion for adequate theorizing from scientific demonstration to plausible argument. An *argument* dependent on a logically flawed construct is as problematic as an alleged demonstration dependent on the same construct.

Cappella and his primary resource Miller (1987) could preserve most of the very fruitful metaphor that theories are like arguments without the freight of their claims about causality. Cappella is clearly right, for example, that "settling honest disagreements through rational argument is notorious for its imprecision and lack of closure," and that "real debates over scientific theories are debates over incomplete, imprecise, and circumstantial accounts of phenomena just as is the case in legal, political, and public advocacy." Thus it would be a short distance to the claim that, in all four of these discursive worlds—legal, political, public, and social scientific—causality in anything like the natural sense is neither a possible nor a necessary part of human understanding and the theorizing that embodies it.

In brief, some of these authors' theorizing efforts might be even more precise and productive if they were to sort out more clearly the distinctions between the goals of explanation and understanding, and if they more thoroughly considered the degree to which their approach to communication theory can produce adequate causal accounts.

Process or Product?

On the one hand, if my initial model of these writers' views is accurate—Empirical Observations $\longleftrightarrow$ Concepts $\rightarrow$ Theory—then theory is being viewed here as a product. On the other hand, if Cappella captures any consensus in his account of theoretical debates, then the central focus is on "incomplete, imprecise, and circumstantial accounts of . . . phenomena," that is, on the ongoing processes rather than what they produce. As with the distinction between explanation and understanding, this difference can be consequential. One who views theory as product is more likely to emphasize the first interpretation of this book's title—that communication theory is produced incrementally, and in particular ways—; to strive for the three c's of certainty, closure, and control; and to rely on what I have called a classical view of validity as a measure of the *correspondence* between a theoretical formulation and the features of the "objective" world it purportedly represents (Stewart 1994). On the other hand one who views a theory as process is more likely to emphasize the second interpretation of this book's title—that theorizing is an ongoing conversation or struggle; to acknowledge the uncertainty, openness, and descriptive rather than normative nature of theoretical formulations; and to rely on interpretive approaches to validity (Stewart 1994).

In this volume, Berger and Philipsen appear to view theory most clearly as product. Their end-goal seems to be to produce a set of explanatory axioms, corollaries, and/or propositions that can be tested for validity against the phenomena they allegedly explain. Cappella also identifies a hoped-for product, which he labels "a theory of face-to-face interaction," one version of which is discrepancy-arousal theory. In the spirit of his interpretation of theory-as-causal-argument, he contends that evidence exists to support the plausibility of his theoretical formulations against its competitors and that he and his colleagues can aptly and effectively respond to their critics. He concludes, however, that although theories themselves ought to be well-defined and clearly-explicated products, theory construction and theoretical debate are characterized much more by the hurly-burly of human intercourse than by closure and certainty. O'Keefe is also working on a specific product that she labels "the theory of message design logic." But she acknowledges that the definition of the problem this theory addresses has changed as the process of theorizing has unfolded from "understanding social inference processes and their role in communication behavior" to "finding the best account of variation in message design." This is important, because, insofar as process actually redefines product, one may argue that process is being foregrounded in her work. O'Keefe also finally characterizes her theory or model as a "way of looking at communication," which could be understood as a "lens" (product) or "approach" (process). Albrecht articulates a perspective that is closest among these authors to theory as process. She identifies system theory as the guiding metatheoretic orientation for her research program, but then borrows from various types and levels of theory in her research design and data interpretation. She presents findings as fruitful though rather tentative, and does not project her work toward any goals of comprehensive coverage or completion. Her efforts appear aimed primarily at incrementally developing improved understanding of parts of a complex and loosely-defined set of cognitive and communicative activities.

In addition to identifying some similarities and differences among these theorists, I want to argue that the process perspective is plausible, and that these two orientations—process and product—can limn a dialectic that can be productive for the communication theorist. Philosopher of history Eric Voegelin (1956, 1957, 1974, 1978) develops an apt interpretation of *theoria* as process, as theorizing. One of Voegelin's fundamental claims is that one ground of human reality is what he calls "the tension of existence." By this he means that human life can most fruitfully be understood as a complex of tensions between, for example, ignorance and knowledge, poverty and riches, sickness and health, death and life, immanence and transcendence. This perspective highlights the point that a given human always knows some things and yet does not know enough, has wealth and yet does not have unlimited resources, is alive and yet is moving inexorably toward death, is embodied and yet cannot wholly be described in spatio-temporal terms. Anaximander, Plato, and Aristotle recognized all this, as did Augustine, St. Thomas, and Kenneth Burke. One could also argue that Leslie Baxter and others (Baxter 1992, 1993; Baxter and Montgomery 1996) are pursuing a similar basic as they develop their "dialectic" or "dialogic" perspectives on interpersonal communication.

Voegelin maintains that the human who lives in these unresolvable tensions can develop two kinds of knowledge. Epistemic or existential knowledge "refers to an experience in which one is wholly involved" (Webb, 107). It is the kind of knowing that emerges in full, dense, rich, and reflective living. Doxic knowledge, by contrast, is distanced and reduced; it is paradigmatically logical knowledge expressed in propositions. Importantly, both are legitimate; as Voegelin puts it, "they are two aspects of one world that is given in two kinds of cognitive experiences of the same human being" (Voegelin 1957, 216–217). Both are knowledge, but they differ in the degree to which they acknowledge and embody the *tension* that is the ground of human reality.

As Voegelin primarily uses the term, "theory" refers to the former, to "knowledge that is the conscious expression of immediate experience and that has become explicit . . . " (Webb 1981, 109). He emphasizes that, since immediate human experience is tensional, any adequate explication of it must preserve this tensionality. Thus, those who theorize risk falling into two main errors. One, which Voegelin calls a "transcendentalizing gnosis," is to claim an ineffable intuition of ultimate reality—as religious mystics, cultists, and "true believer" theorists often do. The other, an "immanentizing gnosis," consists of claiming "that one's articulated understanding captures the real perfectly" (Webb 1981, 110), that is, that a theoretical formulation is valid because it fully corresponds to the reality it allegedly explains. The theorist is often led into this kind of error by turning away from experience in an effort to look at what presumably lies outside it, for example to "sense data" or psychological data.

As Eugene Webb points out, "It is a necessary corollary of this analysis that theoretical understanding, in Voegelin's sense of the term, makes existential demands of the inquirer" (1981, 112). Voegelin writes, "theory cannot be developed under all conditions by everybody. The theorist . . . must, at least, be capable of imaginative re-enactment of the experiences of which theory is an explication. . . . theory as an explication of certain experiences is intelligible only to those in whom the explication will stir up parallel experiences as the empirical basis for testing the truth of theory" (Webb 1981, 113). This means that the theorist in Voegelin's sense must be a person who "dwells consciously and freely in the tension of existence, and this means that he [or she] must experience the tension and be willing to acknowledge it and the demands it makes on his [/her] existence" (Webb 1981, 113).

One of the most important features of the original colloquium invitation was that it encouraged these theorists to reflect on the connections between their theorizing and their personal experience. In varying degrees, each author reported on the always-present but often-overlooked connections between biography and theorizing that marked his or her work. Philipsen's account is perhaps the most candid and illuminating. Before and during his experience as an undergraduate, he writes, he internalized a coherent and experientially-verified understanding of communication anchored in the writings of Carl Rogers, Irving Lee, and Kurt Lewin. This understanding was directly challenged by the people he encountered in Teamsterville, and his first theoretical efforts were focused on responding to this challenge by explicating the coherence of their alternative ways of speaking. As often happens, this experience in another culture sharpened his interest in his own. "And so," Philipsen continues, "I set about the task of discovering and describing what I have come to call Nacirema communicative conduct as a cultural system." His effort in this volume is to add to the series of propositions that make up his resulting theory of speech codes. Voegelin's analysis clarifies why these biographical insights are important for Philipsen's theorizing. Voegelin might also caution Philipsen not to forget the biographical roots of his original inquiry motives and to beware of the tendency toward immanentizing gnosis which threatens any research program designed to develop a complete enumeration of propositions that purport to enable one to predict, explain, and control "the form of discourse about the intelligibility, prudence, and morality of communicative conduct."

Each of the other theorists might also profit from reflecting on how their work embodies the tension between theory as product and theory as process. Berger and O'Keefe, for example, could be encouraged to continue to trust and pursue their experientially and intuitively (not just "scientifically") developed hunches that they have identified something approaching a universal of human communication—in O'Keefe's case the universal feature of message variation and adaptation, and in Berger's case the feature "that in all social interactions some measure of uncertainty exists and that the potentially negative effects of this uncertainty must be hedged against in order to avoid such undesirable interaction outcomes as failing to reach instrumental goals, being misunderstood, or angering, hurting, or embarrassing others." Cappella might be reminded that his view of theory as argument can privilege either product or process. Individual arguments can be viewed either as parts of a *case* that will ultimately be closed by a decision about who won and who lost, or as contributions to a *conversation* that is evolutionary and ongoing. I read

Cappella's personal modus operandi as conversational rather than adversarial in the legal sense, but his colleagues and opponents may sometimes fall into the other model or argument. This distinction raises the issue of the ramifications of treating theory as argument or story, to which I turn next.

Theory as story or argument

My goal in this section is simply to argue that this is another difference that makes a difference. In other words, the theoretical work in this volume may also be partially assessed and usefully sharpened by noting the chapter authors' positions on this issue and exploring some ramifications of their choices.

As has been amply shown, Cappella treats theory explicitly as argument. Berger refers to his essay as a "narrative," and as I have already noted, Philipsen includes some personal narrative in his description of this empirical work. Albrecht foregrounds the notion that her chapter "reveals a story," especially with her epigraph from *Children of the Holocaust,* to which she returns in her final paragraph. Only O'Keefe is noncommittal on this issue, preferring "account" to either "story" or "argument."

Both the "argument" and the "story" metaphors for theorizing are consistent with criticisms of narrowly scientific approaches to the human studies. For at least half a century, researchers have acknowledged that theories neither consist of demonstrations that reflect ultimate truths of the objective universe nor posit universal laws of human behavior. They are human constructions, accounts of one sort or another that reflect their author's biographies, biases, agendas, cultures, blind spots, methodological preferences, and political affiliations. But may they most aptly be termed "stories" or "arguments"?

Several of the distinctive features of stories are illustrated in Albrecht's epigraph. First, stories are populated with *characters,* individual, identifiable people. The quotation from Epstein's book that begins Albrecht's chapter is a description not just of anybody, but of "the Herbens, Willi and Liza" and the specific people around them. Second, stories occur in and help define particular *contexts*. There is a time—"the fifties and early sixties"—a place—"the state parks around New York city"—and palpable details—sights, smells, sounds, tastes. Third, there is an agon, a tension or struggle that develops as the story unfolds—in this case the tension between coping with everyone else and living with one's own community made up of other children of the Holocaust. Stories also have identifiable structural components—the setting of the scene, character development, intensity that builds toward a climax, a more or less complete resolution of the agon in a conclusion or denouement. All these elements contribute to the point of a story, which is to capture some important dimensions of human *meaning*. Stories remind teller, listeners, and readers of how they are similar to and different from each other, what is to be valued and condemned, and how one ought to behave. And when a story is evaluated, when its "validity" is assessed, it is measured primarily against the experiences of its tellers and listeners which, as Fisher (1987) explains, are standards of coherence and fidelity. Critics of a story ask whether it "hangs together," whether the characters think, feel, and behave as "people like that do," and whether the events low coherently. They also test the story against relevant aspects of their own experience, checking whether the story reflects life as they have lived it.

"Story" is a powerful metaphor for theory, and *Children of the Holocaust* tells a powerful story of a unique communication network, a social organization that profoundly affects the lives of those who populate it. I completely agree with Albrecht's claim in her final sentence, "Theories and data about individuals and their communication networks are remarkable vehicles for revealing to us the essential stories of personal identity, institutional development, sheer survival, and life."

In order fully to exploit the story metaphor, however, Albrecht would have to alter significantly the methods of data gathering and analysis that characterize the research she reports here. Consider, for example, the studies he discusses that are more fully reported in Albrecht and Hall (1991). She and her colleague were interested in how experiences of, for example, "shame," "trust," and "support" affected communication about innovation. They conducted interviews and administered network surveys and then statistically analyzed the survey data to produce correlations between communication frequency about innovation and perceptions of relationship uncertainty, satisfaction, and compatibility. When a problem concerning aggregated vs. unaggregated data arose, Albrecht and Hall responded by "demeaning the data," by subtracting the average reported judgments on a given variable such as "trust" from each score on that variable for the relationship reported.

In this study, the research questions, the setting in a radiation oncology department, and the focal constructs "shame," "trust," and "support" all point toward the possibility of recounting a compelling *story* about the human *meanings* of communication networks and innovation. But the decision to focus on survey data rather than the descriptions, complaints, anecdotes, and other stories told in the interviews, and especially the decision to "de-mean" the data run fundamentally counter to the assumptions inherent in the "story" metaphor. In order actually to "storify" these empirical data into a theoretical narrative, Albrecht and her colleagues would have had to treat the data much differently. It may be possible for readers intimately familiar with these data analysis strategies and tactics to move from the graphic and tabular displays in Albrecht's chapter to understandings of "the essential stories of personal identity, institutional development, sheer survival, and life." But I do not believe that most readers will readily and fully accomplish this translation.

In short, the story metaphor demands its own set of data gathering, data analysis, and theorizing moves. If a theorist is to take the metaphor seriously she or he might want to work toward developing an account that reads and may be assessed as, a story.

On the other hand, a theorist might find the "argument" metaphor more compelling, as Cappella does. Assuming this metaphor is construed as what Dan O'Keefe (1977) calls Argument 2 not Argument 1—as process of arguing not a specific case constructed to win a debate—then the theorist will approach his or her enterprise very much as Cappella does. There will be relatively little emphasis on closure—treating a question as no longer needing to be asked—certainly—accepting an answer as absolute and final—or control—privileging accounts that appear to be successfully deterministic. Instead, theory-building will be viewed as operating "in the realm of the circumstantial, the plausible, and the argumentative;" theoretical claims will be assessed by content- and context-bound "standards of accepted knowledge within the field of study;" and theoretical formulations will ultimately be accepted or rejected as a result of "deliberations not unlike those carried out . . . in serious debates of public policy." Whichever metaphor is employed, however, it seems reasonable to expect that theorizing follow its lead. When theory is viewed as a narrative, then data and analysis should be used to storify; when theory is viewed as argument, then works should be designed to contribute to at least one of the relevant ongoing, unfinished conversations.

SOME FRUITS OF THIS THEORIZING AND SOME REMAINING ISSUES

The previous paragraphs raise issues related to these theorists' *philosophies* of inquiry. Whether contemporary social science should emulate the natural sciences, the humanities, or critical and postmodern perspectives; whether theorists should foreground the processes they engage in or the products they produce; and whether theories ought to be assessed as stories or arguments are all questions about the presuppositions guiding theoretical work, and philosophy has traditionally been viewed by many as the systematic critique of presuppositions like these. The same philosophical lens that offers a view of how these theorists do their work can also provide some insight into the claims they make. In the remaining pages of this chapter, I want to identify one or two of what I believe are each chapter's most significant theoretical contributions, contributions that emerge when this work is viewed philosophically. In addition, I propose to highlight one theoretical issue that I believe each chapter leaves incompletely addressed.

Communication Networks and Cognitive Structure

One of the most exciting moves made by Albrecht and her colleagues was to link the construct of face with decisions individuals make about the interactions in which they engage. As Albrecht explains, her research group was trying to figure out how people managed the uncertainty that the risk of innovation engendered, and they found that this risk was experienced as a threat to "one's self concept [which] is thus precariously exposed to others in the same political arena." This finding led them to extend their conceptual frame to include Goffman's (1967) analysis of face.

This move aptly exploits a trend in the contemporary human studies to explore the meaning and flesh out the significance of the claim made by, among others, philosopher Charles Taylor that all social theory both is anchored in and problematizes persons' *self-understandings*. Taylor (1985) treats this feature of theory as one which clearly distinguishes social from natural science. As he puts it,

> the big disanalogy with natural science lies in the nature of the common-sense understandings that [social] theory challenges, replaces or extends. There is always a pre-theoretical understanding of what is going on among the members of a society, which is formulated in the descriptions of self and other which are involved in the institutions and practices of that society. A society is among other things a set of institutions and practices, and these cannot exist and be carried on without certain self-understandings. (P. 92–93)

One reason why sociologist Erving Goffman's theorizing has had such a pervasive interdisciplinary impact is his awareness of this phenomenon, which he terms "face." Albrecht and her colleagues appropriate this construct and Scheff's (1990) extension of it to the claims that pride and shame are the principal social emotions operant in a social system. In a communication network, they reason, these manifestations of face may be managed by multiplexity, because multiplexity" can be a signal of the level of trust, certainty and stability multiplexity, between two people." The certainty provided by a multiplex tie can offset the uncertainty generated by an innovation message, so that the existence of multiplex ties in a network may enhance the network's ability to cope effectively with innovation. And the lynchpin in this connection between multiplexity and innovation is face, the communicators' self-definitions or self-understandings.

This is an exciting theoretical claim, at least in part because of the way it connects social structure and the phenomenological experience of organizational members. As Albrecht's and her colleagues' work demonstrates, network theory alone offers some important insights into how organizations cope with innovation. But it is difficult fully to exploit the story metaphor Albrecht proposes with only sociometric data, tables of talk frequency, and work compatibility scores. Rich and thick stories could be told, however, about organizational members' sense of the levels of trust, pride, and shame that characterize their relationships with superiors, subordinates, and co-workers.

On the other hand, one issue Albrecht's theoretical work leaves unaddressed concerns the political dimensions of organizational life. Increasing numbers of organizational scholars (Alvesson 1987; Deetz 1982, 1986, 1990, 1992; Deetz and Mumby 1990; Fischer and Sirianni 1984; Greenburg 1986; Mumby 1988; Stablein and Nord 1985) are insisting that any examination of organizational life must centrally acknowledge the power relationships inherent in human systems and should provide at least scholarly consumers—and preferably lay readers—tools for criticizing and resisting the dehumanizing effects of corporate hegemony. Deetz (1992) connects this critical thrust directly to issues of "face" and morality. "Organizational decisions, products, and practices," he argues, "have major effects on human development. Anything that influences the continued formation or deformation of the human character has ethical implications. . . . *Representation, communication,* and *morality* become mutually defining terms" (1992, 3).

Deetz appropriates from Foucault (1972, 1980) the distinction between the power *of* knowledge and power *in* knowledge, the latter of which enables one to view critically efforts to generalize and theorize about organizational communicating. From this perspective, he echoes Voegelin's argument that theory must "be an intrinsic part of experience itself" (66). Any efforts to test hypothesis or refine quantified methodologies "need to be complemented by a more basic understanding of the relations between theories and the world, relations of power and knowledge, and the relation of theories to real human communities" (68). In sum, Deetz maintains, communication theory

> should be grounded in the present social-historical context aimed at enhancing useful social responses to contemporary social issues that are themselves partially theoretically constructed. Such a theory is ultimately answerable to real community of actors rather than universal standards of truth. It must also grow out of that community's struggle to understand and respond to its actual historical context, though it cannot simply end there. In this sense neither a formal reconstructed normative science nor an ethnography of everyday-life theorizing will do . . . A necessary interactivity of social science, researched subjects, and audience community must be assumed. (Deetz 1992, 79)

From this critical perspective, organizational scholars and other intellectuals have the responsibilities to make explicit the political presuppositions that ground their research, to engage reflexively in self-critique, to collaborate with rather than exploit the organizational members they study, to challenge privileged interests, and to help organizational members create potent responses to problematic situations they experience.

Clearly, this critical research agenda contrasts sharply with much of what appears to motivate Albrecht and her colleagues. Just as clearly, there is room—and a need—in the discipline for diverse research programs, each of which wears its own set of blinders. But the larger community might at least ask all stripes of theorists more fully to take into account fundamentally different voices. As the comments by Deetz indicate, critical theorists offer arguments to support their decisions to privilege interpretation, critique, collaboration, and application over, for example, hypothesis testing and the development of propositions and axioms. Theorists employing non-critical perspectives might legitimately be expected similarly to explain their rationale for bracketing political concerns, deemphasizing power relationships, privileging objectivity over critique, and leaving application to teachers, consultants, and other "consumers." In short, if proponents of various approaches to theorizing could do a fuller job of taking into account the others' arguments, theoretical accounts of organizational life could be greatly enhanced.

Uncertainty Reduction

The most powerful aspect of Berger's and his colleagues' theoretical work is also the most basic: their research indicates that uncertainty reduction is a truly pervasive social phenomenon. As Berger notes in his introduction and conclusion, whether communicative activity takes place in face-to-face interaction contexts or mass-mediated venues, this activity appears clearly to consist at least in part of efforts to manage uncertainty. And since uncertainty has such potentially negative effects as "failing to reach instrumental goals, being misunderstood, or angering, hurting, or embarrassing others," "managing" such uncertainty most often means *reducing* it.

Berger's report of the development and testing of his theoretical perspective illustrates its remarkable range of application. Earkt studies focused on a narrow data base consisting of transcripts of initial conversations that were filled with what Altman and Taylor (1973) termed "superficial" questions about home towns, role identities, and current living situations that seemed to coalesce into a kind of extended greeting "ritual." Berger and his colleagues persuasively argued that such patterned exchanges were in fact consequential and convenient social moves that were designed to develop "the level of control necessary to achicvc one's instrumental and interaction goals" and that functioned to reduce initial uncertainty. Then the theory branched out in various directions. Some studies examined the role uncertainty reduction plays in established relationships. Others identified the "passive," "active," and "interactive" strategies persons' use "on line, as interaction episodes unfold" to acquire information to reduce their uncertainty. Still other studies focused on strategies individuals use to avoid revealing information that interlocutors want to acquire in order to reduce their uncertainty. But the most challenging and productive recent direction of development has been toward how cognitive plans function to reduce uncertainty.

This move links Berger's and his colleagues' research efforts, not only with those of other communication researchers (e.g., Greene 1990; Tracy and Coupland 1990; Cappella, this volume), but also with the research programs of some of very highly-respected and widely-cited cognitive scientists (e.g., Miller, Galanter, and Pribram 1960; Schank and Abelson 1977). As Berger explains, he and his colleagues have studied effects of plan complexity on fluency and the aversion to contingent planning. They have also tested the applicability of the *hierarchy hypothesis* to planning to determine "how individuals go about altering plans when their plans fail to bring about desired end-states." Some of their studies suggest that individuals may make adaptations to goal failures that are relatively conservative, and that framing and reframing are used to help cope with frustrated plans. In pursuing this line of research, Berger and his colleagues have appropriated insights from the facework studies of Goffman and Brown and Levinson, cognitive development research, urban and transportation planning studies, and research on "group think." All of these extensions and appropriations demonstrate the powerful range of applicability of uncertainty reduction theory. No developing communication theory I am aware of has this breadth of scope.

At the same time, a look at the other side of the scope "coin" can highlight one of the questions left open by the current state of this research program. Contemporary metatheorists emphasize, as I have already noted, that theories are perspectives or approaches rather than representations of objective truth. This means that theories reflect their authors' cultural, epistemological, methodological, professional, and even personal biases, and that theories can most appropriately be evaluated by assessing their utility, productivity, credibility, and consequent plausibility rather than the degree to which they accurately capture "the way things really are." There is a significant difference between the claim that a theory is highly "accurate" (that is, that it closely corresponds with some features of objective reality) and the claim that it offers a fruitful interpretation or account of a range of significant and puzzling phenomena. Partly because of the intuitively broad scope of uncertainty reduction theory, Berger and his colleagues sometimes fail to acknowledge this distinction, and the result is that they sometimes rather idiosyncratically read some sources and overstate some claims.

Early in Berger's chapter, he asserts the "*postulate* [italics added] . . . that in all social interactions some measure of uncertainty exists." A "postulate" is defined as a proposition taken as self-evident without proof as a basis for reasoning. Thus, technically speaking, at this point Berger is appropriately tentative; theorizing has to begin somewhere, and he chooses this claim as his starting point. But later he maintains that "the assertion that individuals involved in social interactions . . . must reduce their uncertainties about each other . . . seems unassailable," and he concludes that his chapter "attempted to *demonstrate* [italics added] that uncertainty is a fundamental feature of communicative activity. . . ." An "unassailable . . . demonstration" is considerably more than a "postulate," and the reader may legitimately ask whether Berger's and his colleagues' research and their interpretations and appropriations of other theory and research warrant this level of claim. In other words, from inside the uncertainty-reductions system, the facework, politeness strategies, compliance-gaining, urban planning, and cognitive structures research might all look as if it is in fact focused on uncertainty-reduction strategies. But one might legitimately wonder how Goffman (1967), Brown and Levinson (1978), or even Greene (1990) would respond to Berger's appropriation of their work. Discursive efforts to preserve self and other's face, for example, may conceivably be interpreted as uncertainty reduction efforts. But only from inside this perspective, only given Berger's initial *postulate*. If one begins from Goffman's starting point, and uncertainty-reduction reading of the relevant observations is both reductive and distorting. As a result, some important insights of the original theoretical and empirical work are lost and others are reconfigured in terms the original theorist might find difficult to recognize. This problem could be minimized were there a more consistent acknowledgment in Berger's and his colleagues' work that they are constructing an argument or story rather than a demonstration.

Berger does sometimes phrase his conclusions with appropriate tentativeness as, for example, when he summarizes, "it would seen premature to dismiss uncertainty as a potentially important correlate or relationship outcomes." But at other times he appears to have become so powerfully convinced of the efficacy of his perspective that some of his claims dangerously approach True Believer status. I would find his theorizing even more powerful if he were to present it more consistently and clearly as *one* fruitful perspective, *one* plausible and even sometimes compelling argument about how some aspects of communication may be understood to unfold.

Automated Patterns of Face-to-Face Human Interaction

As I have already indicated, one of the most useful and productive features of Cappella's chapter is the frame he crafts around his description of the current status of discrepancy-arousal theory. As he explains, the theory itself focuses narrowly on the cognitive activation aroused by a perceived discrepancy between one interlocutor's expectations and his or her perceptions of his or her partner's behavior. A perceived discrepancy triggers arousal, which in turn causes affect, which then leads to approach or avoidance behaviors that can be read as adaptive strategies. So even though the theory is narrowly focused, it has ultimately to do with mutual adaptation, "arguably the essential characteristic of every interpersonal interaction."

Cappella could have begun his chapter with the literature review that supports his argument about the centrality of mutual adaptation. Or he could have emphasized what he calls "the minutiae" of discrepancy-arousal theory. But instead, he first explained in some detail important features of his philosophy of inquiry and his approach to theorizing. This compositional strategy provided his reader with a perspective that can be applied not only to his chapter but also to other theoretical formulations. Robert Craig (1993) has explained why such a move is today a necessity rather than an option or luxury: When scholars in the human studies believed in the unity of science, presuppositions were relatively straightforward and widely understood and accepted. But today, fundamental questions about theorizing are so open—in both communication and the other human studies—that readers are confronted with a wide range of philosophies of inquiry, even within a compactly-defined research tradition. As a result, they usually have to scan reference lists and read between the lines of introductory and concluding remarks in order to determine what the theorist believes about, for example, the role of causality in this theoretical program and the connections between these and rival theoretical claims. As a result, theoretical discussions without any metatheorizing risk considerable misunderstanding. Cappella uses the early pages of his essay to minimize this problem. A reader may disagree with the position he takes, but at least one can be confident that extensions, questions, or criticisms address relevant concerns in terms the theorist would readily understand. All this can materially enhance the fruitfulness of the ongoing conversation.

One important shortcoming of Cappella's and his colleagues' theoretical program, at least at this stage of its development, is that its tight scope often decreases the significance of its findings. These researchers have applied formidable intellectual and methodological energy to the task of narrowing their focus to the molecules, or even atoms, of cognitive functions that allegedly cause communication behaviors. Partly as a direct result of this narrowing, they have often produced findings of limited newsworthiness. Consider, for example, what a layperson might predict about speech tempo or personal space invasions. If one questioned a random sample of members of the cultures who participated in Cappella's research, how many different answers would one likely to get to the following questions:

> "When one conversation partner talks faster, is the other member of the pair likely to talk faster or slower?" And
>
> "When one partner invades the other's personal space, is the person whose space has been invaded likely to move closer or father away?"

Do communication theorists need a research enterprise as powerful as the one Cappella and his colleagues have designed to confirm that "speech tempo between partners is typically reciprocal while invasions of personal space typically produce strong compensatory reactions," that "when the partners are intimates, the region of acceptance [of personal space violations] is widened and violations of personal space norms are experienced as effectively positive and approach results," and that "people adjust certain of their behaviors (the automatic ones) to those of their partners and that these adjustments are consequential to the individuals and their relationship"?

Of course, one can argue that "obvious" findings only appear so *after* they have been confirmed by careful research, or that although lay intuitions about tempo and space may have been confirmed, other lay intuitions won't be. But one can also argue that the situations or contexts that humans inhabit are not experiences as made-up-of-atoms-or-molecules and therefore cannot most efficaciously be explained, understood, or modified primarily via *analysis*—the process of dividing them into their constituent parts. It may be preferable to study human communication from various molar, rather than molecular, perspectives, especially if one ultimately views communication as, in Craig's (1989) terms, a *practical* discipline, one ultimately concerned with *application*. In other words, one could argue that, when theorizing about human communication, there is an inescapably direct correlation between narrowness of focus and potential triviality of findings.

It also appears that, as the experimental designs Cappella describes were refined to take into account more variables, findings got less conclusive. When the self-monitoring personality variable was introduced and Cappella studied high and low self-monitors' compensations to proximity, "the fully crossed interaction between distance and self monitoring did not obtain." In other words, some results confirmed the theoretical predictions, but some did not. A test using high and low sensation seekers produced similar results: "the desired interaction between sensation seeking and distance on nonverbal affiliative response did not materialize, although the means were in the correct directions." Cappella argues that partial confirmation is often an outcome of testing "networks of propositions." But this rationale may be viewed as acknowledgment of the limitations of a theory focusing on cognitive and behavioral atoms or molecules. Just as with Berger's and his colleagues' work, scope conditions cut at least two ways.

In short, discrepancy rousal theory still faces formidable challenges of application. Cappella notes that psychologists Levinson and Gottman (1983, 1985) have studics the degree to which "convariation in arousal during interaction is predictive of marital satisfaction and stability several years later." Perhaps it is reasonable to hope that cognitive communication theorizing in the late-1990s could make similar moves toward pragmatic applicability.

Adaptation via Message Design

Two sources of the power of O'Keefe's theorizing are her willingness and ability to attend to *context*, and her focus on the "negotiation of social selves."

Early philosophies of mind and social scientific theories linked human behavior to invariant structures—e.g., "faculties of the mind," "psychological needs," or "attitudes"—that allegedly were accessed or functioned to produce desired outcomes. One mark of late twentieth-century social theorizing is sensitivity to the context in which cognitive structures or response strategies are applied. Theorists are increasingly aware of human adaptive abilities, and theories increasingly take into account how decision making, persuading, informing, greeting, promising, developing intimacy, arguing, and other consequential human activities are modified to fit their specific contexts. O'Keefe explicitly develops this line of reasoning to its culmination in what she views as the developmentally most sophisticated "design logic," the "rhetorical," which involves a unique kind of reasoning: "The speaker (a) projects a state of affairs in which both parties play their roles, without conflict or offense; (b) determines the differences between that state of affairs *and the present situation;* and (c) attempts *to change the hearer's representation of the situation to conform to the desired state of affairs.*" In other words, the rhetorical design logic construct helps explain why and how some communicators both adapt to and modify aspects of the context or situation they are a part of.

The significance of context-dependence surfaces at several points in O'Keefe's chapter. For example, before developing her Message Design Model, she explains why she prefers it over the dominant explanation of message variation currently in the research literature, the Strategy Choice Model. According to the latter model, "messages producers have a list of possible types of messages to employ in any type of communication situation; message production is a process of selecting the appropriate type of message and then instantiating the abstract message format as a specific message." One problem with this type of model is that it cannot explain different responses to a low diversity task; another is that it assumes a process of genuinely rational message selection that "cannot be done on the basis of its abstract type," because "what can be said in a given situation depends on what is true (or can be true) of that situation, and so messages must be designed and evaluated in relationship to the specifics of a given situation." By contrast, a primary feature of Message Design Models is that they view "what is actually said, and how it is said . . . [as] a function of processes that modify and elaborate the message so that it will better serve the message producer's [situated] goals."

O'Keefe's observations confirmed the intuitive recognition that these goals vary, and that not everybody adapts messages to specific situations as effectively as everybody else. The focus among O'Keefe's constructivist colleagues on cognitive complexity influenced her theoretical account of these differences in adaptive competence. As she explains, she observed that people who were less cognitively complex used certain types of messages much less frequently than those who were more cognitively complex. She also discovered that some messages appeared to reflect a design strategy "different in kind" from the ones other theorists had described, "a strategy that cannot be described within any model that assumes that communication situations consist of a set of fixed parameters that dictate goals and in turn dictate actions, since it depends on altering the situation to fit the action to be performed."

As she describes this "rhetorical" design strategy or logic, O'Keefe prominently integrates her own version of the same powerful theoretical construct that Albrecht thematized in her chapter: "face" (Goffman 1967), "self-understanding" (Taylor 1985), or, in O'Keefe's words, "social self," and this is a second source of the power of O'Keefe's theorizing. The rhetorical message design logic, she writes, "reflects a view of communication as the creation and negotiation of social selves and situations. . . . For the rhetorical communicator, social reality is created by what and how something is said or written. . . ." So far O'Keefe's research program has not focused on this "negotiation of social selves" process. But her move toward this dynamic does open the door to a connection between O'Keefe's theorizing and several other cutting-edge research programs, including efforts by self-labeled "social" and "radical constructivists." Some of these theorists are closely studying "the social construction of emotions, persons, interpersonal relationships, etc. in the language used by individuals; that is, in their *discourse*" (Krippendorff 1991, 115). Family communication researcher Jane Jorgensen (1991, 1992), for example, examines how research interviewers and family interviewees co-construct one another in the interview situation. She views the identity each manifests as an "interactional achievement" (Pollner and Emerson 1988), worked out in verbal-nonverbal talk.

John Shotter (1984, 1991, 1993a, 1993b) is currently perhaps the leading communication theorist and empirical researcher working out what he calls a "rhetorical-responsive version of social constructivism" (1993b, 2–16). Social constructivism, he argues, focuses "upon people's use of certain ways of talking to construct different kinds of social relationship" (1993b, 6). Part of Shotter's empirical work explores how interactive pronoun use helps accomplish identity in conversations (Shotter 1984). In a move O'Keefe would probably not follow, Shotter explicitly situates his approach as a development *beyond* cognitive science and the behavioral sciences to a kind of "practical hermeneutics" (1984; 1993b, 6), and a development beyond the view of language as referential or representational to an account of language as co-constitutive.

At a much lower level of sophistication, my coauthor and I have integrated a simplified account of collaborative identity development into the basic interpersonal communication course under the heading "negotiating selves" (Stewart and Logan 1993, 1997). Basic course students find it useful to explore how principles and skills of disclosure and listening get applied in the identity-negotiation process. Conversations routinely embody, for example, interlocutors' choices about whether to *attend to* the other's unique features, relevant choices, and affect, and whether to *disclose* aspects of one's own uniqueness, choices, and feelings. The social—cultural—interpersonal quality of the communication between these interlocutors can be usefully understood as an outcome of these interdependent and changing choices. Thus, students can begin to explore relationships between specific verbal-nonverbal identity-negotiation moves and the kind or quality of communication they experience.

In short, O'Keefe's focus on adaptation to specific situations combined with her as-yet-undeveloped thematization of "the creation and negotiation of social selves" connect her theorizing to some other important programs in the human studies and materially enhance the possible range of application of her theoretical and empirical work.

One remaining question I have about O'Keefe's theorizing concerns the degree to which her fundamental view of communication affirms or moves beyond a representationalist view of "message." Issues of this sort that are raised in O'Keefe's work also surface in a variety of related literatures, including not only Shotter's (1993b) discussion of representation but also Hans-Georg Gadamer's comments on the concept of "expression" and some Artificial Intelligence researchers' critiques of "the language of thought." One of Gadamer's (1989) goals in *Truth and Method* is to distance his account of understanding from psychologistic accounts anchored in the construct of "empathy." "Let us remember," he writes near the end of this book, "that understanding what someone says is not an achievement of empathy in which one divines the inner life of the speaker" (1989, 489). Rather, interlocutors (or, for Gadamer, reader and text) engage in a dynamic of linguistic play that leads them to produce (rather than reproduce) a negotiated sense or comprehension. Gadamer underscores his dissatisfaction with psychologistic theorizing in his discussion of the concept of "expression" (Gadamer 1989, 502–4). For moderns, he argues, the term "expression" has a decisively "subjectivist element," in that "an expression is the expression of something interior, namely of an experience (*Erlebnis*)" (503). This account of expression maintains the cartesian dichotomy between body and mind in that bodily actions are often read as "external" manifestation of "internal" states. Gadamer maintains that Aristotle and other early rhetoricians recognized that "an expression is never merely a sign that points back to something else, something within; rather, what is expressed is itself present in the expression—e.g., anger is present in angry furrows in the face" (504). Gadamer's point is familiar to critics of linear, conduit models of communication: It is misleading to view verbal-nonverbal discourse as simply or primarily a manifestation of some internal state that can be transmitted "into" listeners or receivers of the discourse. Such models are parasitic on the intuitively appealing but conceptually problematic divisions between "thoughts or ideas" and "expressions" of them.

In some contemporary Artificial Intelligence literature this same set of issues surfaces in debates over the efficacy of "the language of thought" (LOT) (Fodor 1975, 1987; Davies 1991). Artificial Intelligence researchers who subscribe to what is often termed the "symbolic paradigm" argue that language units (e.g., words, or speech acts) may plausibly and fruitfully be viewed as symbols of some ultimately neural events that they *represent*. On this view, language "expresses" thoughts. The process is much more complex and subtle than John Locke envisioned, but he was basically right about the relationship between mental events and linguistic ones. Connectionist theorists, on the other hand, do not believe that current descriptions of the brain support this view of language; in brief, "the connectionist paradigm is opposed to the language of thought" (Davies 1991, 229).

One central issue in this debate between symbolic and connectionist AI theorists is the efficacy of the fundamentally representational view of cognition that grounds LOT theories. Serious questions about the accuracy of representational models have been raised by some neurophysiological data tracking the status of individual neural nodes. For example, it can be shown that a certain node is always ON whenever the subject being considered is "dogs," and never ON—or ON very weakly—when the subject is "cats," whereas another node is ON for "cats" and not for "dogs." Originally, data like these appeared to support a representational view of cognition, because it seemed that certain neural nodes were representationally correlated with certain semantic features which could then be articulated in discourse—the LOT model. But, as one author explains, "the best reason for *not* calling the dog-active node the dog symbol is that you can 'kill' or disable that node and the system will go right on discriminating dogs, remembering about dogs, and so on, with at most a slight degradation in performance" (Dennet 1991, 24). Moreover, other nearby nodes which appeared to be operating almost randomly picked up some of the disabled node's functioning, so those "noisy" nodes are also involved in the process. Neural system functions, in other words, overlap, or are distributed in parallel and interconnected ("connectionist") networks, not in the simple linear structure prescribed by the symbolic/LOT paradigm.

Partly as a result of data like these, critics of early artificial intelligence efforts argue that the "fathers of AI made a bold conjecture, and encountered an equally uncompromising refutation" (Boden 1991, 11). It has become abundantly clear, some theorists argue, that symbolic AI research cannot model either common sense reasoning or flexible pattern matching. And these are significant failures. In fact, Boden (1991) asserts, rarely in the history of science "has there been such an expensive blind alley. The only comfort to be drawn from nearly 40 years of AI research is that it has finally been shown to be a dead end. The abject failure of GOFAI [Good Old Fashioned Artificial Intelligence] has at least spurred the investigation of alternative computational approaches" (11). Connectionist theorists differ in the alternatives they propose, but many are convinced that the folk-psychology language of thought model is not supported by current understandings of cognitive functioning.

Literatures like these, which are obviously much more complex than this brief review indicates,[1] raise questions about the models of language and communication that underlie descriptions of *message* design and production. The central question, of course, is what constitutes a "message," specifically, to what degree messages are viewed as representationally or symbolically linked to thoughts. On the first page of her chapter, O'Keefe notes that, from the perspective of a Message Design Model, messages "are seen as assemblies of features that have complex relationships to multiple message functions." This characterization suggests what messages "do," but leaves undescribed what they "are." Much later in the chapter, she explains the relationship between messages and the cognitive or logical features of her model as

> like the relationship between an equation and the curve it describes. It would not be proper to say that the equation is one of the "characteristics" of the curve. Similarly, it would not be proper to say that the equation "causes" the curve. . . . what we make explicit in describing a design logic probably has no identifiable correlate under a human skull, but may nonetheless be a true description of the form-function relationships in a set of messages produced by a person. (P. 111)

The specific view of message production implicit in her theory, she continues, sees message production "as the transformation of situation representations into expressions. . . . in general, messages originate in speaker's representations of situations . . . as thoughts that are available for expression." This sounds very much like a LOT perspective.

When O'Keefe reports on empirical work she clarifies that what she concretely means by "message" is a response to the researcher's request that the subject "write out what they would say [for example] to Ron; that is, they [were] asked to provide a message and not just a general description of the approach they would take" (O'Keefe 1988, 93). So "message" in this research means a written self-report of what one would say in a certain situation. The appendix to O'Keefe's study reveals that the messages produced ranged from "You asshole. I knew you wouldn't do your work. I'm going to see that you are fired" (1988, 100) to ten-sentence attempts to save everyone's face and rescue the troubled project outlined in the research scenario. In a report of another study (O'Keefe and Shepherd 1987), much is made of the importance of "exchanges" between interlocutors, but the actual data analysis is performed on "lines of action within arguments (1987, 403), which consist if utterances that one person produced.

The literatures briefly sketched here indicate why O'Keefe's treatment of the construct "message" may be problematic. First, most of O'Keefe's and her colleagues' work studies written data and thus does not take into account all the paralinguistic and physical phenomena that are included in actual verbal/nonverbal (both oral and written) communicating. Another problem as critics of constructivist research have noted, is that these studies focus not on the event of language/communication but on one interlocutor's actions. Thus, they may generate information of psychological or perhaps proto-communicational interest. But they do not focus directly on the event that engages *both* or *all* communicators. This appears primarily to be the result of the assumption that talk consists essentially of individual utterances that are expressions of thoughts and are strategically configured and instrumentally performed to accomplish individual goals—that is, products of message-design logics. This way of approaching communication can clearly generate some important insights. But it is also limited by its biases. Like Searle's Speech Act Theory—which O'Keefe calls "an explicit and formal message design logic"—O'Keefe's program is fundamentally monologic. It views communicating as a series of individual utterances rather than an event that unfolds as it is co-constructed (Leeds-Hurwitz 1992; Shotter 1993b). It also foregrounds instrumentality by treating discourse as a means to its speaker's implicitly or explicitly understood ends. Even if, as O'Keefe notes, the relationship between "thought" and "message" is not causal, messages are still treated as means to (intentional) ends. Thus, questions arise about the role of intent in the model of communication underlying O'Keefe's program (Stamp and Knap 1990). For all these reasons, this research program currently leaves its central construct—"message"—underdetermined, which makes it vulnerable to criticisms about the construct, "expression," the theory's apparent representationalist assumptions, and its picture of the relationship between language and thought.

Speech Codes Theory

Like O'Keefe's theorizing, Philipsen's concentrates on communication that is *situated* or context-dependent. But Philipsen develops this initial orientation into an approach with more social significance than that attached to any of the other theorists represented here, and this is a significant positive feature of his work. In his first sentences he emphasizes that he is interested in connections between people as they "exist in a particular time and place," connections that are "situated" because they "are contingent upon the milieu in which and the resources with which they are constructed." These resources he calls "speech codes." Thus, speech codes are situated, public, and discursive, and a theory of speech codes is a theory of the ways individuals marshal their public, discursive resources to cope with the opportunities and challenges they face in particular situations.

One general strength of speech codes theory is that it functions as a powerful antidote to ethnocentrism. One might argue that this is obvious, and that it is a feature of all anthropological and cultural studies. But each generation of consumers of theory and research appears to need to be reminded of the perspectival and consequently biased nature of widely-adopted views of "the way things obviously are." Philipsen's report about the impotence in Teamsterville of his previously unquestioned, "theoretically and commonsensically legitimated" approach to communication based on Carl Rogers, Irving Lee, and Kurt Lewin underscores this feature of theory-application. And his and his colleagues' studies of Nacirema culture offer liberating insights into widely taken-for-granted and therefore unreflectively privileged ways of speaking.

Philipsen's theorizing can also be understood as support for the most substantive and enlightened versions of the current efforts to honor multiple voices and encourage diversity. The first of his four basic questions "has prompted the search for evidence of distinctiveness, across cultures, in the resources people deploy to invent, characterize, interpret, and rationalize their communicative conduct." And proposition one asserts "that *wherever there is a distinctive culture, there is to be found a distinctive speech code*." To the degree that such codes are located and found to have force in social life, they obviously must be acknowledged, at least in contacts with their users. Moreover, as Philipsen's proposition five indicates, each identified speech code is assumed to control "the form of discourse about the intelligibility, prudence, and morality of communicative conduct." This means that cultures are initially understood as equally systematic, analogously coherent, similarly prudential, and all concerned with issues of morality. This is clearly *not* to say that any (encultured) individual must *value* all other cultures the same way one values one's own. But it is to say that members of each identified culture occupy, as it were, their own argumentative ground and therefore at least initially deserve that this integrity be respected. The social and work lives of both theoreticians and laypersons could be enhanced if we were able consistently to apply this principle.

These socially significant features of Philipsen's theoretical program get efficacy and epistemological purchase from the assertively empirical stance he and his colleagues take. Extensive *in situ* observation is a prominent feature of each study in this program. In the best social scientific tradition, investigators attempt to observe unobtrusively and as objectively as possible. Moreover, researchers move systematically toward focusing observations not just on general features of the culture but on specific uses of "a term or notion about communicative conduct." Ways of speaking are described concretely and specifically, for example, as choices made in the *madre* form of address, expressions of the framing statement, "I'll tell you *dugri*. . . ," or uses of clusters of terms contrasting "real communication" with "mere talk." This drive toward empirical specificity enhances both researcher and reader confidence in member checks and other strategies and tactics applied to test the validity of findings. Philipsen accurately notes that this empirical ground makes formulations of speech codes appropriately subject to empirical disconfirmation, "that is, new fieldwork data or the re-interpretation of extant data could lead to a revision of the formulation that was proposed."

Like some other features of theorizing, however, Philipsen's and his colleagues' objectivist, empirical stance can be said to cut more than one way. Along with Albrecht and her colleagues, Philipsen's group is vulnerable to charges from critical theorists that they incompletely take into account the ways they participate, not in objective observations, but "in a series of multivocal reflexive interactions that are saturated with power relations and struggles over the meaning of cultural identity" (West 1993, 209). Some critical theorists emphasize the claim that the quest for objectivity is naive, even when postulated as an ideal. Jackson (1989) argues, for example, that ethnographers confronted with "the arduous conditions of fieldwork, the ambiguity of conversations in a foreign tongue, differences of temperament, age, and gender between ourselves and our informants" cling to notions of "objectivity" and "specific method" primarily to preserve a threatened sense of self in the midst of disorienting situations (1989, 3). Other critical ethnographers accent the potentially and actually destructive impact that ethnographic activities and reports can have on the cultures and people studied. As Conquergood notes, ethnographic writings "are not innocent descriptions through which the other is transparently revealed" (1991, 191) but *rhetorical* constructions with significant political and social effects (Geertz 1988). From this viewpoint, "The future of ethnography lies in the ability of researchers to understand how Others articulate their sense-making of their lives, while at the same time having the perspicacity to reveal the relations of power in which these Others' sense-making is articulated" (West 1993, 214).

In a contribution to this debate, Philipsen (1991) acknowledges that ethnographers should engage in "the careful study and ethnographic appreciation of many discourses, including, on occasions, discourses of power" (329). But critical theorists argue that such a position overlooks demonstrations by Foucault and others that power inheres in *all* discourse, prominently including "objective" and "scientific" academic writing, and that ethical and humane standards demand that such power relations be acknowledged, thematized, and, insofar as it is possible, equalized. One might say that critical ethnographers are demanding that Philipsen's proposition five be reflexively applied to the objectivist ethnographic enterprise itself, so that both informants in and consumers of this research could determine how these *researchers'* "shared speech code" predicts, explains, and controls *their* "discourse about the intelligibility, prudence, and morality of "their own communicative conduct."

Philipsen concludes that speech codes theory should be tested by assessing whether its use "will continue, as it has in the past, to stimulate discoveries about particular ways of speaking" and whether the generalizations it proposes "stand the test of further work." It seems to me incontrovertibly true that the ethnographic work he reviews has stimulated important discoveries about particular ways of speaking. It also seems true, however, that some critical ethnographic work has indeed tested these studies' methods and findings and has found that some of them overlook important philosophical inconsistencies and entail political and social theses and policies that remain unarticulated by objectivist ethnographic researchers. Perhaps in some future work Philipsen and his colleagues could both respond directly to critical theorists' assessments of the power relationships in objectivist ethnography and integrate more reflexivity into their own practices. The result could be a theory of speech codes that is even more responsive to the breadth of metatheoretical insights now available.

CONCLUSION

The chapters in this volume demonstrate the robust health of communication theorizing by displaying some ways in which creative and insightful people blend concepts and empirical observations into interpretive and explanatory generalizations. Each chapter demonstrates what it means to carry out a research *program,* how collaboration can enhance discovery, and how aspects of narrow, midrange, and broad theories can be fruitfully synthesized. Both inexperienced and seasoned communication theorists can profit from these accounts of how theorizing actually gets accomplished.

For me, four conclusions emerge from a review of the theorizing in this book: First, as most researchers in the trenches readily admit, theorizing is not a neat and tidy, linear process of consistent incremental progress. It is a manifestly human endeavor, which is to say that it is often hit-and-miss, two steps forward and one step back, a process more cluttered by incomplete explorations of conceptual and practical cul-de-sacs than punctuated by Aha! experiences. So why don't virtually all theorists give up the chase? Because they are driven by the moral convictions that increased understanding is genuinely possible and that the topic or focus of their theorizing is too vitally important to abandon. Everyone who profits from their work can be grateful that each of these theorists has been infected or seduced by a compelling vision. We can also be assured that our own, often stumbling efforts mirror theirs.

Second, communication theorists are sometimes leading and often joining a widespread movement in the academy to affirm the ontological significance of speech communication. Postmodern philosophers underscore the tight link between human communicating and human being (Schrag 1986). Sociologists and psychologists explore how humans co-construct "conversational realities" (Gergen 1985; Shotter 1993). Medical researchers correlate physical health with interpersonal well-being (e.g., Lynch 1977, 1985). In short, many scholars and consumers of scholarship are becoming increasingly aware that communication involves much more than the epistemological processes of idea-transmission and emotional expression. Human communication embodies human ontology, which is to say that how humans talk and listen helps determine who we are. As especially Albrecht, O'Keefe, and Philipsen demonstrate in this volume, larger organizations, smaller networks, larger cultures, and smaller speech communities are all sites for the enormously consequential processes of discursive, verbal-and-nonverbal identity-negotiation.

Third, there is a fundamental difference between, on the one hand, studying communication as a series of actions or interactions that are influenced or even determined by cognitive or psychological variables and processes and, on the other hand, studying communication as a thoroughly situated and co-constructed accomplishment. From the former point of view, research and theorizing should work to explain communicatively relevant information-processing strategies and tactics that are *influenced* by perceptions of others, but that ultimately occur "inside" *one* person, or patterns that are reactive and responsive to external stimuli and that in turn cause communication behaviors, but that are clearly and purely *cognitive*. A version of this perspective seems to me to underlie at least Berger's, Cappella's, and O'Keefe's chapters in this volume. From the latter point of view, communication research and theorizing can most fruitfully attend to the co-constructed events themselves, not simply by analyzing them into units of verbal and nonverbal behaviors but by articulated their radically situated, fundamentally collaborative, and thoroughly emergent properties. A version of this perspective appears to underlie Philipsen's program. Albrecht's interest in "patterns of sociation" inclines her in the second of these two directions, while her focus on "cognitive structure" tends her toward the first.

Some communication scholars argue that, until this field's research adopts the second perspective, our theorists will continue to be justly viewed as conceptually and methodologically parasitic on (and therefore subordinate to) our colleagues in psychology and sociology. Others argue that it is short-sighted and naive to attempt to ignore cognitive processes, and that, if and when it is necessary, *communication* research on and theorizing about such processes can easily be distinguished from complementary work in other disciplines. I believe that the goals of scholarship are best served by encouraging multiple theoretical voices. Confronting issues of disciplinary identity, however, may sometimes require a narrower view. In any case, these two perspectives might usefully serve to distinguish among theoretical programs pursued by communication scholars.

Finally, it appears to me to be increasingly difficult to ignore the political dimensions of communication theorizing. As the best public speaking teachers have always known, ideas have consequences, and theoretical ideas can be among the most consequential. I acknowledge that scholarship is clearly different from journalism, even though they are both empirical, and that part of the difference has to do with the critical distance and "objectivity" that marks scholarly observation. But it also seems apparent that, insofar as theories are human creations that are interpreted and applied by other humans, they are imbued by the biases of their creators and affect the lives of those who consume them. This means they embody power differences and, in their interpretation and application, they help preserve or change power relationships. All this is to say that they are *political.* Since the Enlightenment, the myth of the objectivity of science has enabled communication and other social theorists to avoid confronting these political dimensions of their work—which helps explain why no theorist in this volume clearly acknowledges the politics of his or her theorizing. Yet, it is probably time, as critical theorists insist, to replace the Enlightenment myth with a more responsible, active acknowledgment of the human consequences of developing communication theories.

NOTE

1. For example, some connectionist theorists view their paradigm as also representational. See Boden 1991.

REFERENCES

Albrecht, T. L., & Hall, B. J. (1991). The role of personal relationships in organizational innovation: Communication patterns among scientists and professionals. *Communication Monographs 58,* 273–288.

Altman, D. A., and Taylor, D. (1973). *Social penetration: The development of interpersonal relationships.* New York: Holt, Rinehart, and Winston.

Alveson, M. (1987). Organizations, culture, and ideology. *International Studies of Management and Organizations 17,* 4–18.

Apel, K-O. (1984). *Understanding and explanation: A Transcendental-Pragmatic Perspective.* Georgia Warnke (Trans.) Cambridge, Mass.: MIT Press.

Baxter, L. (1992). Interpersonal communication as dialogue: A response to the "social approaches" forum. *Communication Theory 4,* 330–337.

Baxter, L. (1988). A dialectical perspective on communication strategies in relationship development. In S. Duck (Ed.), *Handbook of personal relationships* (pp. 257–273). New York: Wiley.

Berger, C. R. (1991). Communication theories and other curios. *Communication Monographs 58,* 101–113.

Berger, C. R. (1992). Curiouser and curiouser curios. *Communication Monographs 59,* 101–107.

Berger, C. R., & Chaffee, S. H. (Eds.) (1987). *Handbook of communication science.* Newbury Park, Cal.: Sage.

Boden, M. (1991). Horses of a different color? In W. Ramsey, S. P. Stitch, & D. E. Rumelhart (Eds.), *Philosophy and Connectionist Theory* (pp. 3–20). Hillsdale, N.J.: Lawrence Erlbaum Associates.

Bohman, J. (1991). *New philosophy of social science: Problems of indeterminacy.* Cambridge. Mass.: MIT Press.

Brown, P. & Levinson, S. C. (1978). Universals in language usage: Politeness phenomena. In E. N. Goody (Ed.), *Questions and politeness* (pp. 56–289). Cambridge: Cambridge University Press.

Conquergood, D. (1991). Rethinking ethnography: Towards a critical cultural politics. *Communication Monographs 58,* 179–194.

Craig, R. T. (1989). Communication as a practical discipline. In B. Dervin, L. Grossberg, B. J. O'Keefe, & E. Wartella (Eds.), *Rethinking communication 1: Paradigm Issues* (pp. 97–122), Newbury Park, Cal.: Sage.

Craig, R. T. (1993). Why are there so *many* communication theories? *Journal of Communication 43,* 26–33.

Dallmayr, F. R., & McCarthy, T. A. (Eds.) (1977). *Understanding and social inquiry.* Notre Dame: University of Notre Dame Press.

Davies, M. (1991). Concepts, connectionism, and the language of thought. In W. Ramsey, S. P. Stitch, & D. E. Rumelhart (Eds.), *Philosophy and connectionist theory* (pp. 229–257). Hillsdale, N.J.: Lawrence Erlbaum & Associates.

Deetz, S. (1982). Critical-interpretive research in organizational communication. *Western Journal of Speech Communication 46,* 131–149.

Deetz, S. (1986). Metaphors and the discursive production and reproduction of organization. In L. Thayer (Ed.), *Organizations and Communication: Emerging perspectives, 1,* (pp. 68–182). Norwood, N.J.: Ablex.

Deetz, S. (1990). Representation of interests and the new communication technologies. In M. Medhurst, T. Peterson, and A. Gonzales (Eds.), *Communication and the Culture of Technology* (pp. 43–62). Pullman, Wash.: Washington State University Press.

Deetz, S. (1992). *Democracy in an age of corporate colonizations: Developments in communication and the politics of everyday life.* Albany: State University of New York Press.

Deetz, S. & Mumby, D. (1990). Power, discourse, and the workplace. Reclaiming the critical tradition in communication studies in organizations. In J. Anderson (Ed.), *Communication Yearbook 13* (pp. 18–47). Newbury Park, Cal.: Sage.

Dennet, D. C. (1991). Mother nature versus the walking encyclopedia: A western drama. In W. Ramsey, S. P. Stich, and D. E. Rummelhart (Eds.), *Philosophy and Connectionist Theory* (pp. 21–30). Hillsdale, N.J.: Lawrence Erlbaum.

Fischer, F., & Sirianni (Eds.) (1984). *Critical studies in organization and bureaucracy.* Philadelphia: Temple University Press.

Fisher, W. R. (1987). *Human Communication as Narration: Toward a Philosophy of Reason, Value, and Action.* Columbia, S.C.: University of South Carolina Press.

Fodor, J. (1975). *The language of thought.* New York: Crowell.

Fodor, J. (1987). *Psychosemantics.* Cambridge, Mass.: MIT Press.

Foucault, M. (1972). *The archaeology of knowledge.* A. Sheridan Smith (Trans.) New York: Princeton University Press.

Foucault, M. (1980). *Power/knowledge: Selected interviews and other writings, 1972–1977.* C. Gordon (Ed.) New York: Pantheon.

Gadamer, H-G. (1989). *Truth and Method,* 2nd rev. ed. J. Weinsheimer & D. G. Marshall (Trans.). New York: Crossroad.

Geertz, C. (1988). *Works and lives: The anthropologist as author.* Stanford: Stanford University Press.

Gergen, K. J. (1985). The social constructionist movement in modern psychology. *American Psychologist 40,* 266–275.

Goffman, E. (1967). *Interaction ritual.* Garden City, N.Y.: Anchor Books.

Greenberg, E. S. (1986). *Workplace democracy: The political effects of participation.* Ithaca: Cornell University Press.

Greene, J. O. (1990). Tactical social actions: Toward some strategies for theory. In M. J. Cody & M. L. McLaughlin (Eds.), *The psychology of tactical communication* (pp. 31–47). Clevedon, England: Multilingual Matters.

Hempel, C. (1965). *Aspects of scientific explanation.* New York: Free Press.

Jackson, M. (1989). *Paths toward a clearing: Radical empiricism and ethnographic inquiry.* Bloomington: Indiana University Press.

Jorgensen, J. (1991). Co-constructing the interviewer/co-constructing "family." In F. Steier (Ed.), *Research and Reflexivity* (pp. 210–225). London: Sage.

Jorgensen, J. (1992). Communication, rapport, and the interview: A social perspective. *Communication Theory 2,* 148–155.

Kanter, R. M. (1982). The middle manager as innovator. *Harvard Business Review 60,* 95–105.

Kanter, R. M. (1983). *The changemasters: Innovation and entrepreneurship in the American corporation.* New York: Simon & Schuster.

Knorr-Cetina, K. & Mulkay, M. (Eds.) (1983). *Science observed: Perspectives on the social study of science.* London and Beverley Hills: Sage.

Krippendorff, K. (1991). Reconstructing (some) communication research methods. In F. Steier (Ed.), *Research and Reflexivity* (pp. 115–142). London: Sage.

Kuhn, T. S. (1962). *The structure of scientific revolutions.* Chicago: University of Chicago Press.

Leeds-Hurwitz, W. (1992). Forum introduction: Social approaches to interpersonal communication. *Communication Theory 2,* 131–138.

Levinson, R. W., & Gottman, J. M. (1983). Marital interaction: Physiological linkage and affective exchange. *Journal of Personality and Social Psychology 45,* 587–597.

Levinson, R. W., & Gottman, J. M. (1985). Physiological affective predictors of change in relationship satisfaction. *Journal of Personality and Social Psychology 49,* 85–94.

Lynch, J. J. (1977). *The broken heart: The medical consequences of loneliness.* New York: Basic Books.

Lynch, J. J. (1985). *The language of the heart: The body's response to human dialogue.* New York: Basic Books.

Miller, R. W. (1987). *Fact and Method.* Princeton: Princeton University Press.

Miller, G. A., Galanter, E., & Pribram, K. H. (1960). *Plans and the structure of behavior.* New York: Holt, Rinehart, & Winston.

Mumby, D. K. (1988). *Communication and power in organizations: Discourse, ideology, and domination.* Norwood, N.J.: Ablex.

O'Keefe, B. J. (1988). The logic of message design: Individual differences in reasoning about communication. *Communication Monographs 44,* 80–103.

O'Keefe, B. (1993). Against theory. *Journal of Communication 43,* 75–82.

O'Keefe, B. J., & Shephard, G. J. (1987). The pursuit of multiple objectives in face-to-face persuasive interaction: Effects of construct differentiation on message organization. *Communication Monographs 54,* 346–419.

O'Keefe, D. (1977). Two concepts of argument. *Journal of the American Forensic Association 13,* 121–128.

Parsons, T. (1971). Value-freedom and objectivity. In F. R. Dallmayr & T. A. McCarthy (Eds.), *Understanding and social inquiry* (pp. 56–65). Notre Dame: University of Notre Dame Press.

Philipsen, G. (1991). The forum. Writing ethnographies. *Quarterly Journal of Speech 77,* 327–329.

Pollner, M. & Emerson, R. (1988). The dynamics of inclusion and distance in fieldwork. In R. Emerson (Ed.), *Contemporary Field Research: A Collection of Readings* (pp. 47–61). Prospect Heights, Ill.: Waveland Press.

Schank, R. C., & Abelson, R. P. (1977). *Scripts, plans, goals and understanding.* Hillsdale, N.J.: Lawrence Erlbaum Associates.

Scheff, T. J. (1990). *Microsociology: Discourse, emotion and social structure.* Chicago: University of Chicago Press.

Schrag, C. O. (1986). *Communicative praxis and the space of subjectivity.* Bloomington: Indiana University Press.

Shotter, J. (1984). *Social accountability and selfhood.* Oxford: Basil Blackwell.

Shotter, J. (1991). A politics of relational forms: The sociality of everyday social life. *Cultural Dynamics 4,* 379–396.

Shotter, J. (1993a). *Cultural politics of everyday life: Social constructionism, rhetoric, and knowing of the third kind.* Milton Keynes: Open University Press.

Shotter, J. (1993b). *Conversational realities: Constructing life through language.* London: Sage.

Stablein, R., & Nord, W. (1985). Practical and emancipatory interests in organizational symbolism: A review and evaluation. *Journal of Management 11,* 13–28.

Stamp, G. H., & Knapp, M. L. (1990). The construct of intent in interpersonal communication. *Quarterly Journal of Speech 76,* 282–299.

Stewart, J. (1994). An interpretive approach to a validity in interpersonal communication research. In K. Carter & M. Presnell (Eds.), *Interpretive Approaches to Interpersonal Communication* (pp. 45–82). Albany: State University of New York Press.

Stewart, J., & Logan, C. (1993). *Together: Communicating Interpersonally,* 4th ed. New York: McGraw-Hill.

Taylor, C. (1971). Interpretation and the sciences of man. *The Review of Metaphysics 25,* 3–51.

Voeglin, E. (1956). *Order and History. Vol. 1: Israel and Revelation.* Baton Rouge: Louisiana State University Press.

Voegelin, E. (1957). *Order and History. Vol. 2: The World of the Polis. Vol. 3: Plato and Aristotle.* Baton Rouge: Louisiana State University Press.

Voegelin, E. (1974). *Order and History. Vol. 4: The Ecumenic Age.* Baton Rouge: Louisiana State University Press.

Voegelin, E. (1978). *Anamnesis.* G. Niemeyer. (Ed. & Trans.) Notre Dame University of Notre Dame Press.

von Wright, G. H. (1971). *Explanation and understanding.* Ithaca: Cornell University Press.

Warnke, G. (1984). Translator's Introduction, *Understanding and Explanation* by Karl-Otto Apel. Cambridge, Mass.: MIT Press.

Webb, Eugene (1981). *Eric Voegelin: Philosopher of History.* Seattle: University of Washington Press.

Weber, M. (1968). Basic sociological terms. In F. R. Dallmayr & T. A. McCarthy (Eds.), *Understanding and Social Inquiry* (pp. 38–55) Notre Dame: Notre Dame University Press, 1977.

West, James T. (1993). "Ethnography and Ideology: The Politics of Cultural Representation." *Western Journal of Speech Communication,* Vol. 57., pp. 209–220.

Winch, P. (1958). *The idea of a social science and its relation to philosophy.* London: Routledge & Kegan Paul.

CONTRIBUTORS

Terrance L. Albrecht, Department of Community and Family Health, University of South Florida, Tampa, Florida

Charles R. Berger, Department of Rhetoric and Communication, University of California, Davis, California

Joseph N. Cappella, the Annenberg School of Communication, University of Pennsylvania, Philadelphia, Pennsylvania

Barbara J. O'Keefe, Department of Speech Communication, University of Illinois, Urbana, Illinois

Gerry Philipsen, Department of Speech Communication, University of Washington, Seattle, Washington

John Stewart, Department of Speech Communication, University of Washington, Seattle, Washington

INDEX